Also available at all good book stores

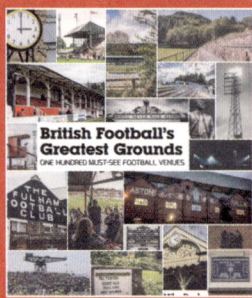
9781785316470

9781785313929

9781785315466

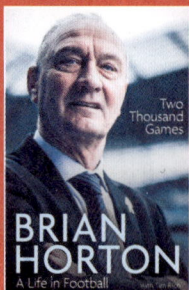
9781785316685

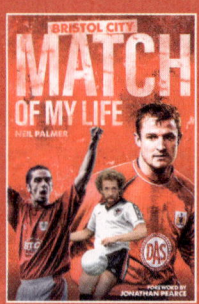
9781785315480

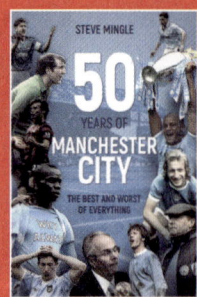
9781785313288

9781785316326

9781785316678

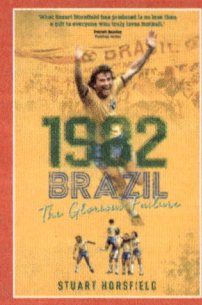
9781785316869

He's Here, He's There...

NEIL PALMER

He's Here, He's There...

First published by Pitch Publishing, 2021

Pitch Publishing
A2 Yeoman Gate
Yeoman Way
Worthing
Sussex
BN13 3QZ
www.pitchpublishing.co.uk
info@pitchpublishing.co.uk

© 2021, Neil Palmer

Every effort has been made to trace the copyright. Any oversight will be rectified in future editions at the earliest opportunity by the publisher.

All rights reserved. No part of this book may be reproduced, sold or utilised in any form or transmitted in any form or by any means, electronic or mechanical, including photocopying, recording or by any information storage and retrieval system, without prior permission in writing from the Publisher.

A CIP catalogue record is available for this book from the British Library.

ISBN 978 1 78531 765 1

Typesetting and origination by Pitch Publishing
Printed and bound in India by Replika Press Pvt. Ltd.

Contents

Acknowledgements 9
Foreword 11
Introduction 15
  1. The Boy From The Drum 20
  2. Taking A Chance 34
  3. Sillett's Boys 46
  4. Making Your Mark 64
  5. Julie 81
  6. Comings And Goings 92
  7. We Have Ourselves A Team 109
  8. I'm Not Coming Off 127
  9. Let's All Get Up The Concorde 140
10. Survival 152
11. Silverware 166
12. End Of An Era 180
13. The King Of Maine Road 190
14. Dad 200
15. Wembley 208
16. Moving On 225
17. A Club Too Far 238
18. New Challenges 247
19. Where's Gerry Gow? 264
20. Joolz 275
Career Statistics 283
Bibliography 284
About The Author 286

'Loving you changed my life
It should come as no surprise
That losing you has done the same'

Acknowledgements

BOOKS LIKE this stand or fall on the memories and opinions of the people who knew, or shared, a pitch with its subject. Therefore I am forever grateful to the vast number of family, team-mates, opposition players and friends and supporters who gave up their time and spoke honestly about Gerry Gow. The list has been endless and again I am grateful to have been able to share and listen to their memories. In truth a couple of words by me in this section really cannot properly thank them.

Writing about any sporting hero carries a responsibility and at times the weight of getting it right for Gerry's family and the supporters seemed too much. Without the help of the Gow family the task may not even have got off the ground, so again I am in their debt. Chris, Willie, Rachael, Jenny, Julie and Joolz, you are all very special people.

Writing any book can be a very solitary experience so I would like to thank my wife Sally for the endless back up she gave me during this project. Support is a very important thing during the process of a book and again I thank Paul and Jane Camillin and their incredible team at Pitch Publishing who produce wonderful books all year round. Hopefully this will be one of them.

THE GERRY GOW STORY

Thanks must also go to Garry Bray, Gary James, David Woods and Matt Stevens for their incredible knowledge of their respective clubs. A special mention must also go to Chris Bradfield and Jonathan Pearce, whose enthusiasm for the project and love for Gerry was plain to see from day one. And also to Sean Donnelly for always supporting anything Bristol City.

Most of all I thank you, the reader, for taking the time to pick the book up and give it a go. I hope that through these pages you will discover a bit more about the Gerry Gow who was loved by us all.

Foreword

THE SUMMER of 1970. The hippies were hanging on. The punks had yet to find their tartan bondage gear and safety pin piercings. Pre-teen rebellious angst was stirring in me.

England had lost the World Cup quarter-final to West Germany. Peter Bonetti, one of my earliest heroes, had gifted them the winner. I'd cried. I wanted a new hero to believe in.

I already had my Bristol City favourites. Pictures of chunky midfield maestro Bobby Kellard, craggy, old centre-forward John Galley and blond Bristolian pin-up boy Chris Garland had adorned my walls. But there was something missing.

Georgie Best had been banned by the FA in January for his 'disreputable behaviour'. My grandmother loathed him. I loved him. But he didn't play for Bristol City.

Saturday, 15 August. As always I took my little transistor radio to Ashton Gate to listen to Radio One up until the players ran out when I'd switch to Radio Two, as it was then, to listen to the other scores. Elvis Presley was singing the last number one of his lifetime, 'The Wonder of You', and out they came from the little tunnel in the old main Ashton Gate stand. Bristol City and Sunderland. Ninety minutes later I had found my footballing James Dean with the Robins badge on his chest.

THE GERRY GOW STORY

I had first met Gerry Gow when he arrived in Bristol as a teenager from Glasgow and spent time at the home of manager Alan Dicks in Ormerod Road, Stoke Bishop. It was a leafy street where we played football around parked cars and dodged moving ones. Once or twice, Gerry came out to have a kickaround. I didn't really know who he was. I understood few words of his Glaswegian growl but one thing he saud has always stuck in my mind.

'When you tackle make your body low like a boulder. They don't move. Don't stand tall like a tree. They fall over!' He was seven years older than me. Too old to consider a friend. Then.

Bobby Kellard had been sold to Leicester a few days earlier. The number ten shirt was up for grabs. Gerry seized it in a breathless 90 minutes, which resulted in a 4-3 for his side. Two goals for Gerry Sharpe, one each for Ken Wimshurst and Alan Skirton. But it was the 18-year-old in only his second league game who stole the show. He snapped into tackles against rock-hard Colin Todd and Bobby Kerr. He wanted to outdo the great former Arsenal goalscorer Joe Baker, who did net two for Sunderland that day, but was certainly not outshone.

I worshipped Gerry from then on. I modelled myself on him. He had the glint in the eye of one who mocked the establishment. I became an anti-school dissident. The hair became longer and more unkempt. So did mine. Detention followed! I tried to play like him. I tackled like fury. But I could never pass the ball like Gerry.

That's what people forget. Yes! He was a piratical buccaneer with the whiplash challenges that were to put Bremner and Giles or the dreaded Rovers enemy Frankie Prince, among countless others, on their backsides. But he could play. Really play.

FOREWORD

He could pass like a dream, read the game, lead by example and score goals. He should have played for Scotland. He should have played in more cup finals than just the one with Manchester City.

When people ask me who my favourite all-time footballer is from my 50 years pf being involved in the game they expect to hear Best, Cruyff, Messi or Ronaldo. Perhaps Beckenbauer or Moore. I admired them all and many others.

But unashamedly I always say Gerry Gow.

For me he was more than just a footballer. He became my mentor in my teenage years when I was filming Bristol City games for the club with my dad. We were the first club TV analysis team in Europe. I got close to the players. They became like older brothers. I still adore them all. But Gerry was special.

When I got my first job with Radio Bristol, Gerry was always the first to do an interview and the first to point out the mistakes I had made in reports. He still had the Glasgow growl.

When he was about to leave for Man City he came to the commentary position and did one final interview. We both cried. I was heartbroken.

I am ashamed that we lost touch for many years. There was a phone call or two when he was at Yeovil and messages from mutual friends. Wilderness years. I won't forgive myself for that.

One day out of the blue I was asked to host a testimonial evening for him. We had a pint in the bar beforehand. It was as if the missing years had never existed. True friendship is like that.

Only a few too short months later, he called. He told me he was ill. That he wasn't going to get better.

THE GERRY GOW STORY

The end of the story. Except it isn't.

Christopher Reeve, the Superman actor, once said, 'The hero is an ordinary individual who finds the strength to persevere and endure in spite of overwhelming obstacles.'

Neil's text will tell the story of the barriers Gerry had to cross in life and in football. I am so pleased his story is in the hands of a good writer and a good Bristol City fan who has tirelessly spoken to the people who knew the man so well through so many landscapes of his remarkable journey …

I never met James Dean of course. I'll never get to meet Bruce Springsteen, I guess. But I was a friend of my greatest hero.

Everywhere I go, I know – he's yur, he's there. He's every fucking where.

Jonathan Pearce

Introduction

THE MORNING, 10 October 2016 was like any other day for me. I was at home making a coffee with a few thoughts of what I would do in two days' time for my birthday. There wasn't a lot to choose from as my 54th birthday beckoned; reminding me of how the years were flying past. I contemplated the options for my wife and me as after all, the days of going on a massive bender and ending up in a nightclub were long gone, so I took a look at what was on the TV that night.

I then became aware of the radio as the BBC Radio Bristol announcer stated, 'Former Bristol City footballer Gerry Gow has passed away after a battle with cancer.'

The news stopped me in my tracks. I was immediately transported back to the images of Ashton Gate in the 1970s and Gerry, with his wild perm and even wilder moustache, slaying all before him as the crowd sang, 'He's here, he's there, he's every fucking where, Gerry Gow, Gerry Gow, 'I have to admit I have a little couple of verses of it myself as I went and sat in the living room.

The song is and always will be iconic to a certain generation of supporters. Many fans of my era would without hesitation name Gerry Gow as the greatest player ever to wear the red shirt of Bristol City. Only a handful of players have been loved by the supporters of the club in the way the man from the Glasgow suburb of Drumchapel was. Even today, as you pick your way through the obvious 'Sack the manager/keep the manager' posts on Bristol City forums, whenever a midfielder is signed he will always be deemed 'not as good as Gerry Gow', or if the club is struggling in some way there are always the 'what we need is 11 Gerry Gows' posts, which just shows you the high esteem he is held in even today.

I got a few messages on my phone asking if I had heard the news as I sat down at my computer to look at the hordes of comments online at the various forums of clubs that Gerry had played for. It was overwhelming for anybody to see the outpouring of love towards a footballer who had connected with the fan on the terraces, yet the posts probably came as a wonderful comfort for his family. I found myself wondering how they must be feeling at such a terrible time.

I had always wanted to write a book about Gerry, mainly due to his legendary role in Bristol City's most triumphant era, but things just never fell into place. When my first book, *Derby Days* was released in 2007, I spoke to 11 Bristol Rovers and 11 Bristol City players about the Bristol derby. The one omission from my City XI was Gerry as nobody knew where he was and despite my investigations, all I and his team-mates could find out was that he was possibly in the Portland area at the time.

Writing other books, whenever I have spoken to his team-mates or opponents I have always ended up asking them a particular question, 'What was Gerry Gow like?' The stories relayed back have lengthened my initial interviews at times by hours as players spoke with such affection for him.

INTRODUCTION

Gerry was a player brought up in a time where every club had their own 'hard man'. Some even had three or four such players as did Leeds United at the time. All of those teams would have loved to have had Gerry in their side. He could mix it with the best and he usually did, shining during a career in which he outfought and outplayed the Leeds United double act of Billy Bremner and John Giles. While later wearing the blue of Manchester City he played the Spurs midfield duo of Glenn Hoddle and Ossie Ardiles off the park in the FA Cup Final, showing that he was much more than a hard man; he could play a bit as well and certainly did not care for reputations. But you don't need me to tell you that – just read some of the comments on Gerry contained within the pages of this book, from people vastly more authoritative about the game than me.

So in 2019 I met Gerry's son Chris through a mutual friend in Portland in a pub called The Punchbowl. The pub was plainly football-orientated with various club shirts on the wall and Sky Sports on the TV. While waiting for Chris I looked at all the memorabilia and found a picture of Gerry in his prime, along with other Bristol City and Manchester City items on the wall. At that moment, Chris entered and I started to pitch the idea to him. We spent a few hours chatting and I was elated that he wanted the book to happen as he thought it would be a great thing for his kids and grandchildren to read in years to come. We agreed to keep in touch and I stepped outside into the pouring rain. Although the meeting was successful, it wasn't the bests of starts as beautiful though Portland is, it rained from the moment I left my house in Bristol to the time I arrived back home some three hours later, but the meeting was great and we reminisced about Chris's dad.

On the drive home, all I could think about was the book and how it would be constructed in terms of Gerry's career. Chris was happy to help in any way he could and told me that he was still touched by the receptions he received at all of Gerry's old clubs when they find out who he is. But I had massive reservations, mainly due to the weight of responsibility of getting it right for Chris and the family, and also the various supporters of all his clubs, especially Bristol City.

I had a few things that I didn't want the book to be. I didn't want it to be an analysis of every detail of his life, or a blow-by-blow account of every game he played. I wanted it to be a footballing journey through his life and for him to be brought to life by the memories of the people who knew him. They would be the ones who told the story. And I was at pains to make sure Gerry's illness didn't take up too much space at the end as I didn't feel there was anything to be gained in documenting all of his fight with that terrible disease.

I also did not want Gerry, especially from a Bristol City perspective, to be held out as some kind of 'cult hero' which I'm sure he was at Rotherham United and Manchester City but that did not apply at Ashton Gate. Invariably that term is used for players who are loved by the fans but have a career that burns brightly but only briefly at a particular club. That was not the case for Gerry at Bristol City. He was loved as he gave 100 per cent and supporters saw something of themselves in him, partly due to the way he played the game. He was one of them but on the pitch he shouted and screamed at team-mates, wound up the opposition and felt the same pain as they did when the team lost. All players feel that but there are only a few who convey that spirit to the fans on the terraces. Gerry truly was one of

INTRODUCTION

those players. This was also matched by his consistency in the red shirt of the Robins. He was always in the side driving them on through their glory years in the 1970s.

During my research I never had one player refuse an interview even though Gerry had kicked half of them up in the air at some point in his career. Everyone spoke with love and mutual respect for him, although many were reserved at first, telling me that they had some stories that could never be printed. They told me some of them anyway but the tape machine stayed well and truly turned off.

Gerry's family and friends knew what a special man he was and I know supporters have a perception that he was a wild man on the pitch and a wild man off it. Sure, he was no angel off the field but I just hope the pages in this book will give supporters a brief glimpse not only of Gerry the footballer but also of Gerry the man and if this is the case then the objective will have been achieved.

1

The Boy From The Drum

LIKE ALL major cities, Glasgow was an industrial heart that needed feeding, London had the Thames, Liverpool had the Mersey and Newcastle had the Tyne. Glasgow was supported by the Clyde. Ships were built and the world's goods were imported to the port, from the exotic fruits of distant Asia to the coal mined from across the United Kingdom, keeping the heart of the city beating. Shipyards sat shoulder to shoulder along the length of the Clyde and at one point a fifth of all the ships in the world were built on the river.

From as far back as the late 1800s, the population of the city kept on growing as industrial workers arrived from Italy, Ireland and across Scotland to fill the much-needed jobs and start a new life. As the city grew, there was a real need for housing and by 1931, 85,000 people were crammed into an area of one square mile. It was a tough city that needed to change.

The Drum, as its affectionately known to the locals, was born as a result of those decaying living conditions from the heart of the city to the nearby areas in the south, east and west. Following the Second World War, areas of Glasgow needed rebuilding if the city was to prosper and accommodate its industrial workers in a more respectful environment.

The 1954 Housing Act, brought in by the Government, was a scheme that many people regarded as a 'slum clearance'. But the act instead called it 'urban regeneration'. Across many areas of the city, people were living eight to a room and around 30 to a toilet, a situation that could not go on. Large high-rise blocks, separated by green open spaces, and smaller terraced estates consisting of two- or three-bedroom houses, many with gardens, were constructed at the start of the 1950s. New areas such as Drumchapel, Pollock, Castlemilk and Easterhouse appeared on the sprawling map of the redeveloped Glasgow.

People flocked to get one of these new homes. In Drumchapel alone, over 30,000 people moved into the area and many loved it. There was decent housing and open space for the kids to play but due to its infancy there was nothing in the way of infrastructure such as shops or even pubs early on. All this would come a few years later. Others felt dumped there. They struggled with being a few miles outside Glasgow and in their eyes communities had been torn up and knocked down to make way for a new city. The Gow family looked upon the move as a bright new start.

There was also plenty of work for people in the shape of the docks and the Goodyear tyre factory, along with the Beatties Biscuits factory and the large Singer sewing machine plant nearby in Clydebank. Having said that, Drumchapel was essentially still filled with people on low incomes and living in a certain level of poverty, but it was a place where a tight community quickly formed, as one resident put it on a BBC documentary on the area broadcast in 2000, 'We didn't know we were poor as everybody around us was the same, we only knew we were poor when people from the telly told us.'

In the same documentary another resident spoke about what the neighbourhood meant to them, 'The Drum always felt like home even though we lived there or moved away and came back to visit you cannot leave the Drum, it follows you all through your life.'

It is a place that over the years has produced many famous faces, all of whom have credited the Drum with being something that runs through their very soul. People like comedian Billy Connolly, actor James McAvoy, and footballers including Andy Gray, Danny McGrain, John McDonald, Alex Miller, and our own Gerry Gow, all enjoyed their formative years there. Like those before him, the Drum shaped every facet of Gerry, from being a tough no-nonsense footballer who was afraid of nobody and nothing to the loving family man who cared about people he loved and the community around him. The area gave him and his family a good grounding in life.

Jimmy Gow was what you would think of as a man's man. A docker who hailed originally from the Govan area of the city, he was a tough man of average height without an inch of fat on him, mainly due to the tough, backbreaking work on Glasgow's docks. Jimmy had experienced terrible tragedy in his life early on. He had previously been married and had a daughter called Agnes but when she was no more than a toddler Jimmy's wife Sarah died of pneumonia, leaving him as a one-parent family which would be a terrible struggle in today's world let alone the 1940s. Jimmy was unable to cope and after many sleepless nights and long discussions with his wife's family, it was decided that Agnes would be better off in terms of stability and opportunities if she went to live with her mum's family in Lisburn, Ireland. It was a heartbreaking decision for Jimmy but he knew it was for the best. Years later he met and married Helen, who would become the love of his life. They would visit Agnes in Ireland over the years, making her welcome and part of their family.

Jimmy and Helen had their first child, Gerald, on 29 May 1952 at Glasgow's Stobhill Hospital. They were both overjoyed and it coincided with them moving from Helen's parents' house, which they shared in Balornock, to their brand new home in Drumchapel. They soon added to the family group with Willie two years later and then Catherine. Helen stayed at home looking after the children while Jimmy worked all hours on the Glasgow docks. It was a hard life; many dockers were not expected to live beyond the age of 50 due to its tough nature and many a time Jimmy would come home with black eyes or cuts and bruises from accidents on the docks involving carts and booms.

The docks were a gateway to the world beyond Glasgow, dealing with wool, coal, fish, cloth, wine, fruit, pottery, iron, wood and tobacco and items would regularly find their way back to Drumchapel where the rest of the family would despair at the strange things they would find sitting in their living room.

To research this book I travelled to Glasgow to meet Willie and his wife Janet. It was a freezing December day and I was wrapped up as though I was on my way to the Arctic. I agreed to meet Willie at a bar in the centre of the city. You could certainly see that I was from out of town as most of the clients walked in off the streets without even a coat. I was waiting for a couple of minutes when a white-haired guy came up to me and asked if I was Neil. Straight away I could see it was Gerry Gow looking back at me since Willie was the image of his older brother.

We talked about Gerry and their life growing up. Willie recalled, 'Dad would always bring stuff home when he could, it was just the sort of thing dockers did back then. I remember he brought a massive bunch of bananas home once and we had not seen a banana before, they were all green and not ripe yet and still on a massive vine, we didn't even think they were bananas as we had heard they were supposed to be yellow. He must have looked a right sight walking through Drumchapel with those over his shoulder. Mum put them in a cupboard to ripen but she didn't really have a clue as to what to do with them, but they got eaten in the end by us kids and all our mates.

'Mum also went into the kitchen to do breakfast once and found a white dove sat in the kitchen. Dad had been on nights and there had been a shipment of birds through Glasgow that night and, lo and behold, one had found his way into Dad's pocket. Mum went mad but us kids wanted to keep it as a pet. In the end I think Dad gave in to Mum and released it. You really didn't know what he was going to bring home next.'

Gerry and Willie were inseparable as they ran and played around Drumchapel with the other kids. They would jump dykes, chase rats and swing about on rusty poles and climb the roofs of buildings. They would stay out late playing football in the dark shrieking and laughing and they would eat everything put in front of them, sharing a bottle of pop between several friends and only wiping the rim with their sleeve to clear away left-over saliva. But it was a world where adults commanded authority and were respected.

As a family they would have trips to Ireland. This was always at the time of the Glasgow Fair when the whole of the city shut down for the last two weeks of July and all the workers would head off to the coast. Gerry loved the open spaces of Ireland and particularly the long, windswept beaches where he, Willie, Agnes, and Cath would play for hours in the sand dunes. The whole family loved going there, especially Jimmy, and it's a great testimony to him that he never lost touch with Agnes even though they had both been through some tough times after her mum's death.

Gerry was popular with everyone, mainly because he seemed to be good at most things, although he certainly was no big-head and the fact that he had no airs and graces about him even at an early age made his peers feel comfortable around him and that led to his popularity. He was a real sportsman who loved football but he also excelled at school in most subjects, particularly Maths. Both boys were Celtic supporters although their dad Jimmy loved Queen's Park Football Club.

As far as Willie was concerned, Gerry was his hero. Having Gerry around gave him a certain kudos, particularly around his brother's mates who were that much older. When Willie was joining St Pius Secondary School, many of his friends were worried as the rumour was that new boys got their head put down the toilet and had it flushed, but that never happened to Willie because of the reputation of his brother. Gerry always looked out for his young siblings and when he had a milk round he would give some of the money to Willie and Cathy. He did the same when he got a paper round but he could also have a bit of devilment within him, like the time he convinced Willie to climb out of the bedroom window of their four-story tenement block and stand on the window sill for a laugh.

Willie remembers that incident well, 'We were just mucking about in the bedroom when he just convinced me it would be a good idea. I was always trying to impress Gerry so I just did it. Mum and Dad never found out thank god as they would have murdered both of us. I laughed about it years later with Gerry but he didn't think it was funny and couldn't believe how stupid he had been sending me out on to the ledge.'

The close-knit nature of the Drum gave a certain safety to the children of the area as everybody knew each other and that would be great for times when neighbours would share things among themselves. That community support was particularly important considering that most people had very little, so food would be shared within the family. The flip-side to this was that if somebody broke a window or was cheeky to an adult their parents would know within minutes and the guilty party had to face up to what they did and take any punishment on the chin. It certainly was a lesson for later in life about standing up and taking responsibility for your actions.

There was plenty of industry around the area and although it wasn't particularly well paid, kids growing up knew that they would have a natural progression from school to work and would no doubt be working with people from their own area, which again led to a certain level of security for them. Although Gerry showed great promise with different sports, particularly football, he never really spoke about what he would do when he left school, thinking deep down that maybe the chance to be another Billy Bremner was nothing more than a pipe dream. Jimmy thought it would be a great idea if he took

Gerry to show him the docks. Gerry was aged around 12 at the time and was really excited by the prospect, although he was a little concerned when Jimmy told him not to tell his mother where they were going as Gerry knew from experience that if his dad said that, it was usually something she would not be too pleased about.

Gerry recalled later in his life how he couldn't believe the noise of the place with hundreds of men pushing large handcarts around the site. All of these carts had metal wheels so the sound of them on the concrete floors was deafening. There was also the noise of the steam pumps and cranes belching out steam every second. He saw men in pits shovelling large amounts of coal or grain into sacks at backbreaking speed, and was fascinated by the jokes and banter even though he didn't really understand most of it, but he could tell the men loved being together. Gerry thought it was exciting but whether he considered it a career, that was a different matter. He remarked years later that he thought it was 'bloody hard work'.

When the pair got home, a career in the docks for Gerry was never going to happen as his mum was waiting for the pair of them and she gave Jimmy what for, telling them, 'No son of mine is going to work at the docks, what the hell were you thinking?' Jimmy had no reply although Willie, with years to reflect, now feels there may have been method to Jimmy's madness at the time, 'Dad knew Gerry was a clever kid who always looked like he would go on to bigger and better things. I remember being gutted that I was too young to go to the docks at the time. I am sure dad took him to show him the reality of the place, in a way hoping he would never come back again, but still showing him the importance of mates and friends and how they all worked together. It worked as Gerry often spoke about the community at the docks years later.'

Both Gow brothers loved Celtic, as did most of the boys in the area. They would always play football in the playground or on the Drum's open spaces, pretending to be Stevie Chalmers or Tommy Gemmell. All the boys would play and whatever age they were they would all muck in and start up little street teams. Gerry was tenacious in getting the ball irrespective of the age of some of the lads he played against. He had a determination to win that many of his peers lacked, getting genuinely upset if his team lost. Gerry would also read the local papers so he could keep tabs on the Scottish players like Denis Law, Billy Bremner and Jim McCalliog who were doing well in England. Gerry always told his mates how much better the game was south of the border and how the football was tougher. The young Gow was in his element when Scotland beat England 3-2 at Wembley in 1967. England had won the World Cup a year previously and the whole of Drumchapel partied through the night, as according to every Scotsman at the time this made Scotland world champions.

Jimmy also loved football and although he never really had the money to go and see his favourite team, Queen's Park, or even treat the boys to a day at Celtic Park, he got involved in the game by helping coach the lads at St Pius. Although his football coaching experience was limited, his huge enthusiasm went a long way. He would also take on the responsibility as trainer and would carry a large bag in case the boys got injured. The bag still haunts Willie to this day, 'If we were playing and went down injured, Dad would run on with this huge bag. Its contents were a sponge and a large bottle of smelling salts. All

Dad would do was thrust the smelling salts under your nose; whether you were knocked out or had a cut leg you got a nose full of salts. After a while all the lads including Gerry became aware of this, so it was always a last resort going down injured and if you did you had to get back up before dad got to you. We never let him forget it in later life.'

St Pius was a relatively new school as it had been built as part of the Drum area for the Catholic children to attend. It was a large establishment built at a low level and its concrete construction meant it was visually uninspiring, but the community spirit there was immense.

Because it was new, it had virtually no history either academically or from a sporting point of view. That however changed in 1967 when the school team, led by Gerry, qualified for the prestigious Under-16 Scottish Schools Shield. It was a competition for schools across Scotland, culminating in the final at Firhill, the home of Partick Thistle. St Pius were scheduled to play St Mungos, who were based in the Gallowgate area of Glasgow and had a rich history in the tournament having won it three times as well as appearing in many finals. The game was played on a Thursday night and all the children and their families boarded buses to make the four-mile journey from Drumchapel. Gerry, at the time, was playing for Queen's Park Strollers, who were associated with Queen's Park which made his father immensely proud but on this night there was a lot of pressure riding on young Gow's shoulders as he had almost single-handedly got them to the final with his displays in the middle of the park.

The final was a tense affair with few chances at either end. Willie was sat in the stand along with Jimmy and the other parents. They screamed and shouted with every attack St Pius made. The game was 0-0 at half-time and it was hard to predict a winner, although Gerry had started to get hold of the midfield and with the second half in progress he fought for every ball and covered every inch of the pitch. Professional coaches would say he was undisciplined as he found himself in the back four, clearing a looping St Mungo header off the line or out on the wing putting crosses in, but Gerry showed an incredible desire to win for his school and himself and that was plain to see for those around him.

With minutes left, Gerry won the ball in his own half and raced forwards, side-stepping challenge after challenge on his way. From about 30 yards out he looked up and drove a powerful shot into the top corner of the St Mungos goal which the keeper never even saw. The crowd went crazy and Gerry was swamped by his team-mates.

With around ten minutes to go, Gerry ran the whole show, spreading balls in all directions. When the final whistle blew a huge roar went up into the night sky as St Pius supporters ran on to the pitch and mobbed the team. Jimmy grabbed Willie and held him to his chest.

The coach journey home was chaotic as parents, families and friends sang with pupils. They partied long into the Drumchapel night and the next day the talk at school and around the area was all about young Gerry Gow and how he had made history for St Pius. Willie remarked, 'Gerry achieved many things throughout his footballing life but I will never be as proud of him as I was the night of that game.'

When the dust settled, Gerry was still Gerry as far as his parents were concerned. He still had to tidy up around the house and run his errands, but they took longer as local people wanted to chat to him about his footballing exploits. Gerry being Gerry, he was was very low key and if anything he became a little embarrassed by all the attention. The game though had sparked a lot of interest among the clubs around the area and beyond, aided by a clipping in the local Glasgow paper calling the young lad from the Drum 'a star of the future' after the game. There was interest from Queen's Park, Partick Thistle, Celtic and English club Derby County, who were managed by the great Brian Clough. Scouts approached Jimmy and he had long talks with Gerry about what he wanted to do. He was approaching 16 and he was being offered a chance to do what he had always wanted with an apprenticeship at some of these clubs.

Gerry wasn't interested in Queen's Park, who were amateurs, or Partick Thistle, who were a small Division One club. There was no bigger team than Celtic who had Jock Stein in charge and he was putting together a side that would eventually conquer Europe. A scout had approached the family to ask if Gerry would play for one of their youth teams. Gerry was torn as it was his club, but he wanted to see if he could have a crack down south like many of the Scottish players he admired so he and Jimmy made arrangements to go to Derby to see what they had to say, particularly as the Derby scout told them that if he liked things down there the club would offer Gerry a chance.

Derby were on the cusp of something special with the young management team of Brian Clough and Peter Taylor in charge. They had just won the Second Division and were full of great Scottish players like John O'Hare, John McGovern and the great Dave Mackay, so on paper it seemed this young lad from

Glasgow would fit right in. The whole of the estate wished them well as they made the long rail journey to Derby. Willie remembers it well, 'Mum was worried about Gerry and there were a few tears as they left. We went to the station to see them off and I did think I would never see him again.'

The plan was for Jimmy and Gerry to meet somebody from the club, stay overnight, then meet Clough and Taylor while being shown around the place. The reality was that after their six-hour train journey there was nobody to meet them at the station initially. Frantically Jimmy found a phone box and phoned the scout in Scotland, and after a long wait somebody arrived. The pair were taken to the training ground and shown around, although there was never any meeting with Clough or Taylor which they were very disappointed by. They received no concrete offer from Derby so they felt that the whole visit was a bit pointless, especially considering the effort made in travelling all the way down. Disillusioned, angry and upset, they came home to Glasgow the next day. Jimmy was very disappointed at the way Derby had treated his son, and although Gerry was upset, a lot of the family and neighbours rallied round him. Later in his life Gerry still never found out what had happened with Derby County and the scout did say that arrangements had been made to offer him something.

As far as Helen was concerned, that was it for football but instead it only made Gerry's resolve tougher when it came to wanting to make it in the game. He continued his career with Queen's Park Strollers although the interest from other Scottish clubs became more and more intense with offers coming after almost every appearance. Jimmy took all of them with a certain degree of scepticism and his feelings towards football clubs, especially English ones, had been tarnished after the Derby County experience, although all that was about to change when after a evening youth game in which Gerry had excelled as usual, a dark-haired gentleman approached him and said, 'Hello, Mr Gow. My name is Tony Collins. I am from Bristol City and I would love to talk about your son, Gerry.' It was a conversation that would change Gerry's life forever.

2

Taking A Chance

WHEN IT came to spotting potential footballers, Tony Collins was considered something of a genius. Over the years football's 'Master Spy', as he was called, has worked with many big names in his role as chief scout at various clubs. Tony has advised the likes of Don Revie and Brian Clough at Leeds United, Jim Smith at QPR and Derby County, as well as Ron Atkinson and Alex Ferguson at Manchester United. His opinion has been trusted by the very best in the game and when Revie became England manager in 1974 Tony even scouted opposing international sides.

Born in London in 1926, Collins had a tough start to life, being mixed race in an intolerant society. With no father to call on, he was brought up with the help of his maternal grandparents. Tony excelled at football and became a gifted left-winger, playing for York City, Watford, Norwich City, Torquay United, Crystal Palace and Rochdale during the 1950s. After manager Jack Marshall left Rochdale for Blackburn Rovers, Tony was encouraged by his team-mates to apply for the job, which he got in 1960, becoming the very first black manager in the Football League. Collins even took the Fourth Division outfit to the 1961/62 League Cup Final where they were beaten 4-0 by Norwich City over two legs.

When Tony eventually left Rochdale in 1967, he applied for various managerial vacancies but with no success. Still looking to stay in football, Tony met the young boss of Bristol City, Alan Dicks, at an Oldham Athletic game, where Alan asked Tony to look at his team the following week. Tony agreed and produced a full no-holds-barred report, so it was then that Dicks knew he had found the perfect scout he had been looking for. Collins would become the eyes of the club throughout the country and also provide the experience that Dicks needed alongside him.

Dicks had been appointed by Bristol City chairman Harry Dolman after the sacking of popular manager Fred Ford. Dolman was determined to get the Robins into football's top flight and didn't think Ford was the man to do it, although he faced huge opposition to the sacking from not only supporters who vented their anger towards the decision by writing letters to the local paper but also from a deputation of players who visited the businessman's home in Chew Valley on the outskirts of Bristol to try and persuade Dolman to give Ford another chance.

Dolman was originally from Wiltshire. He was an astute businessman who was self made, earning a fortune with his engineering company. A forward-thinking man, through his company he invented many things, notably the automated ticket machines he then sold to London Transport and across the world. He was unmoved by the move to reinstate Ford and his choice was Dicks, who by his own admission was an average player who learnt his trade at Chelsea and Southend United in the 1950s and 1960s. Dicks had been assistant manager to Jimmy Hill at Coventry City and had been recommended for the job to Dolman by Hill. Although a complete unknown to the majority of City fans, the 33-year-old joined up with his new backroom staff of former Chelsea team-mate John Sillett, who would be his assistant while also looking after the youth team, and the extremely knowledgeable Collins. The trio became a formidable team in the rise of the West Country club.

Tracking Alan Dicks down for this book was certainly easier than I first thought. The last I had heard he was living in the USA and with his CV of coaching covering a large part of the world I wondered if I would need my passport to speak to him. Further research provided me with the news that he was living in Bristol, so I got his number and arranged to meet him at his home. As I approached his door I am not ashamed to say I was nervous as when I was growing up in 1970s Bristol, Alan was a large personality. He always seemed to be on the TV and radio and also gave the city top-flight football, which nobody else had done since at the time of writing this book.

Alan, who is well into his 80s, was enthusiastic about a book about Gerry, and he said, 'He was like a son to me.' Alan remembered his early days at Bristol City, 'It was a big move for me, I had learnt so many things under Jimmy Hill and I was overwhelmed when I was given the job. But I knew it was right for me.'

The new regime started reasonably well at Ashton Gate, finishing the 1967/68 season in 19th place and just avoiding the drop into the Third Division. The following season the club finished 16th as the managerial team started to fashion their

TAKING A CHANCE

own side and brand of football. So with Dicks looking to build a side with youth and a bit of experience Tony was dispatched to scour the country, particularly Scotland, to look for the country's top talent. He was flitting between Glasgow and Edinburgh, organising a trial match for Scottish youngsters, and in doing so Tony found himself on a cold night in Glasgow watching Queen's Park Strollers after a few of his contacts had mentioned a certain young midfielder from Glasgow who was attracting a lot of attention.

Gerry Gow impressed Tony with his tough tackling and constant drive and after speaking to a few of the crowd he was directed into the path of his father Jimmy. Tony introduced himself and told Jimmy he was from Bristol City and said what a talent his son was. They chatted about football and Glasgow but Jimmy seemed hesitant about getting carried away only for another English club to mess them about. While they were talking, Gerry came over to the two men and Tony congratulated him on a great performance. Tony wanted to sign Gerry immediately and asked if he would be able to play in a trial match in Glasgow featuring lads he thought were right for Bristol City. Jimmy and Gerry agreed, much to Tony's delight.

After that Strollers game, Tony called Dicks and was gushing with praise for the youngster. He told Alan he was going to play him in the trial game but said that the lad was exceptional, so the trial in reality would be a formality for the youngster as far as City were concerned. With Tony raving about Gerry, Alan agreed to come up and watch the trial game the following week. Alan recalls today, 'I knew that if Tony thought the lad was good, he was good. And I was not disappointed, he had a drive and enthusiasm for the game that couldn't be coached. He was a bit raw and we could certainly do something about that so it was perfect. Tony as usual did his homework on Gerry. As he did with every player we signed, he found out the area he lived, the background of the family just to make sure he was right for us and he certainly was. He was one of the best players I ever signed in my career.'

Tony had certainly worked hard on the trial match, getting players from all over Scotland. Looking back it was an exceptional approach for Second Division Bristol City to steal the march on many big First Division clubs, let alone Celtic and Rangers, by organising a trial in the heartland of Scotland. Players arrived at an old sports stadium with a cinder pitch just outside Glasgow. Alan stood on some terracing while Tony greeted all the players and their families.

One of the players that day was another Bristol City legend from the 1970s, Tom Ritchie. Tom explains, 'It was incredible really how I ended up meeting Gerry. My brother Steve was picked out by Tony Collins weeks before and Tony asked if he could play in the trial game, unfortunately for Tony Steve was also picked to play for Scotland Under-15s against England at Turf Moor, Burnley, that night so he couldn't make it. Tony then asked my mum if she knew of any other lad that might be available so she told him about me. I was playing for my local boys' club and doing okay, so the next thing I knew I was in the trial game.

'I was gutted at first as I really wanted to see Steve play for Scotland and be with all my family who had gone but I knew this was a good chance for me. I lined up in a midfield along with this youngster Gerry Gow who if I remember rightly made a comment that I was posh coming from Edinburgh, and another young Glasgow boy called Billy Menmuir. I don't remember much about the game but I know we did well individually and as a team. A couple of things stick in my mind particularly the first time Gerry went into a tackle, he slid into it on the cinder track, I remember thinking, "This lad's nuts." He talked throughout the game driving us on and he seemed to have bags of confidence, there were a few occasions where me and Billy looked at each other as if to say, "Who is this guy?"

'When the game ended we chatted in the dressing room and he made us laugh, he even told us how well we had played and if I'm honest most of the team although we were all relative strangers took to him, he had a certain amount of confidence which was infectious. Tony came to see us along with City manager Alan Dicks. They thanked all the lads then pulled myself, Billy and Gerry to one side and asked us if we would like to come down to Bristol for a trial game against some of the Bristol lads. Tony also told me my brother was invited. We were all over the Moon to think the Bristol City manager had been up to see us, so a date was set for us to come down south with our family and look at the city and the club.'

Tony and Alan made their way towards Jimmy. The pair told Jimmy they would like Gerry to come south for a trial but they also wanted to make him an offer over the next few days while they were there as, in their eyes, he was the stand-out player. The men all agreed, along with Gerry who was listening intently to them, and they decided to meet up the next day for a chat. Back in the Gow household Jimmy was talking to Helen and the rest of the family about how well young Gerry had played and they were all trying to work out where Bristol was. Gerry asked his dad about what his initial thoughts were and Jimmy just replied that he was proud of the way they had spoken about his son, but he didn't want them too be messed about with promises like last time. Gerry agreed but deep down he was desperate to get his football career going and the thought of doing it down south really appealed to him.

Tony Collins remembers the time they signed Gerry in his excellent biography, aptly called *Tony Collins: Football Master Spy*. He recalled, 'I'll never forget the night Alan Dicks and myself went up to sign Gerry Gow, the bustling, aggressive midfielder for Bristol City. I thought it would cost us our lives. Gerry's father, Jim, was a docker in Scotland, rough and ready, strong as a lion, with three days' stubble on his face. You didn't mess with that kind of bloke, but he took a shine to Alan and me.

'I had first seen Gerry in a youth team game and what a player he looked. His tackling was tremendous and he looked as though he was not afraid of anything or anybody. I made a remark to Alan when a guy standing in front of us turned round and said, "You can forget signing him, he's tied up … you won't get him." So I replied, "I suggest you mind your own business… I'm having a private conversation." The guy did not know whether to say more or just leave. The warning bells rang loudly and both Alan and myself knew there and then that we would have to act fast to have any chance of signing him.

'We saw Gerry's dad after the game and he told us to go and discuss the situation with him. That seemed okay but what we were not expecting was all the family, relations and some friends to be there, about nine if I remember. We had arranged to meet in a Glasgow pub and pubs tend to be tough places in

Glasgow. This one was no exception! Alan Dicks and I walked in to find sawdust on the floor and some darting, suspicious eyes giving us the old one two up and down as we set foot into the place. I'm not saying it wasn't friendly – just that the stares threatened you with frostbite. Dicks and I walked in dressed to the nines. As soon as we entered everyone stopped talking and turned round to look. Dicks shot an expression of panic in my direction and said, "They think we're police." In that case I replied, "Buy them all a drink, quick." That changed everything, the place lit up and we had our chat. We got our man too; Gerry Gow was a great signing for the club.'

Although Willie was only a young lad he remembers that night fondly, 'Dad was so impressed that the manager of Bristol City came all the way up to see Gerry and his family. He believed they showed tremendous respect to us as a family and he reassured mum that although their eldest looked like he would be moving hundred of miles south, he would be looked after by the club and that went a long way with my parents and all of the family.'

The discussions with Gerry and his family went on late into the night, not due to any type of problems regarding what was on offer but mainly due to everybody wanting to buy Alan and Tony drinks all night. It was agreed that Gerry and his dad would come down to Bristol for another game in a few weeks' time, paid for by City, and have a look at the club and if they liked it they would sign there and then. Jim was happy and he was certainly a man of his word.

It was a real coup for Bristol City at the time; although Gerry had not been recognised internationally at schoolboy level his reputation as a great prospect in Scotland was getting bigger and bigger. Fulham enquired about him after manager Bobby Robson along with one of his scouts took in a schoolboy game while on a Scottish scouting mission. For this book, I was also put in touch with former Tottenham Hotspur scout, Ron Clayton. Now into his 80s, he remembers that Spurs were closely following Gerry, telling me, 'We had a good track record up in Scotland regarding finding the odd youngster. We watched the young Gerry Gow along with another lad from Edinburgh who was a year younger than him called Graeme Souness. They both had similar styles but Gerry was the type of lad that got kicked and gave it back well; Graeme took it but at the time didn't really dish it out. For whatever reason we went for Graeme instead of Gerry, and I remember thinking we had made the wrong choice when things didn't really work out for Graeme at White Hart Lane a couple of years later, but by then Gerry was established at Bristol City.'

Another club to miss out on Gerry was Newcastle United. Jim Lees was responsible for scouting around the Glasgow area and he remembered Gerry and Newcastle's failure at the time to get things moving, 'Gerry Gow certainly from my point of view was the one that got away. I remember sending report after report in about this youngster but we just dragged our heels. I'm sure we could have got him but I was let down by the club a bit. In the end I remember approaching his dad, but he told me Bristol City had signed him. No disrespects to Bristol City but I was astonished a Second Division club had stole the march on everyone. But to their credit they obviously looked after him.'

The four lads and their families arrived at Bristol Temple Meads station after a long train ride. They were met by Tony Collins and taken to Ashton Gate where the families were

TAKING A CHANCE

given something to eat. The players went off to get changed for their game on the Ashton Gate pitch. Tom Ritchie takes up the story, 'When we arrived we were all shown round where our digs would be if we got signed, we met the families who would be looking after us and you have to hand it to Tony Collins. Both landladies were Scottish which made us feel at home. We then went back to Ashton Gate and I remember chatting to Gerry about how different Bristol seemed to the areas of Scotland where we both lived. I knew Gerry was from Drumchapel which could be a bit rough and I was from a small mining town called Boness just outside Edinburgh although Gerry still insisted it was posh.

'We changed for the game and were introduced to what I can only describe as a man mountain in the form of youth and reserve team manager John Sillett. He told us to get out on the pitch and wait for his instruction. The match was a mixture of Scottish trialists and lads from Bristol, lads like Keith Fear, David Bruton and David Rodgers. Some of the lads were in the youth team and some were like us trialists from various regions. I found myself in a four-man midfield along with my younger brother Steve, Gerry and Billy Menmuir. Billy was a real talent, a really cultured footballer. He was never really going to get stuck into the tackle but didn't really have to with Gerry by his side, I remember thinking he will definitely get signed along with Gerry who yet again won every ball and could hit 30, 40 yard passes. In the end we all were signed up. My brother Steve was signed as an apprentice as he was younger but myself Gerry and Billy all got offered a one-year deal.'

The players returned to Scotland with their families, knowing that they had secured a chance to make it as a footballer. Jimmy was over the Moon about how City had conducted themselves and he allayed any worries Helen might have had regarding how they were going to look after her eldest son. As the spring of 1969 drew to a close, it was time for Gerry to move south. All the family wished him well as he set off on a new stage of his life. Helen, like all of the family, shed a tear as he headed for the train station, complete with sandwiches and various dos and don'ts regarding living on his own. Jimmy gave him a massive bear hug on the platform and they waved him quietly away into the distance. Brother Willie remembers it well, 'We were all upset, yet pleased for him, we all knew how much he wanted to be a footballer. When we got home we all went into different parts of the house and had a bit of a cry but then we just got on with our lives. Dad had to get ready for work the next day, mum sorted out the dinner and me and Cathleen had homework to catch up on. That night in bed I just kept thinking about him and what he might be doing and where he was, but I knew one thing and that was he was going to do it and I could not have been prouder.'

All four arrived at Bristol Temple Meads and were met by the imposing figure of John Sillett. Sillett was an intimidating individual to most of the professionals at the club, let alone four wet-behind-the-ears Scottish teenagers. Sillett, or Sills as he would be known to them, was in charge of the youth team and was a man who had taken no prisoners in his playing career, a policy which he had carried over into his coaching. If Sills said to do something, you did it.

Tom Ritchie remembers the meeting, 'We had already met Sills, so we knew what he was like. He met us and said, "Right, follow me." We marched behind him through the station and to his car. On the way he told Gerry to take his hands out of his pockets to which Gerry just mumbled a few things under his breath. We piled into his car with our bags and Sills got in the driver's seat. We didn't really exchanged pleasantries, but he did tell us he was pleased to see us and how important the next year was going to be.

'He took us to Ashton Gate where we met Tony and Alan Dicks and a few of the players who were finishing training. Then he took us to our digs. Steve's and myself were by the Hen and Chicken pub in the Bedminster area of the city. Gerry's and Billy's were a stone's throw away near Duckmoor Road. Both sites were walking distance to the ground. We were introduced to our family, myself and my brother Steve were with a family called the McKendricks and Gerry and Billy were with a family called the McLeods. Both hosts were Scottish, which helped as we were made to feel welcome straight away; it was just another example of how Bristol City wanted to support us.

'We unpacked and answered heaps of questions from our landlady about what we liked food-wise and where in Scotland we were from. Then Sills got us together and said, "Right tomorrow morning be at the ground at nine in the morning, and god forbid anybody who's late." With that he got in his car and left.

'The four of us looked at each other and thought long and hard about our next move. We were in a brand new city full of new pubs to explore not to mention new girls and the evening was just starting. So with that we made a collective decision based purely on our impression of John Sillett and all went to bed early ready for the next morning.'

3

Sillett's Boys

JOHN SILLETT'S mere physical presence would strike fear into most people, let alone a group of teenagers. The tough Londoner stood over six feet tall and had the physique and haircut of a British marine. He had made his name at Chelsea where as a no-nonsense full-back he won the First Division in 1955. It was at Chelsea and Coventry City that he first made acquaintance with Bristol City manager Alan Dicks, and when Dicks needed somebody to oversee the youngsters at Ashton Gate Sillett was the first name he gave to chairman Harry Dolman.

Dolman had seen many clubs like Manchester United and Wolverhampton Wanderers developing their own youngsters, so he decided to give Dicks a budget of £10,000 a year, which would run alongside the first-team budget to produce the very best youngsters both nationally and locally. Sillett grabbed the opportunity with both hands. By Sillett's own admission he was still learning in terms of coaching, but what he did know for sure was that he wanted to give Dolman a group of lads who wouldn't be out of place in the first team and with a bit of luck could go on and win the FA Youth Cup for the first time.

That first morning in Mr and Mrs McLeod's Victorian terraced house could not have come quicker for Gerry and Billy. Mrs McLeod was the perfect surrogate mother for the young footballers. Patient, kind, and understanding, she would cook them breakfast and dinner and serve it on her large mahogany table in the dining room. She would pride herself on finding out her guests' favourite likes and dislikes. It was a relaxing house with a happy atmosphere, and parents could certainly feel safe in the knowledge that their young footballer was in good hands.

The location of the house was perfect for Bristol City as it was walking distance to the club. It was homely with its old armchairs and rugs in front of the fireplace, a fire that Gerry and Billy were both responsible for keeping going. People who remember visiting the house remember a constant smell of beeswax due to Mrs McLeod continually cleaning the oak furniture and the clanking old grandfather clock in the hallway.

On that first day she served them a breakfast of beans on toast, telling them how they would need the energy for what lay ahead and how they were to return after training as there were a few errands she wanted doing. The lads said goodbye and set off for Ashton Gate with the instructions they were given. As they came out on to North Street they saw Tom and Steve coming out of their digs and over the next five minutes it seemed as though there was a succession of teenagers with sports bags making their way to Ashton Gate. Gerry picked out one of them as Keith, adding, 'I'm sure that's the quick lad who played upfront with us in that trial game down here.' Gerry called to him and he joined them. He introduced himself as Keith Fear.

By the time they had reached the ground, there were around ten boys with more to come. When they arrived they were a motley crew. They all waited outside as they had been told to go to the ground, but nobody mentioned anything about going in. In the end it was Gerry who entered, much to the delight of the rest of the group. After a few minutes Gerry trotted out with John Sillett running close behind him shouting, 'And if I want a little Scottish bastard looking for me I will ask for one.' It wasn't the greatest of starts, but it wouldn't be long before Gerry came to Sillett's notice again.

The main day was going to be taken up with running, running, and more running. Sillett would set the times the lads had to be at each corner flag and if one of them missed out they all did it again. As the sessions went on Sillett could not believe the determination that Gerry was showing. He was also getting among his peers, helping them and geeing them up when needed. Tom Ritchie remembers those sessions with terror, 'Sills got at us from day one. I remember some lads were physically sick with the thought of doing the training; he pushed us and pushed us and he would be forever in your face but when I look back on my career he was such an influence, I would run through a brick wall for him.'

After the session Sillett pointed out to them how the club structure worked. They would be playing in the South West League which included clubs locally and Wales. The progression then was to the reserves, playing in the Football Combination, which was an incredibly tough league with rising stars as well as older pros who knew every trick in the book. As youth team players and apprentices, they would be using the away dressing room and at no point were they to go anywhere near the first team's dressing room unless they were invited.

Former youth team player Dave Bruton remembers those days alongside Gerry, 'I was an apprentice at the time but I was in the same team as Gerry. My digs along with another player, Roger Seyburn, were just round the corner so we would always be together. Unfortunately for the likes of me and Steve Ritchie who again was an apprentice we had to stay and do jobs round the ground like painting and clearing up whilst all the other first-year pros like Gerry would have free time in the afternoon. Gerry was a real man's man, he never threw his weight around but if he thought he was right about something he wouldn't let it go. I used to laugh when he was shouting and bawling about something as I couldn't understand a word he said and I used to ask Tom Ritchie for a translation but half the time he didn't know what he was on about either.'

In the early days of the youth team Sillett didn't give the players many afternoons off. When he did, they would be spent in various coffee shops in and around Bedminster or one of the numerous cafés in which Gerry would always order chips and beans without fail. The café would be the hub of everything for the young lads; it was where they talked about getting in the first team, about how they were doing and where the banter among them would invariably start. It also tested their competitive edge due to it having a pinball machine in the corner where everyone tried to get the highest score.

Gerry and some of his fellow Scots would sometimes visit and stay with Alan Dicks at his house in Bristol. It was all part of Alan's philosophy of looking after them. His wife would make them a meal so along with their landlady they could assure the parents they were cared for at the club. It was during one of these visits that BBC commentator and journalist Jonathan Pearce first met the man who would become his idol. Jonathan is a mad Bristol City fan who if he can gets a mention of the Robins into most of his commentaries. He also won *Celebrity Mastermind* with a specialist subject of Bristol City Football Club without getting a question wrong in the process. Jonathan had known Gerry for over 40 years and jumped at the chance to be involved in this book. He said, 'I loved the man, he was my mentor and my idol growing up in what were my formative years. I first met him when my family lived in the same road as Alan Dicks. I would be out playing football with Alan's son Patrick and Gerry who had just come down from Scotland used to have a kick about with us, He was about 17 and we were about eight. I remember him talking to me about tackling. He would say even at that young age, "When you make a tackle don't stand tall, make yourself like a boulder and you will be harder to knock off the ball." I was in awe of him right from then.'

As the years went on, Jonathan and his father would be very much involved in the club as Dicks asked them both to film games, so that the boss and the players could assess the team and pick out any improvement they could make to their play. It was revolutionary and City were the first team in Europe to do this. It also gave Jonathan incredible access to the club and Gerry.

In those initial years, the side were certainly put to the test by Sillett. Striker Keith Fear remembers how Sillett worked everyone hard, 'He got into all of us as he was desperate to get us into a team. He told me I had to run more and for Gerry, well his distribution early on was very inconsistent, so he would work with him over and over on winning the ball and then doing something with the ball. Gerry listened to him intently as we all did.'

Defender Dave Bruton remembers those long, intense chats, 'He used to say to us when you have the ball I want you to be arrogant confident, and the moment you lose it you need to be a dog of war to get it back. Always remember never to stand off a player by two yards as a decent player will murder you. He spoke so much sense that we were all captivated by him. I remember when our keeper Len Bond was out injured for a long time and we had no keeper cover so it was a stroke of genius in bringing Ray Cashley who was a full-back for us in the west of England into the squad as a keeper to deputise for Len. In the end Ray stayed our number one and was arguably City's greatest keeper. That was John people believed in him and we all did.'

As the season progressed and the young team invariably beat most of the sides put in from of them. Away from the pitch Gerry settled down to life in Bristol, visiting various local pubs and cinemas. Landlady Mrs McLeod always kept on at him to write home but Gerry's letters were only now and then, in fact Mrs McLeod wrote directly to his mother Helen regularly and they had become the best of friends. Gerry's mate Billy, though, was struggling with life away from Scotland. He and Gerry would go for walks on their days off up to the Ashton Court estate as it in some ways reminded Billy of the rolling hills of Scotland, but Gerry always mentioned that there were no rolling hills or deer in Drumchapel. Willie Gow remembers, 'There was always excitement in and around the house when we got a letter from Gerry telling us all about Bristol and how he was doing. Mum always said he never wrote enough letters but Dad's stock answer was if anything was wrong he would let us know.'

Back on the field the youth team were scheduled to play in two major tournaments during the summer. One was in Roubaix, France, and then would come a prestigious event called the Blauw Whit Tournament in Amsterdam, Netherlands. The Blauw Whit included the best teams throughout Europe at under-18 level and it really was a who's who of European football. It had been going since the 1950s and it was a real honour for teams just to be accepted into the tournament.

Although the lads were relatively new to each other they were forming into a tough unit and many personalities were starting to come through, particularly Gerry who had become the mouthpiece on the pitch and very much the centre of things in the dressing room. After a long chat with Dicks, Sillett brought in first team starlet Geoff Merrick to give the players a bit of experience. Merrick had just broken into the first team and at only 18 he was being groomed as a rising star within the club. Merrick remembers getting the call, 'I wasn't really that happy to be fair. I had just gone 18 and had already had a season in the first team where I was just establishing myself, so to go and play for the youth team appeared at the time as a bit of a step back. Looking back I can see why Sills wanted it as I was still eligible. I remember hitting it off with Gerry from the start; he was my type of player. Our friendship started from that tournament and I knew it wouldn't be long before he was in the first team.'

The City lads left Bristol (Lusgate) Airport and headed for Lille. It was a fantastic experience for them as it was the first time they had flown, although some of them couldn't wait for the flight to be over. On landing in Lille they travelled by car the 35 minutes to the town of Roubaix. They had a meeting and Sills laid down what was expected of them. He told them they were representing the club and he would have no messing about. They were then expected to join all the other teams in the main hall that evening for the opening meal in club blazer and tie. The other sides in the competition were hosts Racing Stade de Roubaix (France), IC Croix (France), Bradford City, Ajax of Amsterdam, Sporting Lisbon (Portugal), Entente Wattrelos (France), Marseille (France), and Grande Algiers (Algeria).

City hit the ground running and beat the hosts 4-0 with a hat-trick from Keith Fear and a goal from Tom Ritchie. After that they again impressed everyone the following day by beating Entre Wattrelos 3-0 with two goals from Fear and one from Billy Menmuir. City were now becoming the favourites to win the tournament and also were winning over the local press who were in awe of the side, as French journalist Phillipe Norie wrote in his paper *La Voix Du Nord*, 'An English team terribly impressive and possessing all the characteristics of a great team. The ease of the twin centre-forward play of Ritchie and Fear combined with the heart and determination of Gow in midfield mixed with an impeccable defence certainly make these players the favourites for the tournament.'

After the relative ease of the two opening fixtures, next up were Grande Algiers. Tom Ritchie remembers this game in particular, 'I remember lining up against this Algerian team and they were all about six foot plus with massive beards, they didn't look a day under 40. Anyway we were at a corner when all of a sudden this big fella headbutted me on the back of the head. I went down like a sack of shit in a complete daze. With that, apparently all hell broke loose and there was a mass brawl between us. As I came to, I remember seeing Sills run on to the pitch and grab the culprit who headbutted me around the throat he then proceeded to lift him off the ground shouting, "If you ever do that to one of my players I will kill you."

'As I lay there among all this, I remember seeing the Algerian supporters going crazy along the touchline as Gerry was chasing one of their players and every couple of steps he was kicking him up the arse. The game ended in a draw but we needed an escort back to the camp. We all laughed about it after the game although at the time we were terrified but we realised what a unit we were and Sills would always watch our backs.'

With the hostile match against the Algerians out of the way, City found themselves in the final against Bradford City. It was a tough affair and one that former Bradford player Bob Cullingford remembers to this day, 'It was my first proper tournament for Bradford, I was around 15 years of age and although I ended up a defender later in my career I was a midfielder. As a team we were very wary of Bristol City and in particular Gerry Gow. I remember him not giving us any time at all on the ball, he was literally everywhere and although I was young he seemed like a man even though he was only a couple of years older than me. His performance that day stuck with me and I followed his career keenly after that. We drew 0-0 and lost the game on penalties if I remember rightly.' Bradford did indeed loose the final 5-3 on penalties with Fear, Merrick, Cashley, Fry and Seyburn all scoring from the spot. City were presented with the cup and savoured every moment.

From Roubaix the youth team went on to the Blauw Whit where they faced Juventus (Italy), Athletic Bilbao (Spain), Aston Villa, Leicester City, Sheffield United and the hosts, Ajax. For Sills it was a exercise in team building and competition football, and after the result in France he knew he had something special. Again the teams were housed in dormitories on what was Ajax's training ground. Sills laid down the rules as before and the lads stuck to them. Experiences like this one demonstrated the respect the players had for their coach. Tom Ritchie explains, 'We never really had any discipline problems as we thought too much of Sills to step out of line. Yes, don't get me wrong, we mucked about and I remember Gerry taking the slats out of somebody's top bunk so they fell through the bed but there was no creeping out looking for girls or drinking. We just didn't want to let Sills down. Gerry was a nightmare though, always last to sleep and moving about late at night it was the same when I roomed with him later in our careers. Sills would have to shout out from the next room, "Gow, get to sleep."'

Once again City fought their way through the early rounds with some tough, battling performances. Keith Fear remembers how good Gerry was, 'I was scoring and getting a lot of attention yet Gerry battled us through, he was like Sills's voice on the pitch. He was relentless crossing every blade of grass, winning the ball and starting moves. I remember one game where one of the opposition was kicking lumps out of us and Gerry just came up to me and said, "Just leave the ball between me and him, I will do the rest." With that, I did what he asked and Gerry went in with a crunching tackle that only Gerry got up from. The lad played on but was as quiet as a mouse for the rest of the game.'

THE GERRY GOW STORY

I interviewed former Aston Villa man and Welsh international Barrie Hole for another project I was working on. We ended up talking about Gerry Gow and how Barrie first became aware of him. He said, 'I was a professional at Villa after signing from Cardiff City, in the summer I went with a few Villa coaches to a tournament in Amsterdam as I was keen on coaching. The tournament was for youth team players and I recall all of us being impressed by Gerry Gow. He was only a young lad but we told the boys to watch out for him as he was everywhere around the pitch. I think I played against him later in my career, he certainly was a tough, competitive player.'

Bristol City yet again enjoyed the rigours of tournament football and found themselves in the final against Ajax. It's a game Tom Richie remembers well, 'The crowd were incredible. There was around 10,000 in the Ajax stadium. We didn't play that well and found ourselves 2-0 down with about ten minutes left. Gerry kept pushing us as that was his nature, he never gave up and would have been shouting, "We can win this" even if we had been 10-0 down. We pulled one back with a goal from Keith Fear and with minutes left and some of the crowd leaving the ground I popped up and made it 2-2. That meant extra time and Sills told us they were finished, which proved right. Keith got another and we won 3-2. It was probably our best performance throughout the tournaments.'

The last night of the tournament saw the presentation. The teams all shuffled into the sports hall for the ceremony, all of them in their team blazers and ties. The City lads started to get some of the seats at the front of the stage, but they were quickly rebuked by Sills who told them to sit at the very back. Fear explains, 'I was puzzled as were the rest of the lads, after all we had won various trophies but Sills said, "No, you sit at the back and you savour that long walk up to the stage so everybody can see you." I have to admit we really did milk it and he was right we felt ten feet tall.'

When all the speeches had finished they gave out the various trophies, marking a fantastic night for Bristol City. They had the best defence, Keith Fear was the top scorer, and they had won the competition. Sillett beamed with pride and he also turned his thoughts towards the coming season.

After the relative success abroad, the club celebrated the youth team. The lads were pictured with chairman Harry Dolman in the boardroom. The group of young prospects coming through the ranks thrilled Dolman, particularly as he had invested £10,000 into the youth team. Manager Alan Dicks was equally thrilled as he could see some great opportunities for them; he was also overjoyed as all the hard work Tony Collins had put in was now bearing fruit. Dicks also invited the players to meet the first team which they did, the senior players shaking the youngsters' hands and telling them how well they had done. It certainly gave a boost to them showing what they could achieve.

The next couple of games were in the Southern Junior Floodlight Cup. The team had bonded and were doing well but Sills continued to push them, telling them that they had to forget about their success abroad now. The whole point for Sills was to turn these lads into future footballers who could walk into the first team and hold their own. It wasn't even really about getting results at times; it was about creating a physical and mental toughness. This was evident in one SJFC tie at Millwall, which Tom Ritchie looks back on, 'We went to The Den at Millwall and were drawing 1-1. It was a really hard match on an allotment of a pitch. Both sides had chances but for the main we were on top. Then with about five minutes to go Millwall scored to make it 2-1. It was a bitter defeat. I remember thinking Sills was going to let us have it after conceding late on. I remember as we walked off Gerry saying the same. We got into the changing room and Gerry said, "Here it comes," as Sills stormed in. He just said, "Get dressed and get on the coach." Gerry turned to me and said, "Oh well, we are going to get it on the coach then."

'All of us sheepishly got on the bus and hurriedly sat down. Sills got on and sat by the driver, he didn't say anything then about 15 minutes into the journey home he picked up the microphone at the front of the bus. We were all sinking into the seats when he said, "Well done tonight, you all gave everything for the shirt and if you give me that sort of effort this season we will win the FA Youth Cup." We were astonished yet felt ten feet tall; that was typical of Sills and it was the basis of that great Youth Cup run we had.'

Bristol City had enjoyed a relatively chequered history in the FA Youth Cup over the years prior to this group emerging. Their last real success was 1960 when they reached the semi-final before losing to Chelsea, although it was a good side that produced first team players such as Brian Clark, Jantzen Derrick, Terry Bush, and Adrian Williams. The new lads were desperate to do well and kicked off the campaign with a 1-0 victory away at Swindon Town. Their next opponents were Cardiff City, and yet again it was a game in which Gerry Gow left his mark on the opposition. Bluebirds legend Phil Dwyer explained when I interviewed him, 'Wow, Gerry Gow, now there's a player. My first introduction to him was a Youth Cup game at Ninian Park. We knew he was a good player and he had to be watched but I was really impressed with him. We had a corner and I came up for it. While we were waiting I said, "You're a Jock, aren't you?" He never replied, but as the ball broke I won it on the edge of the box and suddenly he came from nowhere and hit me right up in the air, winning the ball in the process. As I lay on the ground he said, "'Ave that, Taffy." We battled all game and as we drew 1-1 it was the same in the replay. He was tough but a really good footballer, he could chase 60 yards to win the ball and never gave up. We battled all our careers when we played against each other but I had real respect for him. I would have loved to play with him instead of against him.'

As City progressed in the competition, several of the players were drafted into the reserve side including Gerry, Keith Fear and Billy Menmuir. The reserves played in the Football Combination against tough opponents such as Arsenal, Spurs, Chelsea and Aston Villa. Not only were they playing against some talented youngsters, but they also faced pros who were maybe out of favour with the manager and had a point to prove or first team players coming back from injury. It was difficult but they knew they were close to getting the nod and joining the senior side. Menmuir got that chance first when he was called in to make his first team debut away in a 3-0 defeat to Huddersfield Town. Gerry was over the Moon for his mate but Billy, for all his talent, was still missing Scotland.

Team-mate Dave Bruton recalls, 'Out of all the lads I think everybody knew Billy would get his chance first. He was a tremendous footballer, really gifted, he could do stuff on the ball that we just couldn't; he was a very cultured player who could hit a pass 50, 60 yards to somebody's feet no problem. He worked so well with Gerry in midfield as Gerry would win it then give it to Billy. Trouble was Billy really missed Scotland and I think that hindered his development at City. Gerry just got on with things and had no real desire to go back to Scotland until he had made it. He talked for hours to Billy about it but I don't think the pain of leaving home left him, it certainly affected his career at the club.'

City gained momentum in the FA Youth Cup and after a 2-0 third round win against Plymouth Argyle and a 5-3 fourth round victory against Bournemouth they found themselves at home against Leeds United in the quarter-finals. Leeds were a massive club and over the years had produced some great homegrown players, so it would be a massive test for John Sillett's side. The supporters got behind the team and a crowd of just under 10,000 turned out to cheer on the future of Bristol City. Many of the first team sat in the stands along with Alan Dicks who ran a keen eye over the youngsters. The Leeds side were a strong one and included John Shaw in goal and Jimmy Mann in midfield, two players who would go on and have great careers with City years later. Sillett recalled Billy Menmuir from first team duty and he sat in midfield with Gerry.

The game was a tense affair as expected, and at half-time the score read 1-1 with City's goal coming from Tom Ritchie. In the end, City gradually got on top and got the winner through a bit of Keith Fear magic. It was a fantastic display and Sillett rewarded the team with a trip to the Bristol Bierkeller in the city centre. Ritchie recalls, 'It was bizarre really. Sills said, "You have played like men so let's drink like men." We all piled into the Bierkeller and some of us had never had a drink before in our lives. Gerry was right in amongst things, starting to sing some Scottish songs, as for me I could hardly lift the pint. We drank until it closed and loads of us were sick in the road outside. Sills was just laughing, telling us we could have the next day off.'

Goalkeeper Ray Cashley also remembers those trips to the Bierkeller, 'He was brilliant, John Sillett, he really treated us as men even though we were really young kids. We had a great young team and Gerry just drove us all the time on the pitch, he was like a bulldog, never giving up. When I look back, those nights out drinking certainly prepared us for life in the first team.'

The success of the youngsters went through the club, as first-teamer Gordon Parr also reflects, 'I remember the youth team doing well, we were really impressed with them and we made sure we told them when we saw them in and around the ground.'

Sillett was planning another trip the following day, taking the lads to watch the quarter-final between Stoke City and Spurs at the Victoria Ground. City knew one of these sides would be their opposition in the last four. Tom Ritchie recalls, 'We sat in the stand and knew one of the teams was going to be our semi-final opponents. Spurs had a really good side that contained Phillip Holder, John Oliver and Steve Perryman. I remember sitting there and watching one player absolutely run the show. I looked in the programme and saw his name was Graeme Souness, a Scottish lad from Edinburgh. I was surprised as I had never come across him in local football but he was fantastic as Spurs won 2-0. After the game we waited outside the ground for our coach. As we were waiting the Spurs lads came out and were hanging about for their coach. Everything was fine until Gerry started goading them with things like "Cockney wankers", "You got no chance against us". With that Souness came out of the staff door and went over to Gerry and said, "Well, I'm Scottish, and you, mate, are a Scottish wanker." Things erupted as we had to keep Gerry and Souness apart. We managed to get him on the coach but all the way home he never shut up about, as he put it, 'That Scottish Spurs wanker.'"

For Spurs, as Steve Perryman said when I interviewed him, it was pretty much the same, 'We spent the journey home calming Graeme down as he was shouting what he was going to do to that Bristol Scottish wanker'.

So the semi-final was set up nicely as Bristol City went to White Hart Lane for the first leg. City kept the same team that had beaten Leeds and Spurs were unchanged too. Perryman takes up the story, 'We knew Bristol City were dangerous, particularly Gerry Gow and Keith Fear. Gerry was going to attack every ball and he certainly was the driving force of the team. We felt if we could come away with a win we would be okay. Graeme had to have a talking to about keeping a clear head and it was difficult as Gerry and he clashed in the first five minutes. From that moment they just seemed to find each other all over the pitch.'

Spurs showed their class and went ahead after 15 minutes but City had a great chance to equalise through Fear, only for England youth goalkeeper Barry Daines to save his shot. Spurs went 2-0 up in the second half and City just had nothing left. As the teams left the field Gerry and Graeme Souness walked off chatting like old friends, as plainly there was a mutual respect for each other. The team were distraught but had high hopes for the second leg at Ashton Gate in a couple of weeks.

Another team bonding night at the Bristol Bierkeller was planned and it had the same effect with many of the youth team being sick in the street, but they were a group that would run through a brick wall for their mentor, Sillett. The second leg once again saw a good crowd of around 8,000 as the Bristol supporters came out to cheer on the boys. Spurs yet again turned on the class and although the game was tighter they eventually went home 1-0 winners and progressed 3-0 on aggregate.

Perryman was keen to be involved in this book when I contacted him and he recalled his early meeting with Gerry, 'Bristol City were a good side. I knew Dave Rodgers from England Schoolboys but I was really impressed with Gerry Gow. After the game in the dressing room we all commented on what a good player he was. Graeme said, "He never gave me a minute's peace, he's a tough bloke." That was praise indeed from Graeme as he never said much about the opposition. I think Gerry got under his skin a bit and Gerry wasn't afraid of anybody; you could see that in his play.'

Spurs went on to win the FA Youth Cup, beating Coventry after a replay. The Robins were on the floor, feeling they had let Sills down, but he gave a rousing speech about how proud he was of them and how they had become men before his eyes. For Gerry, it was a matter of weeks before he got the call to Sills's office for the 'chat' he had been waiting for.

4

Making Your Mark

IT WAS a lovely spring morning as the youth team finished their light training session at Greville Smyth's Park under the ever-watchful eye of John Sillett. As Sillett ran across the road to Ashton Gate he shouted. 'Gowy, see me in my office when you're washed and changed.' Gerry never thought much about it; it couldn't have been a bollocking as Sillett would probably have delivered it there and then.

When he was ready, Gerry made his way along the corridor to Sillett's office. He knocked on the door and Sillett's booming voice rang out, 'Enter.' As Gerry came in he noticed not only Sillett sat at his desk but manager Alan Dicks stood behind him. They told Gerry to sit down and asked how he thought he was doing. Gerry replied, 'Okay, I think,' to which Sillett responded, ' I think you're doing better than okay, lad.'

At that point Dicks took over the conversation, telling Gerry that he had some very favourable reports regarding his performances for the youth and reserve teams, and with that in mind he was promoting him to the first team. Alan explained that this was a momentous development for Gerry's career and he knew that the young Scot was ready, providing he kept up the good habits that had been nurtured in the youth team.

Alan told Gerry to get his stuff from the youth team dressing room and to take his place in the first team dressing room, also reminding him not to forget to knock on the door first. Alan's parting shot was to tell him that he was also in contention for the last game of the season, the following Saturday at Charlton Athletic. Alan shook Gerry's hand as he left. Sillett got up from his desk and told Gerry he deserved his chance, he shook his hand and told him to make his mark. Gerry thanked him then left to get his things.

As he arrived in the youth team dressing room, the lads were all changed but had all stayed on to see what the meeting was about. Deep down a few of them knew that he was moving across the corridor. Gerry told them and they all clapped him and shook his hand. There was the inevitable mickey-taking but to a man they were all pleased for him. He gathered his things and walked along the corridor to the big red door of the first team's dressing room.

Striker Keith Fear remembers going through the same experience, 'I was about six months behind Gerry in terms of getting to the first team dressing room. It really was the greatest moment in my career as it was the one thing you had been working towards. It gives me goosebumps when I think about it today. The feeling that the coaching staff and the manager had such faith in you made you feel ten feet tall, you knew you had a lot of work to do but all you thought about was, "I'm on my way."'

Gerry knocked on the door and defender Gordon Parr opened it. 'A new recruit,' he shouted out to the rest of the players. Gordon welcomed Gerry in and the place was chaotic with players smoking and in different stages of undress. Some were still in the bath singing and some were reading the morning papers. Through the cigarette smoke and the noise, Gerry found himself a spot on the wooden bench that ran around three-quarters of the room. Parr told him where to put his stuff and one by one the first-teamers introduced themselves. There were some big characters in the dressing room at that time such as Bobby Kellard, John Galley, Mike Gibson, Jack Connor Ken Wimshurst, and Alan Skirton. Parr remembers, 'Yes, I remember Gerry coming into the dressing room for the first time. We all knew about him as some of us had played with him at reserve team level. We knew he was a talent. We gave him a bit of stick about being Scottish but he gave us some back which meant he would fit in perfect. Some of the younger lads crowded round him like Geoff Merrick, Chris Garland and Billy Menmuir, they showed him the ropes.'

Midfielder Trevor Tainton also recalls that meeting, 'I had played with Gerry in the reserves and knew how good he was, he fitted in really well, no airs and graces; he was a tough lad who you knew would go far in the game. I was delighted to see him make the first team squad as most of us were. I remember him going out of the dressing room to get something and all of us talking about what a great prospect he was.'

Before Gerry left to go back to his digs he rang his dad back in Scotland to tell him the good news. Jimmy was overjoyed, as were all of the Gow family, and they waited desperately for confirmation of his debut. That came from Gerry a few days later so Jimmy told Gerry he was off to the pub to tell his mates. Gerry's brother Willie reflects, 'I remember the call and dad was over the Moon. After he filled us in on the details he was off down the pub to celebrate. I think it was recognition of him making sure Gerry picked the right club, which he certainly did.'

The big day arrived: Saturday, 14 April 1970 with Gerry, a month from his 18th birthday, lining up for his first-team debut. The team sheet that day read Gibson, Jacobs, Drysdale, Gow, Rooks (captain), Parr, Tainton, Garland, Bush, Kellard, Sharpe. As the players sat in the away dressing room, Dicks gave his team talk, pointing out to Gerry that his role was pretty much the same as with the youth team and reserves: sit in midfield, win the ball and play it. He also said that although City were in mid-table Charlton were at the bottom end and therefore fighting for their life. A small note was left for Gerry on his peg in the dressing room. He opened it and it simply read, 'Good luck Gerry, all the best Tony Collins.'

Bristol City's legendary goalkeeper Mike Gibson looks back on Gerry's debut, 'We just wished everyone well before we went out, we didn't make too much of Gerry's debut as we just wanted to leave him to it although he never seemed nervous, he just wanted to get out there. I do remember within five minutes of the game starting he went into a tackle with Charlton player Graham Moore who had been about a bit in the game and could look after himself. Gerry went right through him along with the ball and a few of us raised an eyebrow. I remember saying to Gordon Parr, "Christ, this kid's fearless." He never looked like a debutant; he was full of confidence.'

The game ended with a 2-1 defeat for City, Chris Garland getting the consolation goal late on following a Bobby Kellard free kick. Parr remembers the dressing room after the final whistle, 'Gerry was phenomenal on his debut, he was raw but he had something about him that to be fair made us all take notice. We had seen some lads come in for their debut then get taken out of the side as a way of letting them in slowly, but not this kid. I couldn't see him being left out of the side on this showing, he had a maturity beyond his years and seemed fearless. I always thought that you really had to make your mark on your debut and he certainly did that.'

As the season started to come to an end, all eyes turned to the Gloucester Cup Final against Bristol Rovers. The cup had become a traditional match between the two teams from Bristol but its origins dated back to 1887 when it was originally a knockout tournament, although that changed in 1900 when it was decided the game was to be played between City and Rovers only. The end-of-season showpiece was popular with the fans and although Gerry had faced Rovers in the reserves a few times, this was for a trophy and being the competitor he was he was going to continue his great start at City. Some 12,000 fans came to Ashton Gate to watch the red half of Bristol defeat the blue half 2-1 with two Kellard goals. Another confident display in midfield by Gerry was witnessed by Rovers' legendary winger Harold Jarman. He says, 'He was a lad beyond his years; his timing in the tackle was second to none. He didn't have that distribution to his game that he had later in his City career, but the strength in the tackle was right there even at 18. A few of us remarked after the game that the lad was a bit special.'

The season didn't come to an end until May when City played a friendly at Ashton Gate against Italian giants Juventus. Juventus were full of internationals such as Roberto Bettega,

MAKING YOUR MARK

Francesco Morini and Fabio Capello. They were touring the UK after the end of the Italian season. It was a real test for young Gerry but to his credit, despite the occasional tug of the shirt and deliberate standing on his boots, he came through it like most of the City team. However, he did realise that the Europeans appeared to have a very low pain threshold when it came to getting tackled. City won the game 2-1 with goals from Gordon Parr and Alan Skirton as 7,000 spectators looked on.

A few days after the Juventus win the first team went off for their various family holidays as City had no end-of-season tour planned. Gerry had a meeting with Alan Dicks and Harry Dolman to secure a three-year contract, which he was eager to sign. There were no agents involved and Dolman told Gerry what he thought he was worth. The extra money along with the security the contract gave Gerry was brilliant, although he felt for his friend Billy Menmuir who was only offered another year.

Excited by the news, the pair made their arrangements to go back to Scotland for a week. Landlady Mrs McLeod packed them some food for the long journey home. They got on the train ready for the long journey back to Glasgow and Mrs McLeod contacted the families to let them know they had left safely. Their fellow youth team players Tom and Steve Ritchie had no reason to head back to Scotland as their family had made the incredible sacrifice of moving down to Bristol to help the boys further their career. The train pulled into Glasgow station late into the night and Gerry was met by his dad Jimmy and brother Willie; Billy Menmuir was met by his family also. The two groups chatted with the lads but the Gows headed for Drumchapel and the Menmuirs headed for the Sandyhills area of the city. Willie was overjoyed to see him,

'It was great to see him, he looked fit and strong and I couldn't stop asking him questions about his life in Bristol. He spent a great week with us, he visited family and went to the pub with dad, everybody around was eager to hear of how things were going. But typically of Gerry he just played things down, he wasn't a big head or anything like that. I just thought he was glad to be home for a bit, among friends and family.'

As the new season approached, things were happening off the field at Ashton Gate. City had finished the campaign in 14th, which was okay. Harry Dolman was finishing the completion of the new stand that replaced the Cow Shed. It would have 8,000 seats and would be state-of-the-art in terms of its design and facilities ... The Dolman Stand, as it was to be called, had an initial cost of £50,000 but over the years it had spiralled to £235,000. Dolman and the club had fought tooth and nail to bring the structure to the club, fighting off the local councillors and residents who were very much against it. He generated money from various channels such as loans, advertisements for the stand, selling some of the club houses dotted around the area, and supporters' club donations. Running alongside this was the news that City's star midfielder Bobby Kellard had asked for a transfer before the season ended. Kellard got his wish and was sold to Leicester City for £50,000. What worried the supporters was not only where the money was going but who would replace him. For manager Dicks, there was going to be only one man: Gerry Gow. The faith Dicks was showing was incredible and good though he was Gerry was not the finished article, particularly when compared to Kellard. The decision sparked many letters to the *Bristol Evening Post* newspaper, including:

Dear Sirs

I find it incredible that it seems the money raised from the Bobby Kellard sale will no doubt end up paying for our new stand. This seems more and more likely when manager Alan Dicks claims that he will use the young inexperienced Gerry Gow as a replacement for Kellard. What we need is an experienced midfielder who will cope with the rough and tumble of the Second Division.

Yours truly,
Brian Simonds
Knowle

Dear Sirs

I cannot believe Bristol City are reluctant to sign anybody as replacement for the talented Bobby Kellard. The youngster Gerry Gow is not the answer and this decision by Alan Dicks shows how naive he is when it comes to football management. Bristol City needs experience in the middle of the park or they will have a tough season.

Yours
Peter Gain
Patchway

The excellent book by Martin Powell and Clive Burlton, entitled *Harry Dolman: The Millionaire Inventor who became Mr Bristol City*, contains a comment piece from the *Evening Post*. It reads, 'Our view is that Bristol City must give serious consideration to buying a new player if they make a bad start to the season. The Bobby Kellard transfer to Leicester City has left a gap that we hope Gerry Gow will plug. But if he doesn't after being given a reasonable run, the club must find money from somewhere to bolster the team.

'It has become increasingly obvious that money is in short supply at Ashton Gate. The Dolman Stand project has fully extended the club's finances and it is clear that the £50,000 from the Kellard sale is going into bricks and mortar and not into team strengthening. There is no doubt that the stand is going to be a magnificent asset to the club. But should it take priority over the team? This is an important question the directors must now ask themselves. For the best appointed ground in the Third Division would be a tragedy for Bristol and the thousands of Bristol City supporters who have tolerated the club's Second Division struggle for four seasons.

'We hope any misgivings about this season's playing standards at Ashton Gate will be unfounded. There is nothing we would like to see more than two promotion-challenging teams in Bristol this season. But if City fail to get the winning start they urgently require the directors must get the message early enough to remedy the situation. And in our view that would mean making money available to Alan Dicks for at least one new player.'

The comments were plainly going to put pressure on Dicks and his backroom staff and it was clear that the faith he had in Gerry was going to be tested. Dicks was aware that Gerry was going to be compared to Kellard but again he believed in the youngster. He and Tony Collins knew that he was capable and they saw the maturity he had in his game right from their first meeting back in Scotland. Alan recalled, 'I had complete faith in Gerry and I think he knew it. I wanted to give him a long run in the side and I knew it was a gamble as if a youngster makes a few mistakes you have to be careful with them, but Gerry just got better and better, he repaid my faith in him over and over.'

The first team reported back for training in early July. Gerry was raring to go and while he had a great time home in Scotland, he realised that his future lay in Bristol. For Billy Menmuir, the break seemed to have done him no good in terms of homesickness as the longer he stayed in Glasgow the more he wanted to go back. Gerry encouraged him to take his chance at Bristol City, telling him that everybody thought he was the one bright prospect and that the following season could be his golden opportunity. Billy agreed but deep down Gerry knew he was struggling.

When the team arrived on the first day they were all weighed to make sure they had not overindulged during the summer break. Although Gerry had loved his mum's home cooking along with a few pints with his dad, he still was around ten stones wringing wet. After the typical banter at certain players who had put on a few pounds, John Sillett was let loose on the team for a few days and that meant running and more running before they flew out to Holland for a pre-season tour, playing a few Dutch teams along with First Division West Ham United. Midfielder Trevor Tainton remembered the tour and in particular Gerry, 'Pre-season tours are great at bringing people together, that's why the youth team go on them for tournaments. They become bonding exercises. It can be difficult when you're new to the first team but I remember Gerry just keeping his head down and joining in when he was asked. He was a lot quieter then compared to the tours I went on with him later in his career.'

The trip was a success as City beat Holstein Kiel 2-0 with goals from rising star Chris Garland. They then drew 1-1 with Go Ahead Deventer, Gerry Sharp getting the equaliser. A 2-1 win over Veendam came next as Garland and Trevor Tainton got on the score sheet. Garland again got the winner against a strong West Ham team and City finished with a 2-0 win over Go Ahead, Garland scoring both goals.

City embarked on the new season with optimism although there were sections of the supporters and media that thought it would be a struggle. The club opened their Second Division account at home to Sunderland, who had been relegated from the First Division the previous season and were tipped to come straight back. Gerry retained his role in midfield and lined up alongside a strong City team of Gibson, Jacobs, Drysdale, Wimshurst, Rooks, Parr, Skirton, Garland, Galley, and Sharpe. It was a great chance for Gerry to show the home crowd what he could do. He knew the supporters were not convinced he was the man to fill Bobby Kellard's boots, but the most important thing to him was that Alan Dicks thought he was, and that's all that mattered to him.

Around 18,000 fans poured into Ashton Gate. The new Dolman Stand was open but it was restricted to about 2,500 spectators. The stand certainly looked impressive, and it was typical of Sillett when he told the team he couldn't wait to get them running up and down it. The Sunderland game was a pulsating start to the season as City won a tough, battling encounter 4-3. Although the side had conceded three goals, Dicks and the fans were happy with a win on the first day. Gerry came in for special praise from *Evening Post* sports writer Peter Godsiff, who said in the local paper, 'The young Gow

MAKING YOUR MARK

gave a mature performance in midfield. He may not have the distribution of the now departed Kellard but you cannot fault his desire to win.' Gerry was pleased but he knew he was only as good as his last game.

It was a decent start for the Robins in the league as they drew 1-1 at Charlton Athletic then beat Cardiff 1-0 at home. Unfortunately pressure built on Dicks after a 4-0 defeat away at Leicester City, particularly as it was Bobby Kellard who scored one of the Foxes' goals. Gordon Parr remembers the occasion, 'Yeah, they outplayed us. I remember we had a goal disallowed from Alan Skirton and Dickie Rooks gave away a penalty. Gerry had a tough old battle in midfield if I'm honest but I remember Bobby Kellard chatting to him as we came off and Bobby came in the changing room after and shook our hands.'

As September arrived, it brought with it a 3-3 draw away at Sheffield United. The fixture was end-to-end but it marked Gerry's first league goal for the club, a shot from outside the box. It was a game City should have sewn up after being 3-0 up with 30 minutes to go. On the pitch it seemed the young Scot had won the majority of the Ashton Gate faithful round with his hard-working displays in midfield, judging by the reaction Gerry was getting on the terraces. Off the pitch, Dicks, under pressure and with no money to spend, decided to bring in some of the youth team players into the first team squad. After one win in seven games Dicks decided to throw Keith Fear in for his debut in a 1-0 away defeat against Middleborough. Weeks later, David Rodgers got his chance in a 2-1 away defeat at local rivals Swindon Town.

With league form looking sketchy at best, the club were at least progressing well in the recently formed League Cup.

Wins against Rotherham United, Blackpool and Leicester City found the Robins in the quarter-finals where they would face Fulham away. Going into the game City had found a bit of form with a decent 3-0 victory over Watford. The quarter-final was a tough affair, and Gerry missed it due to a knock on the ankle in a previous game. Both clubs gave nothing away and it ended 0-0, so a replay at Ashton Gate was arranged with the winner taking on Spurs in the semi-final. A bumper crowd of 23,000 crammed into Ashton Gate as Gerry returned to the side. There was a good indication of how he was starting to be viewed by the Bristol public as a huge cheer went up when his name was read out on the PA system. City certainly rode their luck throughout the game and got the break when Alan Skirton was brought down in the area. Gerry Sharpe took the penalty and put City on the road to the last four.

Goalkeeper Mike Gibson remembers the scenes after, 'We were overjoyed to get to a semi-final and the chance of getting to Wembley. I remember we all went out for a drink, Gerry included, at the Town's Talk just outside Bristol. It was a bar/nightclub and it was a place a lot of us used to go. I was married at the time so I and a few of the older lads went home before Gerry and the younger lads, they certainly seemed to have had a good night judging by the look of them the next day in training. The incredible thing about Gerry though was that he was first out on the training pitch and ran and ran. He may have had a drink but you would never have known.'

With advice from John Sillett, another youngster was brought into the first team squad. Ray Cashley was the full-back turned goalkeeper who was given his debut in the 1-0 defeat against Southampton in the FA Cup as Dicks was looking at a long-term replacement for the evergreen Gibson. Gerry could slowly see Dicks and his backroom staff introducing small adjustments and making plans for the future of the side with youth team players being introduced one by one. Dicks did it without breaking the team spirit he was building and as Gerry slowly moved up in the pecking order he got more and more excited by the future.

There was a full house of 30,000 at Ashton Gate as First Division giants Spurs rolled into Bristol for the semi-final, full of internationals. Their team sheet contained Jennings, Mullery, Chivers, Kinnear, Peters, Gilzean, and Steve Perryman. Steve recalls meeting Gerry Gow again, 'We had a decent side, who could look after themselves, Joe Kinnear, Cyril Knowles and Alan Mullery for example. Although Gerry was a youngster in the Bristol City side our manager Bill Nicholson told us to get the ball around quickly as the youngster Gow would be on us from the start. You could tell Gerry did not care about reputations as within minutes of the start he went into a thundering tackle with Joe Kinnear, won the ball then nutmegged former England international Alan Mullery. He was a real competitor and he had lost none of that drive that he had as a youngster in the youth team. I did notice his passing and distribution had come on leaps and bounds. We spoke at the end of the game and that was Gerry he would compete with you for 90 minutes then when it was over it was over.'

BBC commentator and City fan Jonathan Pearce also looks back on the night, 'I was in the tunnel before the game and I remember looking at the Spurs players, most of whom I had been brought up watching on the TV. Gilzean, Peters, Chivers – they looked like gods in their pristine white shirts. They were all focused as they came out and then Gerry walked past and ruffled my hair and said, "Hello". I remember thinking, "He's just as good as these."'

City took the lead through Alan Skirton but were pulled back by an Alan Gilzean goal to end the first leg 1-1. For the second leg at White Hart Lane, Dicks dropped a bombshell by leaving out the out-of-form John Galley and giving his place to young professional Peter Spiring. Thousands made the trip up from Bristol for the midweek game but as City battled they were undone by two Martin Chivers goal in extra time. A despondent side returned home but the local media and supporters treated them as heroes for getting that far and taking the star-studded Spurs team to extra time.

As the New Year kicked in, Gerry was reminded of how fragile a footballer's career could be. City entertained Middlesbrough on a cold January afternoon. In the second half, with City 2-0 up, Dicks substituted winger Jantzen Derrick, leading to chants of 'Dicks must go' from sections of the fans. Despite the cup run the supporters were feeling frustrated at the poor league form. With the clock ticking and Gerry already having a goal ruled out for offside, the Middlesbrough defender Eric McMordie launched into a savage tackle on City player Gerry Sharpe. The challenge broke Sharpe's leg and many who were standing in the East End behind the goal still talk of hearing the crack. Gerry launched himself after McMordie but was pulled away by defender Gordon Parr, who takes up the story, 'We all remember the day Gerry [Sharpe] got his leg broke. McMordie was a nasty player who liked to leave his foot in. I remember young Gerry Gow going after him but I pulled him back as I didn't want him to get sent off. He got on well with Sharpy and he was really upset by it. Gerry never played for City again; it finished his career. The rumour was that after the game even the Boro players wouldn't speak to McMordie as it was such a terrible challenge.'

The whole business put a downer on the club as the 25-year-old Sharpe was playing exceptionally well and also looked to be going on to bigger and better things in his career. Dicks recalls the whole sorry event, 'Sharpy was in the form of his life and I remember West Ham boss Ron Greenwood, who was also doing some scouting work for England, coming to watch a game at Ashton Gate. "Everyone thinks I'm here to see Chris Garland," he told me, "but it's Gerry Sharpe I'm really here to see." I remember when they brought Sharpy into the physio's room, me and Les Bardsley locked the door as we didn't want the lads to come in and see it. The bone was sticking out of the back of his calf. We had to wait for the ambulance and I was told that when he eventually got to hospital he wasn't operated on until 11pm that night. The morning after, we had a board meeting and I told the board that we must have a surgeon or doctor in the ground behind the scenes for every game. They agreed and we continued to do that as a result of Gerry's injury.'

Dicks really had to stop the rot that had set in. Towards the end of the season he replaced fans' favourite Mike Gibson in goal with Ray Cashley. It was a bold move as Gibson had been at the club since 1962. City's fortunes fluctuated and although they were winless in their final five games, they managed to stay up by finishing fourth from bottom. There were rumours of Harry Dolman getting ready to sack Dicks but although Dolman was unhappy with the league position and demanded an improvement the following season, it seemed the League Cup run had secured the manager's future for the time being.

Gerry had been an ever-present in the side, mainly in midfield and occasionally at inside-right, and had scored five goals in what was his first senior season. He had certainly made his mark.

5

Julie

SEVENTEEN-YEAR-OLD JULIE Yea was from the Hartcliffe district of Bristol, an area where there was only one club you could support – Bristol City. Julie's family were no different, with her father, mother and grandfather all season ticket-holders. The whole family would spend every other Saturday at Ashton Gate during the football season cheering on the Robins.

Julie's aspirations were certainly not to be a footballer's wife at that young age. She had started training for a career as a nursery nurse and that was her focus, although at weekends the lure of Bristol's nightlife in 1969 was always a draw for any attractive 17-year-old. A favourite haunt of Julie and her friends was The Way Inn, a bar next to The Royal Hotel on College Green in the city centre, and she also regularly frequented The Heartbeat Club which was housed in the Mecca Entertainment building. There, Julie would see the odd Bristol City player as they danced away to the songs of the time such as 'Sugar, Sugar' by The Archies, 'Honky Tonk Woman' by the Rolling Stones or 'The Israelites' by Desmond Dekker and The Aces. And it was through this smoke-filled haze that she set her eyes on a young footballer from the Drumchapel area of Glasgow.

Today, Julie is incredibly nostalgic about those times and speaks with such love and affection about Gerry and the life they had together, 'I used to go to The Way, well having said that everybody went to The Way at that time. I would also go to The Heartbeat Club which was in Frogmore Street and it was there that I first saw Gerry. I used to see a few of the City players out and about and as my family were big fans I would nod and say hello to them, they were a great bunch.

'On this one night I first saw Gerry, he was with Billy Menmuir and I think the Ritchie brothers as well as a few others. We got chatting and hit it off; he bought me a drink and we had a dance and that was it. We were both kids really as Gerry was the same age, there was no egos about any of them like there would be today. After all, if you were looking for somebody with good prospects to be your boyfriend you would be better picking a plumber or engineer than a footballer – how times have changed.

'My mates and I would meet up regularly with them and we became a bit of a group really, going from the Way Inn and then into the Heartbeat. I look back on it now with such affection. When we became serious as a couple, my family, particularly my dad, who was overjoyed that I was seeing a City player. When Gerry would come to the house, dad used to hog him a bit asking him all sorts of questions like, "Who's playing Saturday?" "How was training?" Gerry was great with him though, he thought a lot of my dad.'

After the pair had dated for a couple of weeks, Gerry popped the question and they were married at Holy Cross Church at

Bedminster in 1970. Gerry was a Catholic and followed his religion up to a point until football got in the way, but his mum was very religious, hence the choice of venue. The wedding was a small affair along with the party afterwards. Billy Menmuir was Gerry's best man, while Alan Dicks and his wife were in attendance along with various City players and staff from the club. The Gow family came down from Scotland and mixed with the Yeas as the party went into full swing.

Bristol City gave the young couple a gift of £500, which was an incredible gesture and showed the high regard in which they held Gerry at the time. They were probably very keen to see their rising young star settle down. The money was put towards a house the couple had their eye on in the Whitchurch area of the city, where a lot of the players lived. It was a three-bedroomed link detached property costing £4,700. The couple also purchased a car for Julie, as Gerry didn't drive.

Julie remembers the time with affection, 'I was 18 years of age and was pregnant with our first child, Chris. Here I was, I had my own house and my own car, a green Triumph Toledo as I remember, thoughts of a career as a nursery nurse soon went out of the window. I loved the freedom of driving and although we were certainly no Posh and Becks, among my friends we were doing okay. When Chris was born we were both overjoyed. It was everything to Gerry being a dad, he doted on Chris as he did with Rachael and Jen, our two daughters, when they came along a few years later. It was so far removed from his image on the pitch as a "wild man" or the image the fans had of him, they never saw him when he was at home doing the nightly feeds or getting up in the middle of the night to change a nappy. He loved the kids and they were, as I said, everything to him.'

Being a Bristol City player's wife then was far removed from the WAGs of today's football. Much like the players themselves, the wives were a tight-knit bunch who would not only spend their time looking after the children but also doing pottery classes and keep-fit classes organised by the other spouses.

Julie explains, 'We were a close bunch like the players and as couples we all socialised. I relied a lot on the other wives and I had a great relationship with the likes of Lyn Fear [Keith's wife] and Mary Jacobs [Trevor's wife]. I remember when Trevor left to go to Rovers, Mary was distraught. I think she thought we wouldn't be friends anymore which couldn't have been further from the truth, in fact we are still as close today. The wives and my parents were particularly helpful in terms of the children and general support when the lads were away on a tour which always seemed to be pre-season, mid-season and end of season. As a family we would spend our holidays visiting Gerry's family up in Scotland, or we would try and get a holiday abroad now and then. We did buy a place in Spain, but I don't think we used it much. My mum and dad loved it though; they went at least twice a year.'

Julie would go to most home games with her mum and dad and as he got older young Chris would join them. I asked Julie what Gerry was like after games and she explained that once they were gone they were gone and he was like that throughout his career, 'Gerry never ever seemed to dwell on a result, even if he had a bad game the match was gone. He was obviously annoyed when the team lost or he was injured but he never dwelt on anything. If people stopped him in the street or spoke to him in his local about a bad result he would just say, "That's gone now, on to the next" and even when he was injured, he

JULIE

hated it not being able to play but he somehow knew he would get back to playing at some point.'

Bristol City's promotion in 1976 was not only a special time for the club, but it was also a special time for the Gows as daughter Rachael was born. Again, as he had done with Chris, Gerry was the doting father eager to attend to all the newborn's needs and help Julie in any way possible.

Although the family were well known around the Whitchurch area they moved to the Hanham district of the city, which was predominantly Bristol Rovers territory. The four-bedroomed mock Tudor house was somewhat bigger than the one they left in Whitchurch and the Gows became neighbours with one of Gerry's biggest opponents, Bristol Rovers full-back Phil Bater. Phil had a well-cultivated reputation as a player who took no prisoners in the heart of the Rovers defence and he and Gerry had many a bruise and scrape from playing each other over the years.

Phil remembers Gerry both on and off the field, 'God I hated Gowy on the pitch. We had many a battle, he was a tough lad but honest. There were many players around then that would leave a foot in or try to injure you but Gowy was an honest player, he was whole-hearted and what you saw was what you got. The game was like that then; you had to stand your ground and not be bullied out of your position by your opponent and that never happened to Gerry.

'We had some great battles against City. He was instrumental in that City side and I rated him up there with [Colin] Bell, [Graeme] Souness and [Billy] Bremner. He was a box-to-box player who could score goals, and I suppose the equivalent in today's game would have been [Steven] Gerrard or [Frank] Lampard.

THE GERRY GOW STORY

'There was an extra spice in the Bristol derby games as we would have four or five Welsh lads and they had four or five Scots lads so it was like Wales v Scotland. Gerry was a few years younger than me so I didn't really know him. He was around the same age as Lindsay Parsons who for me was the real "hard man" in our side. I know people talk about Frankie Prince but Lindsay was a good player and loved a good battle. When he tussled with Gerry as they often did, it was something special; they went at it hammer and tongs and the crowd were on their feet in appreciation, Like the good pros they were, they shook hands after.

'Gerry was in the midfield and that really suited him as he could have two or three tackles one after another where for me at full-back all I really had to bother with was sorting out the winger.

'When Gerry moved into our road I was a bit shocked as it was the wrong side of town, to be honest, for him. Initially we just gave a nod of the head to acknowledge each other and I think I first got chatting to him at a party at a neighbour's house. I couldn't believe how soft-spoken he was. I think like a lot of people he would have had a loud Glasweigian accent but he was totally different off the field. He was fantastic and a great bloke to be around; we were neighbours and he Julie and the kids were great company. I have to say they were a really glamorous couple as well but really down to earth, everybody liked them.

'We used to go for a drink together in the Elm Tree pub, where they served his favourite tipple of Blue Harp lager. You would see fans looking at us really puzzled thinking, "How can they be mates?" I think Julie was happy they moved from

Whitchurch as he got up to all sorts with the City lads who lived near but me and him would regularly go for a pint and find ourselves in trouble with the wives. The press also loved the fact that these two so-called rivals lived in the same road. They even had us playing head tennis for a photo-shoot over my neighbour's fence which implied we lived next door to each other which we didn't; in reality I was round the corner.

'I really miss him. He was a great bloke, and I'm honoured to contribute to this book.'

The relationship between the two players sometimes could get them into trouble and that certainly was the case when son Chris asked Gerry and Julie if he could go training with Phil. Julie takes up the story, 'Chris asked and it was okay with us and with Phil. I think Chris must have been about eight or nine so off he went to the Rovers training ground with Phil. Unbeknown to Phil and obviously us there was a photographer from the *Bristol Evening Post* who recognised Chris and took some pictures of him with the Rovers players. The upshot was that in the paper the following day was a picture of young Chris with the Rovers lads and a headline of "SPY IN THE CAMP". Now this could have been laughed off but Rovers' next game was against City, so although he was only young it did look like Chris was on a scouting mission. Gerry took the mick out of Phil, but I think Phil was more embarrassed about the whole thing to be honest.'

Another neighbor who was shocked to see Gerry move in was Colin Rapesey, or Freddie as everyone knew him. Colin worked for Imperial Tobacco and was a die-hard Rovers fan. He remembers the day as if it were yesterday, 'They built some nice houses at the edge of our cul-de-sac in Hanham and I remember looking out the window as a green Triumph Toledo parked outside the house. I called to my wife that the new neighbours were moving into the house, then out of the passenger side of the car stepped Gerry bloody Gow. I couldn't believe it, Gerry Gow moving into my road, and here I was, a massive Gas Head. Anyway a few days later we got chatting and he was such a great bloke, not at all as I imagined him to be. I thought he was a bit of a wild man and yes, he loved a drink, didn't we all, but he was a real family man. I remember walking up the street at about 3am on the morning my daughter was born, Gerry called out of his window and asked what we had had and I shouted up to him, "It's a girl." He shouted back that we would go out that night and wet the baby's head. A neighbour owned a club in Colston Street called Chicago's so me, Gerry and Phil Bater went and what a fantastic night it was. I have no recollection of coming home but he was such a fun guy.

'I also remember him in the summer cutting his grass or going for a run. He would be tanned without a bit of fat on him just in his shorts with his wild hair and moustache, he looked like a god and all the women in the road liked to have a quick peak out of the curtains when he was about. I really can't speak highly enough of him. I knew Gerry the man, not necessarily Gerry the footballer, and he was a joy to be with.'

The Gows' time at Bristol will always be precious to Julie and the family, and some would say it was where Gerry played his best football, He came through the ranks as a youngster and held his own in the English top flight, but all good things must come to an end and for Julie and the kids there was a move on the horizon. Julie explains, 'I don't really know how the move

JULIE

to Manchester City came about but I know Gerry wasn't happy towards the end of his time at Ashton Gate. It was a big move for us and I was happy to follow Gerry wherever he wanted to go. Again the wives of other players were so important in us settling in and making us feel at home. We bought a show house on an estate in Wilmslow, not straight away; we stayed in Bristol and Gerry was commuting up to Manchester for a bit on the train. When we did move, Tommy Hutchinson, Bobby MacDonald and Kevin Bond were all neighbours and this really helped us fit in.

'Chris became an instant Manchester City fan, he loved his dad playing for them. The club looked after all the players really well. I remember when they got to the Cup Final all the wives and families went down to London a few days after the players in a luxury coach with free drinks etc., and after the game they laid on a massive banquet for the players and the wives; we even went to Stringfellows which was *the* club at the time. It really was a different world, but Gerry just wanted to get home if I'm honest. It broke my heart to see him lose the final as he was really convinced they could win it. They were also such a great set of lads and the fans were incredible towards Gerry right from his first game at the club. But Gerry was getting trouble from his knees and he became a bit disillusioned that he couldn't train as hard as he used to. I used to tell him the cigarettes didn't help but he just laughed it off.

'The cigarette thing was odd as I smoked and Gerry never did until once he came home from a tour of Spain with Bristol City and he was smoking, like a lot of the side did back then. After his spell at Manchester City he went to Rotherham United. We didn't move as there was no need to. Chris was distraught at this news and I remember when Rotherham manager Emlyn Hughes came round to see us Chris stormed out of the house. He also wore his Manchester City scarf to Gerry's debut as a mark of defiance.'

It was clear to see that Rotherham United and subsequently Burnley later were never going to be the finest parts of Gerry's career as by his own admission he was experiencing pain after and sometimes during games and as he was getting older he started to slow down. His reading of the game was second to none but losing that pace was never going to make playing easy for him.

Julie remembers those last couple of years of his career, 'It was difficult for Gerry. He was still a great dad to our three children as we now had Jan but I think he knew that he was at a crossroads in what he was going to do. If I'm honest, I think we started to drift apart which was sad. He took the player-manager's job down at Yeovil Town and as with all manager's jobs particularly at lower league, it was full-on 24 hours a day, seven days a week with hardly any money to spend.

'After Yeovil we moved down to Portland which is a lovely part of the world so he could become manager at Weymouth. Again it was full-on and we by this time had drifted apart, and some time after his sacking at Weymouth we decided to separate. It was very hard for all concerned. There was nobody else involved; we were just kids when we met and these things happen. He continued to be a wonderful dad and grandfather to his children and grandchildren and continued to be a great friend to me.

'When I had cancer a few years back, Gerry was the first person who phoned me to ask how I was. That was him, and

JULIE

when I found out he was ill it hit me like a hammer. When he died the whole family were heartbroken; he was a massive part of our lives and always will be. We were together for around 22 years and I still miss him.

'Today I am Julie Higgins and I live just outside Weymouth and I have been with my husband Peter for nearly 30 years. Peter himself was a player at Bristol Rovers, Torquay United and Doncaster Rovers. He and Gerry were great pals later in Gerry's life and that meant a lot to me and to Peter. Gerry really was a remarkable man.'

6

Comings And Goings

AS BRISTOL City arrived for the start of the 1971/72 campaign the dressing room was starting to take on a much younger feel. Defender Jack Connor had left at the end of the previous season after amassing over 400 games. Goalkeeper Mike Gibson had now dropped back to being Ray Cashley's number two and many of the younger players such as Geoff Merrick and Trevor Tainton were looked upon as being first choices on the team sheet. As for the youth team, defender Dave Bruton was brought into the fold along with a smattering of other youngsters, notably John Emmanuel, a talented midfielder from Wales.

Gerry was raring to go but there was a real sadness for him and many of the lads from the youth ranks as Billy Menmuir had been released. In total Billy had made two appearances for the Robins but although he had considerable talent, and was tipped for big things, it just never clicked for him at Ashton Gate. Gerry and the Ritchie brothers were gutted for him as he had come down from Scotland with them and it just didn't seem right that Billy was leaving. Maybe it was homesickness, or just simply that a move away didn't work for Billy, but whatever the reason it was probably best that he went back home to re-launch his career. Years later, Gerry told friends that he thought Billy was put into the team too soon and was overwhelmed by it all and never really recovered from the experience.

A year later Billy signed for Hearts, but again struggled to make an impact and appeared only 13 times for them in a two-year spell. He then moved to Dumbarton and then Alloa Athletic before drifting out of the game in 1976. I tried to contact Billy for this book but his old clubs had no knowledge of his whereabouts and I drew a blank on various online fans' forums. It was as though he had just disappeared.

Gerry and Billy are an interesting pair. Billy, on arrival at Bristol City, had a depth of natural talent and was tipped for the top. Gerry had enthusiasm and confidence. Billy thought about home and Gerry thought about becoming a footballer. Sure, he went back to Drumchapel now and then, but Gerry knew what he had to do even though he certainly wasn't as gifted as Billy and that single-mindedness shone through. Billy will always be a lost talent for those who played with him and knew him at City.

In the transfer market, manager Alan Dicks, together with his assistant Tony Collins, had bought wisely with the little money chairman Harry Dolman had given him. The main signing was Gerry Sweeney, a tough midfielder who could also play in the back four. Sweeney had learnt his trade as a youngster with Celtic under the influence of the great Jock Stein. With limited chances available to him at Celtic Park, he was let go to pursue his career with Morton. After glowing reports from Collins, City paid £22,000 for him and he would go on to be another piece in Dicks's jigsaw.

As far as Gerry Gow was concerned, he had just found a friend for life. Sweeney was super fit, a tenacious player who was afraid of nobody and off the pitch he was the dressing room joker who would certainly be involved in most of the things going on. He and Gerry gelled immediately. Gerry Sweeney reminisces about their relationship, 'We hit it off right away. It was probably the Scottish thing at first, that's probably why we were drawn together. I loved him, he was an incredible trainer, an incredible footballer and an incredible man and friend. He really gained my respect straight away. He was relentless in training, giving 100 per cent, and I knew then that I was going to enjoy having somebody of that character in my side.

'I used to laugh when we played together. He hated players who dived, so he used to say to me, "I'll give him something to dive about next time he comes my way." I don't know how he would have fared in today's game. I have never seen anybody win a ball like he did. He never lost a tackle and was so important to the team both on and off the field.'

The Robins started 1971/72 with a bang, drawing a thrilling opener 3-3 at home to Millwall, with goals from Chris Garland, Gerry Gow and Gerry Sweeney. Things got even better in the next game, at Sheffield Wednesday. City tore the Yorkshiremen apart and won 5-1 for their biggest away victory for five years. It also saw a hat-trick for striker John Galley with John Emmanuel and Chris Garland getting on the scoresheet.

The side had seemed to come together, but behind the scenes City had accepted a £100,000 offer from Chelsea for the talented homegrown striker Garland. Garland left after only four games of the season but to Dicks and the players' credit his loss never affected them as they maintained a top-four position through to autumn, much to the surprise of the critics.

Gerry had become an ever-present in the side and his 100 per cent commitment had certainly won over those early doubters who felt he would not be anywhere near the standard of Bobby Kellard. In training he would practise distribution over and over again as this had become very much part of his game, along with being a ball-winner. Goalkeeper Ray Cashley remembers the dedication Gerry showed, 'When Gerry first played for the youth team he was good but his game was winning the ball in the tackle. He could also run all day, box to box, and if he had a weakness it was probably that final pass when he won possession. When he moved up to the first team he worked really hard on his passing and striking of a ball. We would work together sometimes after training. He would strike balls for me from different angles and distances over and over again. Many people think he was some sort of wild man on and off the pitch, but he was really dedicated to improving and becoming a better player and nothing would get in the way of that. I think that's why Alan Dicks thought so much of him.'

At the time the club's training ground was based in the Stockwood area of the city and many of the players, including Gerry, lived there or Whitchurch, which was not far away. The team spirit within the camp was growing as players arrived at training together in various cars, which certainly helped Gerry as he couldn't drive. Full-back Bryan 'Speedy' Drysdale tells his favourite story about giving Gerry a lift, 'I lived in Stockwood and Gerry was about two miles away in Whitchurch. I remember bringing him home one night from either Platform

One or The Town's Talk, which were both regular haunts. To be honest I was a bit pissed off for some reason and I dropped him at the end of his road he said, "Drop me off at my door, Speedy." "No, this will do," I replied. "Oh come on, drop me at my door," he continued. With that I drove up his road up on to his grass and stuck the car outside his door. He shit himself and jumped out telling me I was mad. As I reversed off his lawn there were one or two neighbours looking out of the curtains.

'The next day he went mad in the changing room, telling me that his wife Julie had just planted new plants along the driveway and I had smashed them all up. Apparently she gave him a right ear-bashing. After that the end of the road was fine with him. We had such a laugh with him. Gerry was such a great guy.'

The team started to socialise together after some games or meet up for a pint on the odd Sunday afternoon. The usual haunts were Platform One, which was a pretty select nightclub in the centre of the city, where the doorman looked you up and down for a good five minutes before letting you in; The Town's Talk which was a pub/club on the outskirts of the city near the airport; or The Shield and Dagger, a relatively new pub in Whitchurch which was built as part of the new housing estate. It happened to be a stone's throw from many of the City players who lived around the area at the time and it would not be unusual to find one or two sat among the locals on a Sunday afternoon.

Long-time regular Pete Jeffin remembers Gerry, 'I have always been a City fan and I remember Gerry moving in to our estate. He was a lovely bloke although I was a bit apprehensive to speak to him at first when he walked in as he seemed a right hard nut on the pitch but after seeing him and acknowledging him a few times with a nod of the head we got chatting. Sometimes he was on his own and had a quiet pint and other times there would be a few City lads in there. They were never any trouble and always happy to chat particularly if they won on a Saturday.'

Back in the league the club had a disastrous run from autumn to February, winning only one of 20 matches and being knocked out of the FA Cup by Preston North End. The Robins found themselves in the bottom half and the pressure was very much building on Alan Dicks. But turn it round he did as they rallied round to finish the season strongly, only being beaten once in their final 12 games to finish eighth. The late upsurge showed that they could dig in and show character, but Alan felt that there were improvements he could make to the squad given the right backing.

The season ended with a Gloucester Cup defeat at the hand of rivals Bristol Rovers on penalties after a 1-1 draw. Again it was feisty affair but these games lacked a competitive edge even though there was a cup at stake, as the players on both sides were looking to end their long season. City were looking forward to their end-of-season tour and Gerry Sweeney remembers when the lads were told where they were going, 'We were in the dressing room, I think after the Bristol Rovers game, when Alan Dicks came in and told us we would be going to Italy for a couple of days. The boys were thrilled as we fancied playing some Italian opposition. "Who are we playing against in Italy, Boss?" we asked. "Nobody," he replied. "We will be going to Italy for a few days then on to Iran as guests of the Shah, playing a few games then having a few games in

Cyprus." We were shocked. "Bloody Iran," a few of the lads shouted. "Yes, bloody Iran," replied Dicksy. Obviously Iran was nothing like it has been over the last 20 years but we were still a little apprehensive but deep down couldn't wait to go.'

The visit to Tehran was organised by Alan Dicks, Tony Collins and a British coach called Alan Rogers who was at Persepolis FC, one of the country's top sides. Rogers, originally from Southport, had coached all over the world and contacted Tony through a friend with the idea of bringing a British team over as not only a PR exercise but to pit his team against a good team. Rogers had sold the idea to the Shah as PR for the country and Alan was never going to turn down the chance to top up his tan. So Gerry packed his bags and said goodbye to Julie, who was starting to get a taste of life as a footballer's wife in the 1970s as she was on her own a lot.

After flying to Italy the lads got themselves sorted in the hotel and the two Gerrys roomed together. It was pretty straightforward and Dicks had no problem with the players having a drink as long as they didn't go too overboard, and apart from the usual drunken sing-song late at night the two days in Italy went without a hitch.

Landing in Tehran was a real culture shock. The Shah had been in charge since 1967 and although it was a more open society it was still ruled with an iron fist, mainly with the help of the secret police, the SAVAK, who were used to crush any forms of political opposition. The Shah was obsessed with security after being hospitalised some years earlier due to a failed assassination attempt. As the players drove through the hot, dusty streets, it was if they had gone back 100 years in time. There were men pulling hand carts that were piled up with all sorts of things, and families riding on donkeys, who just stared at the coach as it drove through the city. As far as the Iranians were concerned, foreigners were still treated with a certain amount of suspicion.

The team bus pulled into the four-star Hotel Sina and as the players stepped into the foyer they were treated to soft drinks by the hotel staff. The group looked around as it felt like they were in a palace with gold columns and elaborate ceilings covered with gold leaf. The floors and walls were covered with the most beautiful marble with ornate and plush chairs of velvet everywhere. It certainly took a few minutes for the players to take it all in.

They were shown to their rooms and they were told by Dicks that there would be a meeting in an hour where they would meet their hosts officially. After unpacking, they all congregated in the foyer where there was a real buzz as they all chatted about how fabulous their rooms were, then they were taken to another room and asked to sit. A large gentlemen entered, aged in his late 40s, standing around 5ft 8in and looking like he weighed about 17st. He was flanked by two bodyguards, introduced himself as Ali Abdo and said he was a personal friend of the Shah.

He explained that he would be the club's host during their stay. Abdo was a former boxer and self-made millionaire who made his money in the USA through oil before returning to Iran in the late 1950s. He had founded Persepolis FC in 1963. They were based in Tehran and would be playing Bristol City in one of the matches. The other game would be in a few days against a Tehran select team. Abdo pointed out that this team was mainly filled with players from the other Tehran club,

Esteghlal, and in no uncertain terms he wanted City to beat them very badly.

Gerry Sweeney remembers the meeting, 'We just sat there and he went on about his hatred for the local rivals Esteghlal and how pleased he would be if we beat them. Suddenly Gowy piped up, "Well if we do, what's in it for us?" We all looked around, including Alan Dicks, but Mr Ali did not seem fazed at all. He said, "Well if you win by more than two goals, I will surely be able to reward you with £2,000 between you." So as you can imagine we were buzzing with this news, although Alan looked at Gerry and just shook his head. He said to Gerry after the meeting, "What the bloody hell did you ask that for?" "I just thought we should have some sort of incentive if he wanted us to win so bad," Gerry replied. Alan just walked away and we all laughed. It was typical Gerry. He didn't care who you were, if he had to say something he said it.'

The team found themselves in Tehran for a few days before their first match; most of their time was spent by the pool relaxing, interspersed with some light training sessions. Some of the lads were invited to Mr Ali's private residence where he took great delight in showing off his wealth and stature as a powerful man. Gerry Sweeney continues, 'I went with some of the lads to Mr Ali's house, mainly for something to do. I will never forget he called for one of his servants and handed them a pot to balance on their open hand. Still with his two henchman behind him he produced a gun and proceeded to shoot the pot out of the servant's hand. The poor bloke looked as terrified as we were.

'I remember me Gerry and a couple of the other lads venturing out on our own and stumbling across a bedouin tent away from the main city area. As we went in there were a few city lads in there having a drink, as it proved to be a bar. We couldn't believe our luck. We were drinking some beer and wine and sang a few songs and were thoroughly enjoying ourselves when the flap of the tent opened and in walked Mr Ali with a face of stone. The locals stood to attention.

'Defender Ken Wimshurst got up from his seat and said, "Ah, Mr Ali would you like a drink?" Ali replied, "Mr Ali does not drink and does not like drinking." The atmosphere turned a bit awkward and he left, we then finished our drinks. The next day we decided to go back to the local bar and it had been removed with no visible signs that it had ever been there.'

The Robins' first game was a win against the Tehran select XI in the Amjadieh Stadium. The stadium was built in 1939 and there was a capacity crowd inside of 28,000, all eager to see the foreigners beaten. Much to the delight of Mr Ali, City ran out 2-0 winners with goals from Keith Fear and Peter Spiring. After the game there was a small reception in the hotel for dignitaries and the players. Gerry, admittedly with a few drinks in him like most of the players, started to remind his team-mates that they had been promised a bonus by Mr Ali for winning. The lads chatted among each other and the feeling was that, yes they were due a reward. Gerry decided to then get up and shout across the table in Mr Ali's direction, 'Oi, Ali, you owe us a bonus for the win.' With that his henchmen moved towards Gerry. Mr Ali stopped them, looked towards Gerry and the lads, and said, 'No, I said I would give you a bonus if you beat them by more than two goals.' With that, Gerry shouted, 'Then you, mate, are a bloody liar.'

Midfielder Trevor Tainton takes up the story, 'We all just put our heads down, not knowing where to look. It was typical Gerry though; he wasn't pissed, he just stood up for what he thought was right and he didn't care who you were. After all, this was a man who never had anybody say no to him and Gerry didn't care. He bloody kept on about it all night until we went to bed, but that was Gerry.'

City's next game was against Persepolis two days later and as they won 1-0 with a goal from Peter Spiring, Gerry and all the lads took great delight in rubbing it in to Mr Ali, or 'Mr Bloody Cheat' as Gerry referred to him. The tour ended in Cyprus with wins against Apollon Limassol and Famagusta.

In the summer, Alan Dicks made some changes to the squad, including a few enforced ones. The great Tony Collins decided to accept the role of chief scout at Leeds United under Don Revie. Tony was in real torment over leaving but it was an offer he could not refuse, and typical of the man he spoke with all of the City players individually before he left. His decision was a real blow to the club but Alan promoted from within, moving John Sillett to chief coach and defender Ken Wimshurst was given the role of looking after the reserves along with centre-back Dave Merrington who took over the youth team.

On the playing side, goalkeeper Mike Gibson was given a free transfer and made his way to Gillingham, while defender Gordon Parr left for Waterford in Ireland and popular stalwart Dickie Rooks had to retire due to his continuing knee problems. The Ritchie brothers also joined the first team squad after some great displays in the reserves.

As the squad prepared for the new season it was a more youthful City team that had emerged as Dicks started to piece together the type of side he wanted. For Gerry, the previous season had yet again been one of consistency and, thankfully injury-free, he had made 41 appearances in the league and cup while also chipping in with nine goals from midfield.

As he prepared for the new season he and Julie found time to go back to Scotland to see family and friends. The Gows were now used to having a footballer in their mist but Gerry was more than happy to chat about things happening within the family rather than bringing own tales of his career.

During pre-season he would work on his running and stamina by going up to the Dundry hills which sat at the back of his house in Whitchurch. He and Julie would also spend many afternoons with the regulars at the nearby Shield and Dagger pub just chatting about local events, although there was always the obvious question regarding how City were going to get on this season and maybe where supporters felt that Alan Dicks was going wrong, but Gerry just loved interacting with them.

City opened their 1972/73 account with a 1-1 draw against newly promoted Brighton on a soaking wet August afternoon at the Goldstone Ground. Despite the away point the pressure on Dicks had already started from certain areas of the press as they pointed out that the squad was too weak and lacked experience, although many mentioned that the only plus-point was the presence of Gerry Gow.

City had to wait until September before kicking on with a 2-0 away win against Leyton Orient. They followed this with a 1-1 draw at home to Middlesbrough which centre-forward John Galley remembers well, 'I remember Gerry being very pumped up as always for the game against Boro. He mentioned

Boro midfielder Eric McMordie was in the squad and how he had broken Gerry Sharpe's leg. I remember the incident well and the tackle was nothing short of a disgrace. As we kicked off, within minutes Gerry went into a tackle with McMordie and hit him hard. It wasn't nasty and Eric just got off the deck and had a free kick. That was Gerry; early on he singled out the opposition danger man or player with a reputation and let them know he was there. It wasn't a case of retribution for Sharpey, he [Gerry] was just letting Eric know he was in for a tough day. Funny thing is McMordie scored that day but kept himself very quiet.'

Gerry had another run-in two games later with Cardiff City's Scottish defender Don Murray. Don takes up the story, 'Bristol City played really well that day, beating us 3-1, and I'm sure Gerry Gow scored a penalty. It was quite funny really, my team-mate Phil Dwyer who was injured said in the team meeting that Gow would try and run things and he would make his mark early on. In terms of physicality I was probably one of the biggest in the Cardiff line-up and I received the ball in the back four when all of a sudden Gow came from nowhere to dispossess me and literally hit me up in the air. On the field that is my lasting memory of Gerry who was afraid of nobody and looked for the opposition's biggest player. We had a beer after the game and chatted about Scotland. He was interested in how I had ended up at Cardiff after coming from Elgin up in the Highlands. He was a real hard man on the pitch who could play but a real gentleman off it.'

With a morale-boosting win against Severnside rivals Cardiff behind them, City extended their unbeaten run to nine games before losing 1-0 at home to Luton Town. Two more defeats followed: a 5-1 away hammering at the hands of Fulham when Steve Ritchie made his first-team debut, and a 2-1 defeat at QPR.

City entered December in mid-table and changes were made to the strike force as John Galley was sold to Nottingham Forest for £30,000. On paper it was a good move for the forward as Nottingham was where his family had roots. Galley had been magnificent for City with 87 league goals in 174 appearances. His replacement was to be Bobby Gould who Dicks had signed immediately for a Bristol City record of £63,000. Galley remembers meeting Gould at Ashton Gate on the day of the signing, 'I knew Gouldy and he was a decent bloke. We had both been at Wolves together and he was certainly experienced. I was leaving out the door when I saw him coming towards me. "What you up to, Bobby?" I said. "I am just about to sign so I will be playing with you, John." He replied. "I don't think so, Bob, as I'm just off to sign for Nottingham Forest." His face was an absolute picture.

'Before I left I spoke to the City players and in particularly Gerry. I told him I remembered him coming into the dressing room for the first time and how he had grown on and off the pitch. I told him he had a great career ahead of him.'

On the face of it Bobby Gould was a great signing with a wealth of experience from for Wolves, Arsenal and West Bromwich Albion, his capture excited the fans and press. It didn't take Bobby to get his first goal for the club as City drew 3-3 away at Preston North End on his second appearance. A seemingly rejuvenated team started to climb the league as 1972 became 1973 with a cohesive shape and some good football on display. Gerry was relishing driving City on in what had the potential to turn out to be a decent season for the Robins.

Gerry's character is well documented throughout this book and his will to win on the pitch was second to none. In the dressing room every player knew their job and woe betide anyone who didn't do what they were expected. This philosophy was plain for everybody to see on 17 February in front of 11,000 fans at Ashton Gate. City were playing Brighton and were drawing 1-1. Tom Ritchie, the substitute that day, looks back on what happened next, 'I was sat in between Alan Dicks and Les Bardsley who was our physio. We had a corner to defend and Gerry was like a policeman as he always was in those instants, pointing and shouting for players to get in the right position and mark different players. Apparently he told Bobby Gould to mark somebody and Bobby gave him some verbals back and with that Gerry whacked Bobby around the head. Fair play to Bobby, he never retaliated, but Alan Dicks screamed to me, "Did he just hit him?" I saw it but I replied to Alan, "I don't know." With that, Alan shouted at Les Bardsley who to be honest was just minding his own business, smoking his pipe, "Les, did he hit Bobby?" Les just pretended he hadn't heard him and just looked the other way puffing on his pipe.

'At half-time we went in 1-1 and Gerry apologised to Bobby and the team. Alan substituted him with me. We went on to win 3-1 and I got one of the goals. When we got back in the dressing room Gerry got changed and left. That was him though; he was such a winner and on the pitch he was a colossus but afterwards off the field he was genuinely mortified at what he had done.'

Jonathan Pearce recalled the incident and remembers it as if it was yesterday. He felt it was the moment that really set Gerry apart from other footballers, 'I remember the row he had with Bobby Gould when Gerry struck him. All around me people were saying how terrible it was but for a young lad like me I thought it was brilliant. I had not seen players act like that. Gerry looked really fired up and I loved that side of him. I thought he showed how much he cared.'

For the season's final push, Alan Dicks made another astute signing, a goalscorer from Scottish side Morton for £30,000 called Donnie Gillies who would etch his name in City fans' hearts for ever. It was bittersweet for Gerry as although he hit it off with Gillies straight away the deal involved Steve Ritchie, who he first came to the club with, moving the other way to Morton.

Steve had only had one chance in the side and again, as with Billy Menmuir, maybe a move back home was for the best and it certainly worked out that way as he went on to have a good career, playing for Aberdeen and scoring in the 1978 Scottish Cup Final against Rangers.

Gillies mixed in straight away and the Scots fraternity now in the squad became thick as thieves. He reflects, 'I felt at home right away. My first impression of Gerry was that he was a tough lad and really funny. He was a nightmare when he was with Sweeney as Sweeney was always the joker who gave Gerry the bullets to fire. They were great together. I was put up in digs in Whitchurch with a lovely lady and her husband. I am not sure it was a great idea to be round the corner from him, but my god the takings in the Shield and Dagger must have trebled overnight.'

THE GERRY GOW STORY

City pushed hard towards the end of the season, losing only once in their last nine games to finish a remarkable fifth. Gerry had again only missed one game and had even finished as their top scorer with 13 goals. It was a fantastic achievement for the club and proof that they were moving in the right direction

7

We Have Ourselves A Team

IT WAS another pre-season of comings and goings for Alan Dicks and his coaching staff. Bristol City promoted local youth team skipper Gary Collier into the first team along with the talented winger Clive Whitehead. Centre-half Collier had made a few appearances during the the previous season, but Dicks was planning to elevate him with a view to creating more competition among the back four. Whitehead had shown his talent as an England youth international and City had high hopes for him in his first season.

As far as departures were concerned, Dave Bruton had left to join Swansea Town, Trevor Jacobs went across the city to join Bristol Rovers and Peter Spiring joined Liverpool after an impressive season.

Gerry was looking forward to another season at the club and although there was apparent interest in him from Manchester United, where fellow Scotsman Tommy Docherty had taken over as manager and seemed at the time to be creating a tartan revolution by signing as many Scots as he could, Gerry felt happy at Ashton Gate as he believed he could reach the top flight with the players already present. It was always about whether he felt comfortable and happy at a club which was more important to him than chasing the kind of money as he would have received at United. Gerry wasn't personally ambitious; he was just keen for the team to do well.

In the changing room he was his usual self ahead of the new campaign, telling players what they had to do and chastising them if they didn't do it. He would also get into all sorts of scrapes off the field and would have the lads in fits over things that happened to him. Tom Ritchie remembers one incident in particular, 'He came into training one day after visiting family up in Scotland. I asked him what he had been up to. "I have had a nightmare," he replied. "What's happened?" I said. "Well, I was on the platform at Glasgow station waiting for the Bristol train when I desperately needed a shit, so I went to the gents and sat down in the cubicle and let nature take its course. Halfway through there was a shout from the cubicle next door and a voice said, "Oi, mate, I haven't got any toilet paper, any chance I can have some of yours?" "No problem," I said and I got some and put my hand under the gap to give it to him. With that the bastard stood on my hand and undid my bloody watch and ran off. I quickly opened the door to give chase but my bloody pants were round my ankles." We just fell about laughing, but Gerry was stony-faced, which made it even more funny. That was him though, he got himself into all sorts of bother.

'I also remember him turning up for training one day still in the clothes he had worn out the previous night. He looked like shit and was probably still pissed. Anyway we got him in the shower and he just sat there with the water cascading over him, and with that Alan Dicks came in and said, "Where's

Gerry?" "In the shower," we replied. Dicks went in and took a look at him and just said, "For fuck's sake," and proceeded to walk out. But the thing with Gerry was that within an hour he was on the training pitch running at the front of the group and playing games as though his life depended on it and as if nothing had happened. He was a one-off.'

It's no secret that the culture in the game back then was to go for a drink. It was part and parcel of life for most teams up and down the country and City was no exception. Dicks made a rule that nobody went drinking after a Wednesday up to a Saturday game, and to the team's credit they stuck to it. With Gerry, he just liked burning the candle at both ends now and then.

The season started well and City found themselves top of the table in September after five wins in the opening seven games. One notable result was the 3-1 victory at home to Hull City where goalkeeper Ray Cashley got on the scoreline. Ray recalls, 'It was a really windy night at Ashton Gate and the ball had given me and the Hull keeper Jeff Wealands problems all night. Anyway, if I remember rightly it was 1-1 and the ball came back to me in the six-yard box and I just hit it really for a clearance upfield. I watched it and then lost it in the floodlights and next thing I know the crowd roared and all the lads ran over to me and jumped on me. I took the piss out of the forwards for a bit after the game, telling them, "That's how you do it." We won 3-1 and it was a great night. After I spoke to Jeff as we came off and he just called me a lucky bastard. He said he wasn't expecting it, and I said neither was I.'

Another match against Hull would go down in City folklore weeks after Cashley's goal, but this would be for a tale of what

THE GERRY GOW STORY

happened afterwards. As Dicks's side looked to make the step towards the promised land of the First Division he and assistant John Sillett knew they were not far away from getting it right but inconsistencies drifted back in and City had suffered a 2-1 defeat at Hull which came straight after a 2-0 loss at Middlesbrough. On the evening of the Hull game, the players as usual met for a drink where Gerry Gow and Gerry Sweeney were in good form, piss-taking and letting their hair down in the hotel. As the evening went on, some of the players went back to their rooms to sleep and others stayed drinking. As the early hours approached the few players remaining decided they were hungry and went into the hotel's kitchen to get something to eat. When staff arrived in the kitchen to do the breakfasts they were greeted with an almighty mess, with pots of food everywhere and a few cupboard doors hanging off.

The hotel manager made his way to Sillett and all hell broke loose as he and Dicks rounded up the players, many of whom were still in bed. Dicks placated the manager while the players dressed and got on the coach to return home. It was a long drive back to Bristol, especially knowing that they were in for an ear-bashing. When they eventually arrived back at Ashton Gate, Sillett shouted, 'Dressing room, now.' They all piled in and sat around in a group with Sillett and Dicks stood in the middle. Dicks gave them a real going over, with Sillett joining in on how they were professional footballers and they were a disgrace. Then Dicks said, 'Right, anybody who was not part of that embarrassing, childish behaviour last night in the hotel can leave.' Nobody moved. He said it again, 'Anybody who was not part of it can leave. I know it wasn't all of you.' Again nobody moved. He then said, 'Well, in that case I will fine you all £20.' Then Bobby Gould got up and said, 'You're not fining me as I wasn't there.' He then left. Minutes later the players all trudged off home. Dicks then looked at Sillett and said, 'We now have ourselves a team.'

The story epitomises the success of what Dicks had tried to create at the club – a group of players who would be together and go to battle together. He knew some of them had taken an early night but they stood by their team-mates and in that one instance he knew that his team could do something.

This tale maybe doesn't show Bobby Gould as a team player but that would do him an injustice as he was committed to Bristol City and contributed with his fair share of goals. Maybe that particular dressing room wasn't right for him, however, as weeks later he put in a transfer request and was sold to West Ham United in November.

Two bright spots in the season was the emerging central defender Collier and the skilful winger Whitehead, who although eased in did not put a foot wrong. For Whitehead the influence of Gerry Gow was immense and he couldn't wait to contribute to the book, 'I was only 17 or 18 when I got my chance in the side, and you have to remember I had Gerry Gow to my right in the midfield and Gerry Sweeney behind me at full-back. They shouted instructions constantly and never let my standards drop. Gowy was an intimidating individual on the field and I'm sure some lads who maybe didn't have the desire I had to succeed would have crumbled under the pressure of it. I have to give him his due though, there was many a time when I got more confident in the side where I bollocked him for not winning a ball and he took it. That was Gerry – he gave as good as he got. He bossed games from the midfield, he was all about the 90 minutes, but once the game was over it was over, he never seemed to dwell on a win or a defeat or a particular opponent.

'Alan Dicks handled him brilliantly. Gerry was very vociferous, if he had something to say he would say it and Dicks let us all have our say at times. He was a joy to play with in midfield. I remember Alan Dicks explaining that he wanted us to play in midfield as though we were all joined by an imaginary string: as one went forward the rest covered and as one went back we did the same. His influence on me in my early years was immense.'

As Christmas and the new year approached, City's form nose-dived particularly after a 5-0 defeat away to Oxford United and a 1-0 loss at Luton Town. To try and stop the rot Dicks went back to the transfer market and brought in the experienced Ernie Hunt on loan from Coventry City for two months with an option to buy, alongside a young rising star called Paul Cheesley from Norwich City. Cheesley was a Bristol lad who had turned down his two local clubs to make his name with the First Division Canaries. After scoring on his debut for Norwich against Liverpool, many thought he would be given a run in the side, but the Ron Saunders signing was told by new Norwich manager John Bond that he wanted to bring his own players in. He soon found himself back home at Ashton Gate in a £30,000 move and immediately ruffled up the squad.

After a 2-0 New Year's Eve defeat at home to Leyton Orient, Dicks called a meeting at the ground to go through the game, relying on the filming that Jonathan Pearce and his dad had done. The practice had proved invaluable to Dicks and the team in terms of studying previous performances to iron out mistakes. Dicks went through the goals and asked them what they thought. Cheesley certainly pulled no punches and recalls the meeting, 'I was only a young guy but I had been brought up at Norwich City under manager Ron Saunders and he was a man who believed in having his say and if you didn't like it, tough. There was silence and I said, "Well, I think Geoff [Merrick] was at fault for one of the goals." There was a silence then Geoff said, "What do you mean?" "You should have got across your man quicker," I replied.

'Geoff, who was our captain, was not happy, then Gerry spoke up and agreed with me. From there, people argued with me and against me. I remember looking at Alan Dicks during the debate and he seemed to love the fact that we were all giving our opinions freely. From that moment I knew I was going to love it there and I knew me and this little Scottish guy were going to hit it off, not just because he agreed with me but because he spoke so passionately about players doing their job. I would have been deeply disappointed in the squad if nobody had given an opinion and just let Alan Dicks talk. That's how we were. It also shows the mark of Geoff Merrick as he never bore a grudge and said that I was entitled to my opinion.'

Cheesley and Gow not only hit it off on the field but off it too and that led to the birth of F Troop, the drinking and entertainment group of the squad. The members were Cheesley, Gow, Sweeney, Cashley, Drysdale and Gillies. They were the players' entertainment committee and would organise trips out on a Sunday afternoon for a few beers to local pubs or nights out in the centre of Bristol, usually visiting Platform One. Whenever the players all went out certain ones would be going home relatively early but you could put money on F Troop being the last to leave the bar. The whole thing created a unique bond among the City team where they always had each other's back.

The players all seemed to grow together and as it was a relatively young squad they feared nobody. Training sessions up at Stockwood would be tough but also have that injection of light-hearted piss-taking that comes with a solid group. Dicks would run the legs off them, concentrating on fitness as well as organising the different areas of the team. The one thing the players always looked forward to were the Friday morning five-a-sides which were always England v Scotland and at times were so passionate that Dicks or Sillett had to stop them before somebody got injured, such was the passion and commitment.

Forward Keith Fear remembers, 'We really got stuck in at training and I remember Gerry playing as though his life depended on it. I swear in the those five-a-sides he thought he was at Hampden Park. Many a time I remember getting smashed into the bushes when going for a ball with him.'

Donnie Gillies also looks back on those games with affection, 'We really did kick lumps out of each other in those England v Scotland five-a-sides but we also had a laugh. I remember Alan Dicks playing on our side once and he loved to play in them. A ball went out of play into the hedge and I ran to retrieve it, and as I picked it up it was covered in keck [dog shit]. I shouted, "Jesus, it's covered in keck," but all I could hear was Alan shouting, "Quick, Donnie, on my head." I replied, "But it's covered in keck." Not really knowing what the bloody hell keck was, Alan continued to shout, "On my head." So I thought okay, I picked the ball up and threw it towards Alan who then headed the ball upfield. As the ball hit his forehead the shit splattered all over his face. We just all stopped and pissed ourselves laughing. Alan got cleaned up and told me what he thought of me. It brought training to a stop but we were all crying with laughter driving home thinking about it."

City were inconsistent and were knocking around the lower regions of the Second Division but they had put together a bit of a cup run, beating Hull City after a replay, then winning away at Hereford United. And it was on the way home from Hereford's Edgar Street that the team heard who they would face in the next round while listening to the draw on the coach radio. As the draw was made they were chatting and laughing about who they might get when all of a sudden out popped the news that they would face Leeds United.

The players were stunned before they all let out a massive roar and started to jump up and down with excitement. Don Revie's Leeds had a team of internationals and sat top of the First Division, unbeaten in 29 games and the previous season had appeared in the FA Cup Final as well as the European Cup Winners' Cup Final. The first thing Gerry thought of was the arrival of Billy Bremner. Gerry had followed Scotland international Bremner throughout the whole of the Leeds captain's career as he had done what Gerry wanted to do – come down from Scotland and make a name for himself in the English game. Bremner was a true icon in the sport and all the lads wound Gerry up about how he might have met his match in midfield … Typical of Gerry, he replied, 'Bremner will be shitting himself coming to play against me.'

The tie not only caught the imagination of the local press and media but also the national outlets, who descended on Bristol eager to capture a fixture that epitomised the very

THE GERRY GOW STORY

essence of the FA Cup. City were looking forward to the cash windfall they would make from the arrival of Leeds, who at the time were arguably the best team in Europe. While researching this period in the club's history, I stumbled across an old programme I had in the loft at home. It was for a home game against Cardiff City, two weeks before the cup tie. In it vice-chairman Robert Hobbs, in an interview with journalist Peter Godsiff, pointed out how City had to increase prices to maximise the financial potential of the game. He went on, 'Leeds are the top team in the country so we have had to increase prices to fall in line with what Leeds would charge so both stands will now be £1.50, enclosure 75p, covered end 60p and open end 50p. With these increases we feel the club can break our existing record of gate receipts which stands at £13,963 which was for the League Cup semi-final against Spurs in 1970.'

It's safe to saw that City did break the record and brought in £27,000 gate receipts from this match. The interview with Hobbs is a wonderful window into the football finances of yesteryear.

As the scramble for tickets continued, Gerry spent hours on the phone to his brother Willie, chatting about the tussle against Bremner. The family were so pleased that Gerry would get his chance to pit his wits against some of the best in the game.

Alan Dicks remembers a conversation he had with Norman Hunter years later about the tie, 'Norman told me that they knew all about Bristol City. Don Revie was a master in getting as much information about the opposition as he could so they were all told about whoever they were facing. Obviously with

Tony Collins as our chief scout they had tons of info. Hunter told Alan that Don Revie remarked how Gerry Gow was the engine and he was the man that they had to subdue in the game as he set the pace for City and if he won the midfield they would find it difficult.'

Leeds certainly had gained a reputation as one of the toughest sides in the country, and with Hunter, Bremner and Johnny Giles they were a team that could look after themselves. The game was a tough affair in front of a 35,000 crowd and Gerry clashed immediately with Bremner and Giles. It was as though they were just letting each other know they were there. The tussle for the midfield was pretty even when Bremner put Leeds 1-0 up in the first half to silence the City faithful. Rather than dwell on the setback, the Robins came out fighting for the second half and equalised through Keith Fear, sending the players, fans and staff crazy. Jonathan Pearce, who was filming the game with his dad in the gantry above the Williams Stand, reflects, 'When the goal went in I jumped for joy and I nearly fell off the gantry, only the quick thinking of another guy who was filming the game for TV stopped me falling off the edge. He grabbed my arm and saved me.'

City kept going after the goal and started to get on top. As Dicks says, 'I was really confident and supremely proud of how they had equipped themselves against the best team in the country. Gerry never stopped and I did laugh when Revie shouted to Bremner from the dugout, "Stop Gow, Billy. Stop Gow." With that, the ball fell into space and Bremner came in high on Gerry, but Gerry came in higher and put Bremner on his arse. With that, Johnny Giles appeared and Gerry went face to face with him. He did not care for reputations'.

The game ended 1-1 and a replay was needed at Elland Road. It was scheduled for midweek and due to the miners' strike and the need to conserve electricity the kick-off was set at 2pm. Nobody gave City a chance as they were 9/1 with the bookies and to all intents and purposes they'd had their chance at Ashton Gate. But again Gerry was immense in the midfield and although the game was like the Alamo with Leeds' 11 internationals battering them the whole team defended as though their life depended on it. With about 8,000 Bristol City fans cheering them on, the miracle happened as Gerry dispossessed Bremner and fed the ball to Keith Fear who in turn played a lovely ball to Donnie Gillies and he swung his left foot through his shot to put City 1-0 up with about 15 minutes to go. City hung on and that was it: they had achieved the unthinkable, beating Leeds at Elland Road. The players became the talk of the country and man of the match Gerry had walked off having outfought and outplayed one of his idols in the shape of Bremner. The Leeds captain, clearly disappointed, shook his hand and said, 'That was a tough battle, mate, good luck in the next round.'

The scenes in the dressing room were ones of pandemonium. Jonathan Pearce was there with the players, 'It was a great atmosphere. I was sat between Ernie Hunt and Gerry. I couldn't take my eyes of Ernie who had a full set of teeth, yet in the game he had been challenged by Leeds midfielder Peter Lorimer. When Ernie hit the ground he went to the referee to complain and he was missing his two front teeth, claiming they had been knocked out by Lorimer in the challenge. The ref duly booked Lorimer and it appears Ernie just put his false teeth back in for the perfect smile. I remember thinking, "Wow, sometimes they cheat."'

The dressing room was buzzing, especially when Liverpool boss Bill Shankly walked in and congratulated the side as Liverpool were their opponents in the next round. Earlier on, Shankly had said what a great game it would be against Leeds United in the next round. The players gave him some light-hearted banter before Shankly left. As he went outside the City lads asked Jonathan to go out and ask him how they were going to get on against his side. Jonathan did and returned. 'What did he say?' they asked. 'He said we have nae chance,' Jonathan replied, to which all the lads laughed. Man of the moment Donnie Gillies recalls, 'It was incredible. I remember Tony Collins coming in to see the lads which was great. He made a bee-line for Gerry, telling him what a game he had. I don't really remember a lot as F Troop organised the celebrations but I know the lads had a great night.'

The celebrations went on well into the night for players and supporters, some of whom had got into the City changing room to join in. Dicks called one of his favourite pubs back in Bristol, The Robin Hood Retreat, to tell them they were on their way home and the team started the party there, although not everybody was a fan of the performance. The great John Atyeo, a legend at the club, in the 1950s and 1960s, declared in a *Sunday Times* article which featured in his biography *Atyeo: The Hero Next Door* that professional football disgusted him with its 'yob culture'. He said he had been appalled by the feuding of the likes of Billy Bremner and Gerry Gow on the pitch. The article did not go down too well with Gerry who said in his defence that he always gave 100 per cent for the Robins.

After all the excitement and celebrating, City tried to pick up some league form before welcoming Liverpool to

THE GERRY GOW STORY

Ashton Gate, the high point being a deserved 5-2 win at home to Millwall. Liverpool arrived as a another team full of internationals and Gerry immediately homed in on the Merseysiders' defender Tommy Smith, calling him 'a fat old bastard' after a tackle. Smith then tried all game to kick Gerry up in the air, without success.

City's cup run ended with a John Toshack goal for the visitors as Liverpool won 1-0. It had certainly brought the players to a wider audience, particularly for the performance against Leeds, which led to Scotland Under-23 call-ups for Donnie Gillies and Gerry. Donnie recalls, 'We got letters to the club and we couldn't believe it. Gerry was over the Moon, I remember he phoned his family up in Scotland. We were picked to play against England at St James' Park, Newcastle United's ground, in midweek straight after the Liverpool game. We went up by train to Edinburgh where we met with our team-mates. It was quite funny to see Gerry and Graeme Souness together on the same side. To be honest I expected a few fireworks, and I didn't help matters when I told Graeme that Gerry was better than he was, but they were fine together.

'We had a night in Edinburgh at a hotel on the outskirts where we trained and me and Gerry with some of the other lads had a few drinks in the bar until late. It was an important time for Scotland as this was a couple of months before manager Willie Ormond picked the squad to go to the World Cup in West Germany. Obviously it would be incredible to be in his thoughts but there were so many great players around the full squad that we didn't really have a chance, but it was a cap and that was amazing. Gerry was named sub and he was gutted but was guaranteed to come on. I remember picking up that blue shirt in the dressing room and looking at that badge. Me and Gerry both looked at each other and we had to look away before the tears welled up. There was around 25,000 in the ground as we lined up for the national anthems, our chests puffed out, it was such a proud moment.'

This is how Scotland lined up that evening: Jim Brown (Sheffield United), Alex Bruce (Preston North End), Jimmy Calderwood (Birmingham City), Tommy Craig (Sheffield Wednesday), Donnie Gillies (Bristol City), Frank Gray (Leeds United), Derek Johnstone (Glasgow Rangers), Alan Lamb (Preston North End), Ian McDonald (St Johnstone), Willie Miller (Aberdeen), Jim Pearson (St Johnstone), Graeme Souness (Middlesbrough), Gerry Gow (Bristol City), Jim Stewart (Kilmarnock).

They faced a very talented England side consisting of: Alan Stevenson (Burnley), John McDowell (West Ham United), Alan Sunderland (Wolverhampton Wanderers), Ian Gillard (QPR), Gerry Francis (QPR), Willie Madden (Middlesbrough), Barry Powell (Wolverhampton Wanderers), David Mills (Middlesborough), Bob Latchford (Birmingham City), Roger Davies (Derby County), Steve Perryman (Spurs), Alan Hudson (Chelsea).

Donnie remembers the night well, 'They had a really good side full of talent and beat us 2-0 with goals from Latchford and Mills. I had a bloody goal disallowed, and I was fuming. Gerry came on with about half an hour to go and I remember he got stuck straight into Gerry Francis and the two of them squared up. I know I always say it but that was Gerry, 100 per cent, all or nothing totally committed. Francis was having a good game except for the last half-hour when Gerry rattled him.'

THE GERRY GOW STORY

There was to be no further call-ups for either player as Scotland went on to the World Cup that summer. Gerry was in among some of the greatest midfielders of their generation, including Billy Bremner, Peter Cormack, Jimmy Johnstone, Lou Macari and David Hay, let alone the players coming through the Scottish system such as Souness, Archie Gemmill, Bruce Rioch and Asa Hartford. It may well have been due to the fact that Gerry was at an unfashionable club in the Second Division, but that was to be his only time in a Scotland shirt.

City's league campaign fizzled out after the early-season optimism with the club finishing in a lowly 16th place. The FA Cup run had certainly kept manager Alan Dicks in a job and for Gerry those performances against Leeds United and Liverpool had cemented his place in the hearts of the City fans. This was the season we first heard the chant of, 'He's here, he's there, he's every fucking where, Gerry Gow, Gerry Gow.' It was a season where Gerry suddenly clicked with the supporters on the terraces and they knew he was one of them; they demanded effort for their entrance fee and he provided it in spades. Gerry was very proud to be voted the supporters' club's player of the season.

With the campaign over the players embarked on a trip to Greece for games against Olympiakos, Agrinion and AEK Athens, but these were merely distractions for the team, especially F Troop. Gerry packed his bags, kissed Julie and the kids goodbye and went on another holiday with the lads. Donnie Gillies remembers nothing about the three games played but does remember various scrapes he got into with Gerry, 'God, I remember the Greece trip. I spent a lot of time with Gerry and we had a ball, as did all the lads. I remember them all lying out in the sun on a pontoon stretched out to the sea. Me and Gerry were on our own for some reason and to get to them we had two options, go across the beach but you had to pay or swim from the point we were stood across to the pontoon. It was about half a mile. So with us both being Scottish we decided we wouldn't pay so swam for it. I said to Gerry, "It's a bloody long way," but he replied, "It will be fine." We just had our shorts on so we dived in and started to head for the pontoon. We started okay and were chatting to each other giving each other encouragement when, with about a third of the distance to go, Gerry said, "Fucking hell Donnie, I'm drowning, I can't do this." "For fuck's sake, it's a bit late now," I shouted to him. He started to panic and was shouting, "Donnie, help me, help me."

'I am no great swimmer but I managed to get to him and drag him along and at this point the lads could see us on the pontoon and could see we were struggling. As we got nearer I shouted for help and I think Cash [Ray Cashley] and Cheese [Paul Cheesley] jumped in to get Gerry. They dragged him on to the pontoon and he was fine but a bit shaken up. When they saw he was okay, they ripped the piss out of both of us for being tight arses and not paying to walk across the beach.

'We also got so pissed one night and Gerry was sick over the balcony on to the street below, hitting some passer-by, who came looking for us but we just hid in the hotel bar as though nothing had happened. We had a match the day after and he just ran it off like he'd had an early night. His powers of recovery were incredible whereas I was blowing out of my arse.

'He would do things on impulse like the swim or the time we both went out for a walk one evening. I don't know why

I always agreed to go with him. We set off with club blazers on and walked for about 20 minutes just chatting, then we found a bar and had a few drinks with some locals. Gerry loved chatting to them; in fact he would chat to anybody, he was that sort of bloke. As it got dark we then realised we were lost but Gerry said, "I know the way, it's just over that hill." Well, the hill was more of a mountain which was made from white chalk. Anyway, we got back to our hotel eventually and we were covered in white chalk from head to toe. We were pissing ourselves when Gerry found a bucket so he then filled it with water and asked me to hold his legs, again like I fool I did. With that he dangled himself through the window below which was Dave Rodgers's room and threw the water on to his bed. The next morning Dave nearly killed him and me.'

For Donnie's benefit, the games in Greece ended 1-1 against Olympiakos, 1-1 against Agrinion, and in a 2-1 defeat by AEK Athens. Although the season in league terms would be termed a disappointment, in terms of putting Bristol City on the map their stock had risen and there was a groundswell of opinion that the First Division might not be that far away.

8

I'm Not Coming Off

WITH THE season and tours over, Gerry would go back to being just Gerry the husband, dad and neighbour. He would always be seen in and around the Whitchurch area, happy to chat to anybody who stopped him to ask about City's chances for the coming season, which had become the norm in his local the Shield and Dagger or the nearby Concorde.

Fans coming up to him never bothered him while having his Sunday lunchtime pint; he was always willing to answer any questions about the previous or coming campaign, and occasionally he would be joined by other players who lived a few streets away. He was also in his element watching Scotland in the World Cup in West Germany; he would invite the Scottish players at the club to his house when a game was on TV and he couldn't wait to remind the English contingent of their absence from the 1974 tournament.

The players and wives all socialised together, which was always going to be the mark of a successful team as the spirit within the side was second to none. Gerry would also play golf with Donnie Gillies and during one round at Tracy Park Golf

Club, Donnie noticed Gerry having trouble with his knee. Asked if he was all right, Gerry just typically said that his knee was playing up and it was nothing. It was, however, the start of the cartilage problem that would see him miss a large chunk of the coming season.

Over the summer there had been changes behind the scenes. John Sillett had left to become manager of Hereford United and the players were gutted but understood his desire to be number one at a club. The move meant former defender Ken Wimshurst moved up to assistant from reserve team boss, while former Dundee United and Southend goalkeeper Don Mackay was installed to oversee the reserves and youth team. Chairman Harry Dolman was deposed by local businessman Robert Hobbs and became club president. On the pitch, Alan Dicks signed powerful midfielder Jimmy Mann from Leeds United while also landing promising Scottish youngster Mike Brolly from Chelsea.

For City and most of the clubs in the Second Division at the time, the task of getting promotion had just got even harder as Manchester United were alongside them after relegation from the top flight. Although the clubs could guarantee a full house when the Red Devils came calling, Tommy Docherty's team had already been installed as favourites to bounce straight back. Many had looked at City's chances, but the 25/1 odds seemed about right as consistency was always their downfall.

The Robins opened their campaign with a 0-0 draw away at Nottingham Forest and a 2-1 win at home to Cardiff City in the League Cup. The start was promising, but there were far too many draws, with five in the first ten games. Gerry gave 100 per cent as he always did but his knee ballooned after a match at

I'M NOT COMING OFF

Fulham. Physio Les Bardsley looked at it with concern, telling Gerry it looked like it might be cartilage trouble. Gerry sat on the coach home with an ice pack strapped to the offending knee thinking about just how serious this might be after five years of his career during which time you could have counted on one hand the number of games he had missed through injury. When the bus pulled up at Ashton Gate, some of the players went into the supporters' club bar to meet fans but Gerry was bundled into Brian Drysdale's car and given a lift home with Bardsley's instructions of 'ice it, rest it and come and see me at the club Monday morning' ringing in his ears.

That Monday it was agreed that Gerry would be out for the next two weeks to give the knee time to rest. For somebody like Gerry, any time off the pitch with an injury was hell and as a patient he was certainly not great even for just a fortnight, but he stayed at home and rested it, leaving Julie to deal with his disappointment.

The change in midfield gave new boy Jimmy Mann yet another chance. Jimmy had made a good start to his City career since his move from Leeds but found a place in a settled side hard to come by. Jimmy, now working as a tide master at Goole docks, looks back, 'I was really excited to sign for City. Tony Collins had told me all about them and I knew Gerry Gow after having a right old tussle with him in the FA Youth Cup years ago. Gerry had incredible energy, he was like a bulldog. When I played against him as a kid he was good but when I played with him years later he was outstanding. I took his position in the middle of midfield but I knew it [the shirt] was only on loan. I was never going to replace Gerry permanently. He returned after two games. I think we played Portsmouth away and Alan Dicks kept us both in midfield. He had a great game, full of running, tough tackling, he even scored the goal in a 1-0 win. You would never believe that he was out with the early stages of cartilage trouble. I know it came back with conviction later in the season but that day against Portsmouth he was awesome.'

City followed the win at Pompey with a brilliant display at home to beat Oxford United 3-0. As November came, they found themselves in the top eight after a great start to the season and next on the agenda was Manchester United at home, which would be a stern test of any hopes for promotion. A packed 28,000 at Ashton Gate saw a bruising encounter that Gerry Gow relished. United came as the team to beat since they were sitting top of the table, going neck and neck with Norwich City and Aston Villa. City matched United in every department, with striker Tom Ritchie running the visitors' defence ragged. It was an encouraging display by the Robins who gave the crowd the belief that maybe the team could actually get promotion. The game ended 1-0 to City, with Jon Emmanuel getting the winner to the delight of the Ashton Gate crowd. The defeat did not go down well with United manager Docherty, who told the press, 'This Bristol City team is the most defensive home side we have played against this season. They may also be the dirtiest.'

Sour grapes indeed especially as United spent most of the game defending. But as for the dirtiest tag? Donnie Gillies recalls, 'The United game was full of niggles, no real difference to any game but Gerry and United midfielder Sammy McIlroy locked horns early on. McIlroy left his foot in on a few tackles and Gerry was having none of it. Anyway, McIlroy came in on Gerry and cracked into his foot. Gerry went down and McIlroy just walked away even though we were calling him every name under the sun. Les Bardsley came on to treat Gerry and told him he would have to come off as his boot was filling with blood. Gerry just told him to strap the boot, to which Les said, "I can't, you need to come off." Gerry replied, "I'm not coming off, strap it," so Les did. Gerry got back up and the game went on.

'Within minutes Sammy McIlroy was hit by an express train wearing the Bristol City number four shirt. The whole of the United bench got up off their feet to complain as did some of the players, but we just surrounded Gerry. The ref booked him and for McIlroy, well, it was as if every bit of wind in his body had been knocked out. He got up eventually but never made a tackle or went anywhere near Gerry. He even swapped midfield positions with Lou Macari. It was typical Gerry. When we got back to the dressing room his foot looked broken and his boot was literally in half. He never mentioned McIlroy as a lot of players would, he just enjoyed the battle. To be honest he probably admired the Irishman's commitment; that was how he was, once the game was over, it was over.'

After the euphoria of beating the champions-elect, City went three games without a win leading into December. Gerry's foot was badly cut and bruised but he had started to get more pain from the knee, which everybody at the club knew would mean an operation. Things came to a head at home to Aston Villa who were now second in the table. Midfielder Jimmy Mann says, 'I remember beating Villa 1-0. It's etched in my mind as I scored the winner with my head. Again it was a massive win for us at home and against another of the promotion hopefuls.

Similar to the Manchester United game, Gerry was hit on the knee with a late tackle from one of the Villa players. When he was down you could see he was in real pain. Les Bardsley told him he was coming off and yet again he argued that he wasn't as he had unfinished business. He tried to get to his feet with me and Les holding him up, but he couldn't put any pressure on it and there was no way he could carry on. We helped him off the pitch and his participation in the game was over. We all knew it was bad.'

The players were right. It was bad and after a brief examination the club doctor confirmed what Gerry, Les and Alan Dicks already knew – he would need an operation as soon as possible. For Dicks and the team it was a real blow. Their talisman would be out for weeks and as Alan recalls it wasn't just the impact the lay-off would have on the team, it was the impact it would have on Gerry that was the concern, 'I knew weeks before he would need an operation. After all, you couldn't play the way he did – competitive, never shirking a tackle and running across every blade of grass – without it taking its toll at some point. From a selfish point of view I was worried how it was going to affect our promotion hopes as it was now December and we were still in the mix even though United, Villa and Norwich were the favourites. Yet we were going to lose Gerry.

'On a personal note I worried how he was going to cope with not playing. I knew him from the age of 17 and he had hardly ever missed a game, plus I knew what he was like when he wasn't busy on tours. He was always restless and could find himself in all sorts of bother. I also knew Julie would have to play a massive part in getting his recovery right as we all would

I'M NOT COMING OFF

have to. The one thing I did not want was for Gerry to feel not part of things at the club. The surgeon was initially talking months out of the game, but we knew we would have to get him in hospital soon.'

Gerry was booked to have the operation in one of the private hospitals in the Clifton area of Bristol. They would cut open the knee and remove the broken cartilage surrounding the joint and fit new tissue. The operation would take hours and he would have to spend a few weeks in hospital – a far cry from today's operations which are done with keyhole surgery which gets players back on their feet within days.

The squad rallied round and everything was fine, except when Gerry was visited by members of F Troop. Donnie Gilles takes up the story, 'Myself and Gerry Sweeney went up to visit Gerry. We chatted in his room for a while about games etc. and there was an uncomfortable silence when all of a sudden Sweeney said, "Do you fancy a pint, Gerry?" "Not half," Gerry replied, so we went to see the nurse on duty that evening and asked if we could take Gerry for some fresh air. "Of course," she replied. With that we got a coat on him and got him into a wheelchair and proceeded to push him out of the hospital and into the nearest pub. We were there for ages and got absolutely wrecked, we then decided to get him back so we pushed him to the main door and rang the bell for the porter to come, then me and Sweeney ran off leaving Gerry to explain to the nurse why he was pissed. He never forgave us. Dicksy asked us the following day how the visit went and how Gerry was. We never told him he was paralytic.'

Gerry stayed in hospital for a few weeks before returning home on crutches. He was given exercises by the club to do while recuperating which he did relentlessly under the watchful eye of Les Bardsley the physio who would visit Gerry's Whitchurch house. Gerry found the whole thing incredibly frustrating as he couldn't wait to get back on the pitch. He would talk endlessly to Les, Alan Dicks and the players about how he was missing the games that could define their season. When he did get back to the club for rehab, it was agony. The players would all go out training while he was left alone with Les to build the knee up with hours on the exercise bike and being put through various floor exercises. When the lads finished training they would all be together, piss-taking and arranging to go out and socialise, but Gerry just missed playing. Apart from his family it was the other great love of his life and he just felt helpless, especially with City still in the mix for promotion. With every defeat or draw, Gerry always thought that if he was playing he could turn it into a win. It wasn't that he didn't trust his team-mates, but he felt he could control things on the pitch which is one of the reasons he never went to watch City play while injured.

The setback had robbed Gerry of around a third of the season and by early March he started some reserve games with a view to coming back later in the month. Alan Dicks and Ken Wimshust watched every one from the stands and assessed how he was doing. It was massive psychologically for Gerry as he didn't want to lose the 100 per cent commitment in the tackle that was his forte. Alan and Ken knew it too. They understood that Gerry couldn't go in tackles at anything less than 100 per cent or he would get injured again. They and Gerry had to have total confidence in the operation, which as it turned out had done its job.

I'M NOT COMING OFF

Gerry was to return over the hectic Easter break with City still in with a faint chance of promotion. Gerry travelled with the team away to Southampton and although he wasn't in the line-up, he watched City win at The Dell for the first time. The result gave everybody a boost, particularly as Alan told Gerry that he was on the bench for the following day's game at home to promotion-chasing Norwich. Alan says, 'We didn't really want to push him but he was so important to us. Just his presence around the lads was incredible. I knew I was going to give him a run and I also knew he would be on the bench for the next game against Bristol Rovers as again I didn't want to push him although he was raring to go.'

Ashton Gate was buzzing as the East End sang, 'He's here, he's there, he's every fucking where, Gerry Gow, Gerry Gow.' Gerry ran out to warm up and got a great reception. He was back and the fans loved it. He waved and there was a mass cheer around the ground as everybody seemed more confident when Gerry was about.

City struggled against a far superior Norwich side who had not played the day before like the hosts had. Gerry came on for Jon Emmanuel with about 15 minutes to go but they were chasing the game and ultimately lost 1-0 to a Colin Suggett goal early in the first half. Emotions were mixed for Gerry as City had lost pace with their promotion rivals, but he had given the knee a real test and it had come through.

Gerry found himself again on the bench against Bristol Rovers and he was not happy, so he told Dicks in no uncertain terms that he would run Rovers ragged given the chance. He remained there until the final 15 minutes with the score at 1-1, which is how it stayed and there would be no bragging rights for the red half of Bristol. City seemed tired and were finding it hard to score goals.

Off the pitch Alan had received a tentative enquiry from Celtic regarding Gerry. The Glasgow giants were certainly keeping an eye on the City talisman. Alan recalls, 'It was difficult. Celtic were sniffing around Gerry as were Ipswich Town at the time, I knew we could certainly make some money off him but what I needed were players who could get us into the First Division and that was him. Clubs held all the cards then so if we didn't want to sell we didn't irrespective of whether the player wanted to go but I spoke to Gerry about it and he wanted to get us in the First Division, that was all he cared about.'

Unfortunately for City a 1-0 loss at Leyton Orient in the run-in blew their chances of promotion although the fifth-place finish gave a real cause for optimism for the season ahead. City had struggled to score goals but there can be no doubt about the effect of losing Gerry for just over three months. It truly had an impact on the team and results.

Yet again we come to the end-of-season tour and the players from this era recall another memorable trip where Gerry was 'just Gerry', as they put it. As you might expect with the close-knit bunch they were, what happened on tour usually stayed on tour but in this instance many offered up the story. The club flew out to Norway to a place Dicks usually booked for a pre-season trip as the Norwegian teams were still in the middle of their own campaign, so that helped make City sharper going into their own competitive matches. This time they were scheduled to play four games against Molde, Bodo-Glimt, Mjolner FC of Larvik and another team called Mo Idrettslag.

I'M NOT COMING OFF

The players were used to Norway although the flight was in a plane so small it was a case of last one on shuts the door and they usually landed sideways as it got buffeted by the winds. For most of the lads, getting there was one of the most terrifying things they had ever experienced. Gerry was rooming with Sweeney so something was bound to happen. The players had a reception at every club which involved them meeting selected fans and members of the board and their families. Dicks was very relaxed regarding the tours and always stressed that the lads were there to relax, so they could go out and about and enjoy themselves but they should also be mindful that they were representing the club, so at functions they had to have a blazer, collar and tie on.

The tour went well with wins coming against Molde and Bodo-Glimt without conceding a goal. Then City moved on to Larvik, a town on the coast around 80 miles from Oslo. After landing and going to the hotel they had free time to stroll around the small town before a reception later that evening. F Troop immediately found a small bar and went to work on the Norwegian beer. As the players gradually looked at their watches and headed back for the reception, the crowd around their table slowly got less and less until only Gerry and Sweeney were left. It then got to around 7.30pm and all of the side were sat for a meal, suited and booted along with Alan Dicks and the hosts. Two players were missing – Gerry Gow and Gerry Sweeney.

The function room was a large area with a glass wall and doors at the end leading to the hotel lobby and the lifts. As the evening started, Dicks got more and more anxious as to where his missing players were. Their absence didn't go unnoticed by their team-mates either as they were all talking and sniggering about what had happened, and what Alan would do when they appeared. With around three-quarters of an hour of the meal gone, the two Gerrys suddenly appeared in the foyer in shorts and t-shirts. Alan spotted them straight away and leapt up from his table to confront them. The squad could hear bits and pieces of the shouting going on in the foyer and the gist was over where they had been and why they were not wearing their ties and jackets.

Suddenly Alan returned to his table and the boys went into the lift and back to their room, seemingly to get changed. Around 15 minutes later Alan leapt up again from his chair and ran to the foyer and all the boys looked on to see him have Gerry Gow up against the wall by his throat shouting at him. Gerry was wearing his shorts, a tie and a blazer and nothing else. The lads all fell about laughing, and again Alan returned to the table to apologise to his hosts, while Gerry returned to his room followed by some of the lads.

All the way to the room Gerry was cursing and shouting about 'bloody Dicksy', and how he was going to be leaving the tour. When the lads got to the room Gerry said, 'I'm going home,' so he phoned the hotel lobby to see if they could find out how much a flight home would be. In the meantime, the rest of the lads said, 'Well, if you're going home so are we.' They helped Gerry pack and before they went to their rooms to get their clothes the reception called and told Gerry he could get a flight that night but it was around £200. Gerry said, 'Fuck that, I'm not paying that.' When he told his team-mates of the price, to a man they all said, 'Fuck that.'

The next morning at breakfast, Gerry was the talk of all the tables particularly about how they were all going to fly home in solidarity until they knew the price of the flight. Dicks knew the best thing was to leave it there, but also to have a quiet word with both men when the dust had settled, which he duly did.

When I asked both Alan and Gerry Sweeney about the incident, they laughed and said, 'We kept it in house.'

9

Let's All Get Up The Concorde

THE 1975/76 team will always have a special place in the hearts of Bristol City supporters. I would compare it to England's 1966 World Cup-winning side; even to this day, fans can name the entire XI. Under the stewardship of Alan Dicks, City built a team made up of Bristolians, Scots, and other lads hand-picked by the manager himself, Tony Collins and the backroom staff. It was a group capable of adapting to any situation and with the ability to cover each other's positions; they also had the luck not to have many injuries on their rise to the top.

The main man was Gerry Gow. Yes, he wasn't a natural goalscorer like Paul Cheesley or a cool head like captain Geoff Merrick, but what he had was a major connection with the fans. Gerry was always thought of as 'one of them'. His song rang loud at Ashton Gate and also around the Whitchurch area in which he lived as supporters stopped him for a chat at the shops or offered to buy him a pint in his local. Coming into the new season, he had never felt better and there was a real optimism among the squad about the coming season.

On the field there was no change as Dicks felt the squad that had taken City close the previous season would go all the way this time around. Training was the usual running through Ashton Court estate, thrown in with the now famous England v Scotland five-a-side games at Stockwood. Dicks also threw in 'shadow play', which consisted of the whole of the team taking their positions on the pitch without a ball but with no opposition, where they would then move about as they would in a game. The exercise certainly got its fair share of sniggers when Dicks and his coaching team showed the players the concept, which was for them to dictate play and get used to covering each other during a game, but they bought into it and any ideas that could help them in the promotion push would always be considered.

City decided not to go abroad for the pre-season, so instead played two friendlies against Cardiff City and Stoke City, winning both with goals from Cheesley, who was looking as sharp as ever with his strike partner Tom Ritchie. The campaign started away at Bolton Wanderers, another side who were tipped for big things under the guidance of manager Ian Greaves. Peter Reid, a key man in that Bolton side, gave his view of the game in a video played at Gerry's testimonial night. He particularly remembered Greaves's team talk before kick-off, 'Greavsie came over to me and said, "You're up against the lad Gow today, Reidy. Watch yourself. He's strong, will run all day and he can play." Well, he was right, I never really had a kick. Gow was awesome in midfield. He never stopped and every time I had the ball he would be there hustling, trying to get it off me, never giving me any room to make a pass. Yet when I tried it with him he would twist or turn and knock out a ball wide. He was class.'

City full-back Gerry Sweeney also remembers that season-opener, 'We won 1-0 but I just thought we were brilliant. I knew we had something that season that could get us promotion. The team rarely changed and we just knew everybody's game inside out. If someone was not having a great game we would step up to cover them. I knew from the first match it was going to be our season.'

There was also high praise from across the city as Rovers manager Don Megson recalled that, after the Bristol derby ended 1-1 in the August, he felt the Robins looked a different side, 'We drew 1-1 at Ashton Gate and they looked different class to the City sides of old. Don't get me wrong, they were always a good side, but I knew they were going to have a good season, there was a confidence that seemed to run right through the side. I seem to remember our keeper Jim Eadie having a very busy time in goal.'

City's good form continued and although it was still early on they had not been out of the top three. After the Rovers game they went on a seven-game unbeaten run, scoring goals from all parts of the team with sublime football that was clear for all to see in a 4-1 away drubbing of York City. The partnership of Cheesley and Ritchie up front was unplayable, with Cheesley scoring a hat-trick and Ritchie adding the other goal. But it was one of the favourites for promotion, West Bromwich Albion – managed by former Leeds United hard man Johnny Giles – who put an end to City's run. It was a tough battle of a game which Donnie Gillies remembers for a good reason, 'It was a tough game, they beat us 2-0 and they were a side in Johnny Giles's mould – tough and hard. I particularly remember their winger, fellow Scotsman Willie Johnson, elbowing me in the face off the ball. As you can imagine I went after him and I remember Gerry Gow shouting, "Don't do it in the penalty area." Anyway, I never had the chance as I had to go off but I thought when my eye was stitched I would wait in the tunnel after the game. Unbeknown to me, Gerry chased Johnson the whole game and kicked him up the arse every time he got the ball. When the game was over Johnson ran down the tunnel and into the bath so quick I don't even think the bath was run. Yet again, Gerry helped me out.'

As the year progressed City struggled to score and went four games without a goal. All that changed in November as they met York at home in front of the *Match of the Day* cameras. Again the forward line was unplayable, with City winning 4-1, this time Ritchie bagging a hat-trick and Geoff Merrick getting a goal. The whole team were on show nationally and they had set down a marker for the rest of the division that they were the team to beat. Gerry again got the plaudits for his 'magnificent display' in midfield, as the national newspapers called it.

The national exposure certainly created interest in the players, like the FA Cup run had the previous season, and Dicks was fighting off enquiries for Gerry. Celtic were interested, as was Ipswich Town boss Bobby Robson who had been following Gerry's progress right from seeing him as a youth team player in Scotland during his own days managing Fulham. Dicks recalls, 'I spoke to Gerry about the interest but he wasn't interested. To be honest we had the same when Arsenal came in for Tom Ritchie and Geoff Merrick but like it or lump it the clubs held all the cards then. If we didn't want to sell, and we didn't due to the chance of getting promotion, we didn't have to – whether the player liked it or not. It wasn't right but I had to do what was best for Bristol City and at that time with us pushing for promotion we couldn't sell.'

City received a boost before Christmas when Tony Collins returned as assistant manager, much to the joy of the players, particularly the Scottish ones. There had been changes at Leeds now that manager Don Revie had become the England boss, so Tony was happy to accept Dicks's offer to come back and be part of the team. The league was starting to take shape with the main contenders for promotion being City, West Brom, Sunderland, Bolton Wanderers and Notts County who were all fighting for the top three places. With a quarter of the season left to play, the lads decided to have a team-bonding night out in their favourite Bristol nightclub, Platform One. They were regulars and the venue had a certain exclusivity about it, with footballers, and local celebrities often attending.

Peter Williams was a bouncer there for over ten years and he fondly remembers the City lads, and particularly Gerry Gow, 'I worked there for years and there was never any real problems with the lads. The clientele just mixed with them or left them alone. We had one bad incident when keeper Ray Cashley was glassed by what turned out to be a Rovers fan. We sorted it out and I remember the City lads all piling in to help. Gerry was really interesting, he would come up here with his team-mates and sometimes on his own where we would chat about all sorts of things.

'I used to go to the City now and then as the players would sort us out tickets. I was amazed how much of an icon he was to the fans and even today people say, "Wow, you used to know Gerry Gow, what was he like?" He was massive on the pitch. They all sang, 'He's here, he's there, he's every fucking where,

Gerry Gow, Gerry Gow," and speaking to him he just seemed a normal bloke with no ego or anger in him – totally different from the persona on the pitch. If there was any aggro in the club he would just walk away from it yet you would expect from his football image that he would start a fight at the drop of a hat, that's why I found him so likeable. I was really upset when he passed away.'

A good night out was always a great thing for the lads, who would talk about games and take the piss out of each other, making sure nobody was getting too big for their boots. As the final run-in came closer City sat third in the table behind Sunderland and West Brom, with both those teams competing alongside Fulham to play in a ten-day period which would certainly define their season. City's task away at West Brom was just to get something from the game against a good side with a bit of steel instilled in them by manager Giles. A crowd of over 25,000 packed into The Hawthorns and City, although high in the table, were very much the underdogs. Gerry knew that this game could define the season and there was a quiet sense of confidence around the dressing room as every player knew they had to step up to the test. Within minutes of kick-off Donnie Gillies was reprimanded by the referee for a late challenge on Albion winger Willie Johnson. There was no surprise that this was going to happen considering their last meeting, but this was no time to settle old scores as the Robins needed all 11 players on the pitch.

Promotion is never really gained in one match but that night at The Hawthorns did indeed define the season for City. It was the moment that the travelling fans and those at home listening on the radio could truly believe that it was their time. City went

1-0 up just before half-time with a brilliant effort from Gerry Sweeney and the second half, even today, has been compared to the Alamo. City defended for their lives as Albion threw everything at them and Gerry yet again was named man of the match but as he pointed out in the local paper afterwards, 'Every player in a red shirt was a hero tonight'.

The 1-0 win sent a real message to the rest of the clubs fighting for promotion and was a bitter blow for Albion, but it gave City real momentum with eight games to go. A 0-0 draw at home to Fulham came next before another test against top-of-the-table Sunderland. The game also had special meaning for striker Paul Cheesley, 'I had received a letter from the FA telling me that I had been picked for the England Under-23 team to play Hungary at Old Trafford. I was deeply honoured but it clashed with the Sunderland game. I was in turmoil and thought long and hard about it. In the end I decided to give the letter to captain Geoff Merrick to read out in front of the players. My thinking was that if they didn't appear too pleased or try to take the mick I would go to England. If, however, they were supportive and thought it was well deserved then that was good enough for me and I would play at Sunderland and turn down the chance of a cap.'

To a man, every City player wished Paul all the best and said the call-up was warranted, though Gerry wondered why anybody would want to play for England in the first place. The atmosphere under the lights at Roker was incredible as Gerry put in another masterclass in running, tackling and distribution. City yet again defied all the odds and drew 1-1 with Gerry Sweeney finishing off a seven-man move that even had the most fervent Sunderland fan applauding.

City were on track for the top flight and needed two points from the last two games, both at home, with Portsmouth and Notts County standing in their way. Tuesday, 20 April 1976 will always be a massive date for those City fans who were present as Portsmouth came to Ashton Gate for the night that could have sent the Robins to the Promised Land.

Gerry spent the morning relaxing at home with wife Julie and the children before walking to the shop to get a paper which was full of anticipation over the evening's game. It was brilliant sunshine and he stopped to chat to various fans who wished him and the team well. As the day wore on he relaxed, sitting in the back garden of his Whitchurch home before being picked up by Brian Drysdale and Ray Cashley. As the trio drove the three miles to Ashton Gate, they could see City fans on the street with scarves and bobble hats some three hours before kick-off and when they reached the stadium, more supporters were there singing and wishing them well.

The team met and chatted together in one of the club lounges before going down to the dressing rooms. They were all plainly nervous and so Messsrs Gow and Sweeney did their best to lighten the mood by joking and giving their team-mates a few wise-cracks but it soon became clear that tonight was the night and joking was probably best put on the back burner for a while. The task ahead was simple – beat Portsmouth and that would put them in the history books. They had come a long way together and were not only team-mates but were friends too.

There were over 27,000 fans at Ashton Gate that hot spring evening as City ran out with the whole of south Bristol behind them. Their opponents were already relegated under manager Ian St John and although they had the experienced George

Graham in midfield, the rest of the team was mainly made up of youngsters, including a very young Chris Kamara who had just been signed from the Navy. Chris spoke about the game by video at Gerry's testimonial evening, 'I'm sure it was my first season. We had nothing to play for as we were relegated. The atmosphere that night was incredible and it was probably one of the biggest crowds a lot of us in the Portsmouth side had played in front of. I had a crunching 90 minutes against Gerry Gow, he fought for everything and I remember him giving me some stick and also giving his team-mates some stick. After the game, City brought champagne into our dressing room and it was the first time I had ever tried it.'

As games go, it certainly wasn't one of the best as City scored with a Clive Whitehead goal after about three minutes. The Robins were nervous and to a man every member of the team I interviewed about this game said they were awful on the night but just gave everything. As the clock ticked nearer and nearer to full time, the supporters got closer and closer to the pitch and when referee Mr Homewood blew the whole ground erupted. It was the climax of a dream that Harry Dolman, Alan Dicks, Tony Collins, every player who had worn the red shirt of City over the years and every supporter who had gone through the turnstiles over the years had nurtured, of reaching the top flight of English football for the first time in 65 years.

Gerry was ecstatic that he would now be on the same stage as some of the players he had admired for a long time. He was now a First Division footballer; the dream that he had held on to since his days in Drumchapel. He could have left the club and signed for what would have been viewed as bigger clubs when he was a youngster but his heart was always at City. It was where he felt at home and the fans loved him for it.

Chairman Robert Hobbs had ordered bottles of champagne to be delivered to the dressing room and the lads got stuck in straight away, but not before throwing Alan Dicks into the bath. Outside there was bedlam as the City fans all congregated on the pitch in front of the Williams Stand calling for their heroes. Tony Collins, covered in champagne, managed to shout above the noise that the fans wanted them to appear, so in various states of undress the victorious team came out into the stand to a true heroes' reception. When Gerry appeared, the chant of 'He's here, he's there, he's every fucking where, Gerry Gow, Gerry Gow' rang around the stand. As the local TV company filmed Alan Dicks addressing the thousands on the pitch, somebody shouted out, 'Let's all get up the Concorde' in reference to the Stockwood pub that the players occasionally visited. This typified the team perfectly as they were all just ordinary lads who seemed to connect with the supporters. They were not interested in private parties as this was a night they wanted to share with the fans and even to this day the City faithful have never forgotten the gesture.

* * *

For the purposes of the book, I really wanted to find out what the celebrations were like. Many of the players know that they did indeed start in the Concorde and according to several sources they stayed there until 5am before returning a few hours later to carry on. In all honesty they couldn't remember where they had been but they knew that when they played

Notts County at home on the following Saturday a lot of the alcohol had still not left their body. Bravely, Donnie Gillies stepped up to tell me how they were feeling on the day of that match, 'Honestly, a few of us were still pissed. I know it wasn't professional but we had done what we needed to do. There was an open-top bus parade organised for when the season was over, so the fans could celebrate with us. The Notts County match would have been great if we had put on a show for the fans but it wasn't to be and I think the fans didn't care anyway. We had a guard of honour as we ran out but as I said we were a bit the worse for wear. I distinctly remember being in a wall when County had a free kick. They bent it around us and we never moved, and when we turned round Ray Cashley was rooted to the spot and the ball was in the net. We had to tell Ray it had gone in. We lost the game 2-0 but we had made it to the First Division and that's what counted.'

The players were given a fantastic reception by the red half of the city as they toured the south of Bristol. All the areas around the ground were covered with red and white flags and fans were on roofs and lampposts desperate to get a view of their heroes as the coach made its way to the Council House in the city centre where the players would meet more supporters and the Lord Mayor at a function.

City had finished second, behind Sunderland and in front of West Bromwich Albion on goal difference. Alan Dicks had been vindicated in remaining loyal to the players that in the previous years many felt had not been up to it.

It's incredible, especially given how large squads are in today's football and the culture of resting players, that Dicks used 16 players that season and Gerry Gow, Trevor

LET'S ALL GET UP THE CONCORDE

Tainton, Geoff Merrick, Ray Cashley and Tom Ritchie never missed a game.

The squad received a bonus of £1,000 each for promotion and Alan received £5,000, so spirits were high as the squad left Bristol for an end-of-season tour of Spain where they would share a hotel with newly crowned League Champions, Liverpool.

Alan had organised a game with local side Orhuela Deportiva but he knew this stay was about the lads letting their hair down. There was tremendous banter between both clubs and the players really hit it off with each other, as did the coaching staff, who talked at length about the season they had and the teams they had played. Alan was in his element picking the brains of the likes of Bob Paisley, Ronnie Moran and Joe Fagan, particularly when they were explaining the challenges that City would now face in the First Division.

Gerry was in the thick of things as you can imagine although Liverpool defender Tommy Smith reminded him that he called him a 'fat bastard' during the previous season's FA Cup game. Gerry said he still was, to which Tommy and all the players laughed and proceeded to throw him in the pool. It was a brilliant couple of days and deserved for all the effort the whole staff had put together over the season, but they knew that the next campaign would be the toughest they had ever faced.

10

Survival

ACROSS THE summer the excitement for the red half of Bristol didn't diminish and in fact it probably increased as local news stations talked about the various star teams that would be coming to Ashton Gate. Supporters devoured all the column inches of the local paper eager for any new signings or any news from the City camp. The players holidayed with friends and family in anticipation of the release of the new fixtures, and when they came out in July the excitement reached fever pitch as the Robins had drawn Arsenal away. It was a fantastic first game against a team that had never been out of the First Division in its history. Arsenal had won cups and league titles, they were captained by 1966 World Cup winner Alan Ball, and for this season they would parade the most expensive footballer in the country in the shape of striker Malcolm Macdonald who had just signed from Newcastle United for £330,000.

As far as the national media were concerned, it was lambs to the slaughter for the lads from the West Country and in hindsight it was a view held by many of the Arsenal players. Talking to the City players today, they all said that they got the feeling that the Arsenal team underestimated them. Tom Ritchie explained, 'They really thought we were just there for a nice sunny day in London.' In Arsenal's defence who could blame them? City had finished as runners-up in the Second Division and had not really set the world alight in terms of football honours. It was also virtually the same team that won promotion as Alan Dicks had only moved Jon Emmanuel on to Newport County and Mike Brolly to Grimsby Town and although he would like to have brought players in to strengthen the squad, nothing had materialised.

The game caught the imagination of the national media as it was selected to feature on the ITV sports show *On The Ball*, which would be aired the following day. Around 6,000 City fans made the trip along the M4 to Highbury. Reminiscing about the day to friends years later, Gerry Gow called it 'the day we had arrived as a football club'. It was the game that saw the whole of the division take notice of the Robins. Gerry wasn't a player who was in awe of many opponents, maybe Billy Bremner perhaps, but he was relishing pitting his wits against Ball. He rated Ball as one of the best midfielders ever and although he was not the aggressive hard man Gerry had become, Ball had ingenuity, craft and skill and their battle of contrasting styles was mouthwatering to see.

That sunny afternoon at Highbury will always be remembered in City's history as the time a group of players who months before had been playing Second Division football totally outplayed the First Division giants in their own back yard. Striker Paul Cheesley ran rings around David O'Leary, not only getting the winning goal but going close several more times and being denied by the woodwork and

Arsenal goalkeeper Jimmy Rimmer. Full-back Pat Rice pulls no punches with his condemnation of his Arsenal side, 'We were bloody awful that day but you have to give credit to the City lads, they were magnificent and even if we were on form I think we would have struggled to beat them. Cheesley up front was such a threat, and he took his goal brilliantly. On a personal note I really struggled if I'm honest with the young winger Whitehead. He was quick and his delivery of the balls to Cheesley were second to none, but I will always remember the tenacity of Gerry Gow in midfield. He ran the show and he never gave Alan Ball an inch to play in. Not many players did that to Alan, not even on the world stage. I remember those three players were the basis of manager Terry Neil's team talk for the second half, but it didn't seem to do any good. After the game I remember shaking hands with some of the lads and wishing them well for the season ahead.'

The 1-0 scoreline was incredible, for not only the players and coaching staff but for the fans who made their way home from north London. When the team got back to Ashton Gate the players made their way to the supporters' club bar, which was something they had started to do after games regardless of the result. Inside they were given a rapturous reception before some of the lads, including Gerry, made their way up to the Clifton area of the city where they danced and drank the night away in Platform One, again being acclaimed. For the players it was an incredible boost in confidence as they took their tentative steps in the top flight.

Their next opponents were Stoke City three days later and the fixture certainly brought the whole club down with a bump. City carved out a decent 1-1 draw at home to the men from

SURVIVAL

the Potteries but the game will be remembered for an injury to Cheesley. City's big number nine went up for a ball with Stoke goalkeeper Peter Shilton and landed heavily. He was stretchered off. Paul says, 'I went up for a ball with Shilton and I fell awkwardly. The pain was unbearable. I tried to come back some three months later against Birmingham City but the knee was knackered. I had damaged both ligaments and all of the surrounding cartilage of the knee and my career was over.'

The loss of Cheesley hung like a dark cloud over the club. It hit Gerry hard as he was great mates with Cheesley, and what annoyed him was the way the striker was treated in terms of his rehabilitation. Cheese would be running up and down the Dolman Stand on his own, on the advice of the club, yet nobody really knew what was wrong with the knee at the time. In fact he didn't get a proper X-ray until three months after the injury. Gerry voiced his concerns to Alan Dicks and the coaching team but to no avail.

When I interviewed Clive Whitehead for this book he spoke with such passion about what Paul meant to the rest of the lads and to him personally, 'Cheese was immense for us as a team. He was almost our unofficial entertainments manager, organising all sorts for us and our wives. He was a massive part of things off the field and kept that team spirit going. On the pitch he made me as a player. By that, I mean I knew I only had to cross it and Cheese would get on the end of it. It was a massive blow for us to lose him so early on in the season.'

The loss of Cheesley meant that Dicks had to move quickly if his inexperienced side were not to drop to the bottom of the league, but unfortunately injury would strike again as Gerry pulled up in training with an Achilles problem that would need an operation and keep him out for at least three months, although Dicks did specify this time that if anybody went to visit him in hospital they were under strict instructions NOT to take him for a drink.

So as November approached City had lost their two great influential players, and were winless in seven games. Cheese was still trying to get his career back on track and he and Gerry would spend hours together in the gym trying to help each other get fit again with no real light at the end of the tunnel for either of them.

Gerry was not great at keeping himself occupied when injured and although he could potter about the house and help Julie with the kids, playing was everything for him. He became worried about whether he would get back into the side, especially if the board released some cash and Dicks brought somebody in to replace him. All of these thoughts were just going round in his head and the confidence that he had always showed seemed at times to have deserted him. He even wondered if that was it for his time at City as he had been relatively injury-free in his career and with the team in the First Division he wasn't sure if he would ever get the chance to really play in it.

The reality was that the players and Dicks were desperate for Gow to return. Things had never changed – they needed him as much as he needed them and if they were going to give themselves a chance in the division he had to be in midfield. In fact, they needed 11 Gerry Gows.

Dicks reached out to his contacts and as Christmas drew near he got a whisper that somebody would be available who would give the side a lift, much like Gerry did. That man was

Norman Hunter from Leeds United for £40,000. Alan takes up the story, 'Tony Collins got word that Norman was unhappy at Leeds and wanted a change. Manager Don Revie had gone and the whole club was changing. He was going to sign for Southampton but we got there quickly enough to offer him a deal and he jumped at the chance. Deep down I couldn't believe he said yes; he was perfect for the club at the time and I couldn't wait to see him in the same side as Gerry. Like Gerry he had a hard man image which in football at that time was no bad thing but, like Gerry, he could also play. His left foot was incredible and above all else I knew he would be popular with the lads.'

It is with real sadness that I write this part of the book featuring Norman Hunter. I tracked Norman down and we spoke over the phone about his time at City. I was really nervous before the call, after all he was a footballing legend from my childhood, and the last time I had spoken to him was when I was 13 and I bought a pair of football socks from him at his sports shop in Whitchurch. I didn't need them and, like lots of my friends, just wanted to meet Norman. There used to be a steady stream of fans from St Bernadette's Comprehensive spending their dinner hour peering through the window of the shop to catch a glimpse of him.

Before we talked, he told me he was feeling a bit rough with the flu, but nevertheless he fondly recalled his time at City and his early impressions, 'I knew the club from Tony Collins and the FA Cup run back in 1974. They were a great bunch of lads and I was determined that this was going to be a good move for me. Incredibly I was on about £120 a week at Leeds and City put me on £140 which was great but to be honest I would have signed for less. The family moved down and I also opened a sports shop in the Whitchurch area of the city, so as you can see this was not going to be a case of me going out to grass as it were, I wanted to have a new challenge and I got that at the club.

'I played alongside a youngster called Gary Collier who was a great lad and a lad that I tried to give as much advice to on and off the pitch. I really rated Gary. There were big characters at the club and there was none more vocal than Gerry Gow. I remember after my debut against Derby I sat on the bench in the dressing room and threw my boots and socks into the middle. At Leeds United the kit man would pick them up and put them in the laundry box, but Gerry, who was on crutches at the time after his op, said, "Oi, Norman, we take them home and wash them here at City. You're not at Leeds now, mate." It broke the ice as everybody had a good laugh at my expense.

'Gerry was brilliant on the pitch although he never really got going in my first season at the club until near the end after his operation had healed. In the final games he was awesome. The biggest compliment I can pay him was that he was as good as Bremner and I know he was a player that Gerry thought a lot of.'

After our conversation, Norman wished me well with the project and said Gerry deserved to be the subject of the book. Typical of Norman, he added, 'If you need anything, just ring me.' The following week I rang him to see how he was and his wife said he was really ill. A week later he was in hospital and passed away a week after that with coronavirus. He was a legend of the game not only for Bristol City but for Leeds United and England and that phone call, which in hindsight

SURVIVAL

was one of the last interviews he did, will stay with me forever. God bless you, Norman.

Alan Dicks and his coaching staff had not finished there and they also secured the signing of Liverpool midfielder Peter Cormack for £50,000. Dicks explains, 'I remembered Peter from our end-of-season tour of Spain when he was with Liverpool. He mixed well with the lads, probably as he was Scottish, but he was a great player in midfield for the Reds, very skilful but could also put his foot in when needed. Above all both he and Hunter knew the First Division and that was what we needed more than ever at that time.' And as the year came to an end Dicks brought home City legend Chris Garland from Leicester City for £110,000 to provide some much-needed goals. Chris had left Leicester under a cloud after a training ground bust-up had left team-mate Jeff Blockley with a broken jaw.

Gerry returned from injury in January as sub for the trip to Manchester United and it was a very different side to the one he had last played in months earlier. Goalkeeper Ray Cashley had been replaced by Jon Shaw from Leeds, and the arrival of Hunter meant there was no place for full-back Brian Drysdale, his place having been taken by captain Geoff Merrick who in turn had lost the centre-back spot that he had held since he was 17 years old to Hunter. It was testimony to Merrick at the time and backed up by many of the players I interviewed that Geoff wasn't happy at full-back but just got on with things. He never bore any malice towards Hunter and he continued to be at the top of his game even in a position he didn't favour. Geoff was always a man who put the good of the team first.

Gerry returned to his preferred midfield position in the 2-0 home victory against Arsenal where he again ran the show, although Cormack got both City goals. As the season continued things looked bleaker and bleaker for the Robins as they were fighting at the bottom along with Tottenham Hotspur, Stoke City, Sunderland and Coventry City in their own mini league. Unfortunately for City their last six fixtures included meetings with Leeds, Manchester United and Liverpool so the signs were not looking good. Around 29,000 fans packed Ashton Gate for the visit of Manchester United. City needed to get something from the game as time was running out. City took the lead through Chris Garland and then United suffered a setback when full-back Stewart Houston fell awkwardly and broke his leg. The game was physical as always, particularly in midfield where Gerry went toe to toe with Sammy McIlroy as he had done in previous meetings. It was also a fixture that saw United manager Tommy Docherty once again having something to say about City. This time he told the waiting press that the Robins, in his words, 'were far too physical'.

Unfortunately for City Gary Collier conceded a penalty that United's Jimmy Greenhoff converted, and then the game exploded with Gerry and Sammy McIlroy being sent off for fighting. There has been much said about this incident by fans who were there that day, so after some effort I managed to track Sammy down for his take on it. He recalled, 'We were always at it whenever we played against each other. It was the same when I played against him when he was with Manchester City. Gerry was a top player and competitor, he would come looking for you and the midfield was his domain. To be honest that's how the game was back then; every side had somebody like Gerry.

'Anyway back to the game. He came through the back of me and I had just had enough. Some players would go through you then run off but Gerry just stood over you in case you had anything to say. Well, on that day I did. I jumped up and threw a punch at him and he threw one back, and in the end we had to be separated by team-mates. The ref, a Mr Toesland, sent us both off. Gerry went up the tunnel first and I followed. Our manager Tommy Docherty left the dugout and followed us both but only to get to Gerry. As I went into our dressing room Docherty stayed in the tunnel and started to tell Gerry what he thought of him and had to be pulled apart from Gerry before another fight took place.

'In the quiet of our dressing room the magnitude of what I had done hit me. We were due to play Liverpool in the FA Cup Final in a couple of weeks and the sending-off meant I would miss the final. I was distraught. Chairman Martin Edwards came down to see me and assured me I would be playing as they were going to move the game against Stoke City so I could serve that game as my ban.

'My memories of Gerry will always be that he was honest, you knew what you were going to get and I'm glad you tracked me down so I could say a few things about him. He was a hard man who could really play.'

With no Gerry in the side as he was serving his ban, City pulled off another great result with a Chris Garland goal beating Leeds 1-0 at Ashton Gate. With Tottenham Hotspur and Stoke already doomed, it looked like the final relegation place would be fought out between City, Coventry and Sunderland, but with Liverpool due at Ashton Gate for the final home game nobody gave the Robins much hope against a team that had won the league title, reached the FA Cup Final and also the European Cup Final. There was another full house at the stadium with everything to play for and Gerry's job was to stop Jimmy Case in the heart of the midfield. It was a contest he relished as he always preferred to be up against a good, competitive midfielder. Both players were very similar and fans knew it was going to be a spectacle, although Gerry knew he had to keep his head as he didn't want to miss the last game of the season against fellow strugglers Coventry, even if there was nothing to play for. Although the tussle was at times in danger of getting out of hand, the game really belonged to the evergreen Chris Garland whose two goals won it for City and incredibly gave them a chance of survival with one match left.

The scenes at Ashton Gate were incredible as fans spilled on to the pitch to grab hold of their heroes. Whatever happened at Highfield Road three days later, the way the players had performed – especially in the run-in where they had drawn against Manchester United, and beaten Leeds and Liverpool – was phenomenal.

So it all rested on the Tuesday night in Coventry with City, the Sky Blues and Sunderland all sitting on 34 points. Sunderland were away at Everton where success for them would have required Coventry to win due to their inferior goal difference. The game was massive as nearly 15,000 City fans descended on Highfield Road, causing the teams to kick off five minutes after Sunderland, a decision that would certainly favour them both later on in the evening.

The players went up on the same day and knew it was all or nothing. Alan Dicks gave them a team talk that really consisted of just doing the basics right and fighting for everything. The match will go down as certainly one of the strangest last games of the season ever to take place and the whole affair is something

SURVIVAL

that Sunderland fans have never forgotten. City were caught cold early on when Coventry winger Tommy Hutchinson fired the Sky Blues into the lead after 15 minutes.

Defender Bobby McDonald, who would become Gerry's team-mate along with Hutchinson at Manchester City years later, was in that Coventry side that night. He told me when I tracked him down that he didn't really get involved in talking about anything related to his career but made an exception with this book, such was his affection for Gerry as a colleague and as a man, 'We were the better side in the first half and I think the nerves had got to Bristol City if I'm honest. We went in at half-time quite confident and our fans were certainly up for it, and when Tommy got our second we thought we were home and dry but Gerry was relentless. He was magnificent that night and although I was on the opposite side I could hear him shouting to his team-mates that they were not beaten yet.'

This is also backed up by Gerry's partner in midfield, Trevor Tainton, who says, 'Gerry just went round geeing the lads up. We were 2-0 down away from home but he refused to accept that our time in the First Division was over. I honestly feel he would have been the same if we were 5-0 down, he refused to be beaten. He led by example and scored what was his first goal of the season to make it 2-1. I remember him running back to the centre spot shouting, "Come on then."'

Gerry's geeing-up of the rest of the team seemed to have worked when with around ten minutes to go Donnie Gillies got the vital goal to make it 2-2, and as the game went on news broke that Sunderland had lost at Everton which meant both sides were safe. Coventry chairman Jimmy Hill, a good friend of Alan Dicks, decided to put the Sunderland result up on the scoreboard for all the fans and players to see. With both clubs safe, they proceeded to just pass the ball back and forth to each other and if a player strayed into the opposition's half they were told in no uncertain terms to get back to their own territory. The game ended 2-2 and both sets of fans and players celebrated. There was champagne all round in the dressing rooms as both sets of players mingled with each other. The team bus was mobbed by delighted City fans and when Dicks ordered it to stop on the way home so the boys could have a drink, the supporters followed the bus to the pub and drank with the players.

Tom Phillips, one of the travelling contingent, remembers the occasion, 'It was an incredible night. At 2-0 down we thought we were dead and buried but we kept on singing and Gerry Gow pulled us through that second half. I remember waiting for the lads outside the dressing room as they boarded the bus; we hugged them and they were different class, waving and signing autographs. We ran to our cars and we followed the bus to a pub on the way home and went in for a drink with them. It was a great atmosphere and in all the years I have followed City it was certainly the best away day I ever had. Gerry Gow even bought me a drink. I will never forget it. We got home in the early hours and I was up for work next day and couldn't wait to see all the Rovers fans in work who thought we were finished with the First Division. It was a great night.'

Jonathan Pearce also was another of the celebratory group, 'I was in the convoy that followed the bus and I remember it stopped at a pub called The Red Lion just outside Stratford. It was a fantastic atmosphere.'

SURVIVAL

Sunderland lodged an official complaint with the FA regarding the way Coventry had behaved in flashing the score up but nothing was ever done about it, although they never ever forgave Jimmy Hill. City had survived and Dicks had made it happen with some astute signings earlier on in the season. Norman Hunter had been a rock in the side and won the supporters' player of the year award, while Chris Garland's goals in the run-in had saved them from the drop. The season had turned out to be a rollercoaster for players and fans. They had just held on to First Division status and knew they would have to improve.

11

Silverware

AFTER CITY'S last-gasp survival the previous season, Alan Dicks and his backroom staff knew that 1977/78 would have to be when the side got to grips with life in the First Division. Alan stayed loyal to the team and there had been patches during the previous campaign where the side certainly did not look out of place in the top flight.

Norman Hunter had brought defensive steel to the team, along with the emerging Gary Collier at centre-back. Midfield, with Gerry controlling things, again looked okay, but the main problem had been the loss of striker Paul Cheesley at the start of 1976/77, so the club were always going to suffer if they did not get goals. Tom Ritchie and Keith Fear had done well but it was plain that City needed an out-and-out striker, so Dicks put his faith in youngster Kevin Mabbutt, whose father Ray had played at Bristol Rovers in the 1950s, while his younger brother Gary was getting rave reviews in Bristol Rovers' youth team. With his long hair and good looks, young Kevin certainly looked the part of the footballers of the time and it was something he would try and exploit later in his career.

City embarked on a pre-season tour of Scandinavia, winning all six games in the process, and they returned confident for the opening fixture against Wolverhampton Wanderers at Ashton Gate. But yet again they struggled, the only high point in a five-game run being a 1-1 draw at home to Aston Villa, with Mabbutt getting his first league goal. City also embarked on an Anglo-Scottish Cup campaign in August by beating rivals Bristol Rovers 3-1 due to a Ritchie hat-trick.

The competition had been created in 1975 and was a tournament that ran from August to December comprising 16 English teams and eight from Scotland. City had entered in previous seasons but had always been knocked out in the early stages. Gerry loved the tournament as it was a good way of getting back up to Scotland now and then and hopefully seeing the family.

After a win against Plymouth Argyle and a defeat against Birmingham City, the Robins qualified from their group to face Partick Thistle in the quarter-finals. Partick were based in Glasgow and at the time were in the Scottish top flight. The first game of a two-legged affair saw City away and this called for the Gow family to go and see their son play at Firhill for the first time since he turned out for St Pius against St Mungos all those years ago in the Scottish Shield.

Donnie Gillies was excited to be back in Scotland, as most of the Scottish contingent at City were. Hours before the kick-off, Donnie, Gerry and Trevor Tainton decided to have a walk around Partick to show Trevor what their home area was like. Donnie takes up the story, 'We thought it would be good to walk round and show Trevor, so off we strolled and we walked past shop after shop that was boarded up and some houses that had no windows, with a few people knocking about. Me and Gerry were fine as we were used to it, then Trevor asked, "Is it shut?" We just fell about laughing. I think Trevor was glad to get back to the ground.'

In front of 4,000 fans, City surprisingly lost 2-0. Despite the defeat Gerry was delighted to be able to catch up with his dad and brother after the game. In the return City beat a strong Partick team 3-0 with goals from Jimmy Mann and Clive Whitehead, a result that saw them into the semi-finals against Edinburgh side Hibernian. The first leg was a tempestuous affair at Easter Road as Norman Hunter was sent off for a tackle on Hibs player Ally MacLeod and minutes later City midfielder Peter Cormack received his marching orders for a headbutt on Des Bremner.

Gillies continues, 'It was chaos. I remember Bremner having a go at Peter and Peter was ex-Hibs himself. I don't know what he said but I pulled Peter away and then he got out of my sight and duly headbutted him. Bremner was rolling round and off Peter went. When the game restarted Gerry went over to him and told him, "Oi, big man, when you come to Bristol I'm going to kick the shit out of you." Which he did as Gerry Gow was a man of his word. After the game Peter apologised to the rest of us but Norman didn't give a shit as he thought it was a perfect tackle.'

The fall-out from that night at Easter Road carried on with Hibernian chairman Tom Hart calling the Robins 'the Butchers of Bristol' and saying that there was no way that his club would be playing the second leg. He also tried to claim the tie and then threatened to withdraw after paying a £2,000 fine, but City's demands for £12,000 compensation, coupled with an intervention from the Scottish and English league secretaries brought a change of heart. City ran out 5-3 winners in the second leg in front of a crowd of 6,500 at Ashton Gate. The game was a thriller but without the nastiness of the first leg, and there were not many handshakes at the end of the game both from the players and later in the boardroom.

It had been a long time since City played in a final and although the Anglo-Scottish Cup had not really captured the imagination of the Bristol public, silverware was still silverware; players played to win trophies. City's opponents were St Mirren who were in the Scottish top flight and had disposed of Fulham and Notts County on their way to the two-legged final. A young manager called Alex Ferguson was in charge. Ferguson had been at the Saints since 1974 and was just cutting his teeth before going on to dominate Scottish football with Aberdeen and the English game with Manchester United some years later.

Clive Whitehead recalled the first time he saw Ferguson, 'Obviously I didn't know Sir Alex was going to have the career he did at Aberdeen and Manchester United back then, but I will always remember we were at the ground for the first leg a few hours before kick-off and a minibus drove into the ground with some of the players in it and Alex Ferguson was driving it. It makes me smile when I think back to it.'

The first leg was at St Mirren's Love Street ground. City's line-up was: Shaw, Sweeney, Gillies, Gow, Collier, Merrick, Tainton, Ritchie, Mabbutt, Cormack, and Mann. Gerry's family had made the ten-mile trip to see him play. City were on top for most of the game and in front of 8,000 fans they beat the Scottish team 2-1 with goals from rising star Kevin Mabbutt and Peter Cormack. The return leg though was no formality as the spirited Saints drew 1-1 at Ashton Gate with Mabbutt cancelling out the visitors' early goal. When the whistle blew the supporters who braved the rain stood to applaud a City team that had won the club's first silverware since the Welsh Cup in 1934. The players loved picking up the trophy and they milked the ovation from the fans as they ran around the pitch.

Losing manager Ferguson found himself in hot water with the officials after his remarks to them concerning what he believed to be a perfectly good goal that was disallowed for a foul on City keeper Jon Shaw. He was sacked by St Mirren in May 1978 with an industrial tribunal ruling he had 'neither by experience nor talent, any managerial ability'. To Ferguson's credit, when he was approached by the organisers of Gerry's testimonial dinner years later, he certainly remembered the City midfielder and had no hesitation in adding to the tributes on the night. By video he said, 'I remember Gerry playing against St Mirren when I was manager there in the Anglo-Scottish Cup. Gerry was a tenacious tackler; a determined lad with not a massive physique but he was a terrier, a real terrier.' It was high praise indeed from one of the game's greatest managers of all time.

Alongside the cup run was the bread and butter of the league and as the year was coming to an end the club realised they needed a goalscorer. Mabbutt had done wonders in his first couple of months with nine goals in league and cup but Dicks knew he could not rely solely on him and Tom Ritchie, who was playing a more midfield role.

Dicks made a few calls and after a long, drawn-out affair he managed to get former Everton, Manchester City and England centre-forward Joe Royle on loan with a view to a permanent deal later. The acquisition of Royle was a master-stroke by Dicks as the big number nine could help young Mabbutt. Royle's pedigree could only help the team. I asked Joe why he moved to City and for some of his memories of playing with Gerry, 'I came so I could play, it was as simple as that. I wasn't getting a game at Manchester City and they had just signed Mick Channon from Southampton so I knew that was it for me even though I thought I was a better player. I knew Norman [Hunter] and was really looking forward to the challenge ahead as they had a good side

'Gerry was an incredible footballer who would have had loads of caps if not for the likes of Souness and Hartford in his position at international level. I also don't think it helped that he was with what people would say was an unfashionable club.

'He smoked like a laboratory beagle and I was amazed by his toughness not only on the pitch but in training. I remember going for a midweek break in Spain just after I signed permanently. He was swimming in the sea with his sunglasses on and seemed to spend the three or four days we had constantly drinking cheap Spanish brandy; he was pissed all the time. I remember saying to Geoff Merrick and Norman Hunter, "I am worried about this guy, we have an important game when we get back against QPR and he's never going to be fit enough." Norman just said, "Don't worry, he will be fine." Anyway we came off the pitch at half-time at Loftus Road 1-0 down and Gerry was dreadful; he still seemed to be sweating out the booze. I looked at Norman and he just winked. Second half Gerry was incredible; he scored and drove the whole team on to a 2-2 draw. Norman came up to me later and said, "See, what did I tell you, that's Gerry." When he moved to Manchester City I knew they would love him up there, which they did, he was their type of player.'

The signing of Royle certainly gave the fans hope, especially with him getting four goals on his debut against Middlesborough at Ashton Gate.

Gerry was now established at City as one of the main men and senior pros, and during the course of researching the book I was intrigued to find out how he was viewed by this young apprentices at the club. One such player was Martyn Rogers who had spells with Bath City and Exeter City, and now manages Tiverton Town. Rogers was from the Hartcliffe area of Bristol and during Gerry's time was certainly one to watch when it came to getting in the first team. He was a tough-tackling full-back but unfortunately his career at City was ended after a broken ankle.

He looked back on his time at the club, 'I joined as a youngster and worked hard to get a pro contract which I ended up doing. I was a full-back and I remember being asked with a few other youngster to play in the five-a-sides at training. You know what it's like when you're young, you're full of it, so there I am playing with the City squad and I go straight through Gerry Gow. He leapt up and I thought he was going to kill me. Alan Dicks stopped the game and said, "Look, if you're not going to play I will make you run." Well nobody wanted that so we carried on and I forgot about what I had done to Gerry until BANG! He went right through me. The game carried on while I got my breath back and after the match he just shook my hand. I ended up being the apprentice that looked after his boots and he really looked out for me.

'I think after the incident on the training pitch he had a certain respect for me, that I had the balls to tackle him like that. Whenever we were out he would always have a wad of money and he used to get me to go and get the lads drinks, saying, "Here's the money, make sure you get one for yourself."

'I also remember he once had a deal with a boot company who sent him some white boots. Well, they were not Gerry's style and all the lads took the piss out of him for getting them. He said there was no way he was wearing them in a match but if he was wearing them in training I had to wear a pair too so he gave me a pair. When we ran out the lads were dying with laughter.

'He was a great mentor for me. I went on tour with the first team to the USA and as I said he looked after me and he was gutted when I broke my ankle. The injury was complicated and I ended up leaving the club but I will never forget Gerry Gow.'

As the new year started City found themselves in a relegation dog-fight. Their inconsistency was clear for all to see and this wasn't helped when Gary Collier, who was certainly one of the stars of the season, was out for the remainder through injury. Dave Rodgers was an adequate replacement in defence but was nowhere near the player young Collier was.

The team spirit and backs-to-the-wall mentality was still strong and this was never more evident than against Chelsea at Ashton gate. Donnie Gillies takes up the story, 'We won the game 3-0 with goals from Cormack, Gow and Rodgers, and the match was really niggly, especially the two Chelsea defenders Steve Wicks and Micky Droy who could both put it about and particularly Droy who relied on intimidation in his game. Droy was having a go all game at Tom Ritchie. Droy pushed Tom in the box first and that's how we got our penalty early on and that set the tone really.

'We were 3-0 up and Droy's partner Steve Wicks went in nastily on Trevor Tainton so Trevor kicked out at him and got sent off. Then minutes later Droy made a savage tackle on Tom and he grabbed Droy by the throat and suddenly Gowy appeared and grabbed Steve Wicks. It was then a free for all with both sides grabbing hold of each other. As the melee was going on I will always remember Norman Hunter who was a couple of yards away running towards the group who were fighting shouting, "Keep it going, keep it going, I'm on my way." Eventually the ref gained control and sent off Micky Droy although we were lucky not to have a few of us go with him.'

The one for all and all for one attitude the side had was laudable but with Gerry Sweeney getting sent off the following week against Birmingham City and Gerry getting his marching orders the following month after reacting to a challenge by Ipswich Town's Russell Osman by hitting him. It attracted the attention of the authorities. The club were fined by the FA for accumulating more than 175 disciplinary points, along with receiving a severe warning to control their players and a fine of £800. Dicks commented in the *Bristol Evening Post* that 'the players were just committed to the cause'. He may well have had a point as the club finished the season in 17th position with West Ham United, Newcastle United and Leicester City being relegated. Yet again it was a fantastic achievement from Dicks and the players, who were many experts' pick to go down but they had defied the odds and lived to fight another day.

Gerry spent the summer on holiday with the family and living a quiet life. At times like these neighbours and friends got to know the real Gerry Gow – not the tough-tackling Scot whose reputation went before him on the football field, but the Scottish bloke who lived in the road and cut his grass and played football with his kids in the local park or had a pint in the local pub. That side of Gerry kept him sane within the pressure-cooker existence of the football world. Gerry knew how things could easily change for you in the game. One minute you were on top and the next you could be out of favour. His ex-wife Julie remembers, 'When the summer arrived, that was it with football. Gerry liked to relax and forget all about football and what had gone on the previous season, good or bad. He was never one of those players that analysed his game and when he was out he would much rather talk to people about what was on the TV or about their lives than his own and he certainly preferred that to talking about football.'

Gerry worked hard during the summer with running and sprints, but he was carrying a knee problem from the end of the previous season which threatened to carry through to the new campaign.

City went away, yet again to Norway with a few changes to the line-up. Former Leeds United and England full-back Terry Cooper joined for £20,000 from Middlesbrough. Speaking to Terry at a function at Ashton Gate in 2018 he told me how he signed and why, 'I got a call from Norman Hunter, my old Leeds United and England team-mate. He told me that Alan Dicks was looking for a full-back and I fitted the mould, which was a bit of experience. I laughed as I was 34 at the time and told him we might as well go the whole hog and ring Jackie Charlton up for a game. Anyway I talked it over with the wife and Norman said how happy he was and you have to remember it was a First Division side I was going to at the time and believe it or not the money was better at Bristol City. I signed and loved it but I never realised how dear the club would become to me years later.'

Added to the ranks was young wing prospect Howard Pritchard who had come up from the youth team with a glowing reputation. Howard was incredibly complimentary about Gerry when I asked him about his time with him, 'He was a great bloke and he always looked out for us youngsters. He always made sure if there was a night out with the more established players us youngsters got an invite too. As he used to say we are all one dressing room, and us youngsters really looked up to him.

'He was an incredible trainer, he played in training like it was a first team game and when we used to play Bristol Rovers every summer in the Gloucester Cup Final he would tell us how important it was to beat them. I remember him once telling us all that we had to beat them or he couldn't show his face to his neighbours as he lived in the Rovers side of Bristol. Yes, he was a great player and a brilliant guy to know.'

City were due to play six games on the tour but Gerry's knee was definitely in need of rest as it had become inflamed, so there would be no matches for him. The tour was also to be pivotal for long-standing captain Geoff Merrick, who explained, 'It was the start of the tour and we were in the hotel when Alan Dicks asked if he could have a word with me in his room. When I got there he was there with Tony Collins. They both explained to me that with the signing of Terry Cooper and also how well Norman was playing they felt that I would not be getting many games in the coming season so therefore they were taking the captaincy off me and giving it to Gerry.

'I was bitterly disappointed as I had always been captain and I felt I had always done a good job, even when I was moved to full-back I just got on with it, but that was their decision so I vowed to prove them wrong. I spoke with Gerry afterwards and he was uncomfortable with it as he was a good mate and we had known each other a long time, but he knew what an honour it was to lead City out as captain. If you ask me whether he was a good captain, let's just say he had a different style to me. Gerry was very vocal, shouting through games and at players, whereas that was not my style. I could certainly bollock players but I was also the sort of captain who would put an arm round the shoulder and that wasn't Gerry.'

City started their defence of the Anglo-Scottish Cup with a 6-1 demolition of neighbours Bristol Rovers but it was short-lived as they were knocked out in the quarter-final by St Mirren who gained revenge for the previous year. Gerry returned to the side for the 2-0 away defeat to Wolverhampton Wanderers and despite the loss City appeared to be more consistent as they approached the end of the year just outside the top ten after a 5-0 Boxing Day demolition of Coventry City.

One particular bright spark in the season had been the continued form of young striker Kevin Mabbutt who had really taken his chance in the team. Kevin was also somebody who realised the potential of making money outside football, getting himself an agent and also starting the 'Kevin Mabbutt Roadshow' which went around schools selling memberships to fans and in return they would receive a picture of Kevin, a pen and letter from him. Kevin also drove around in a Triumph

TR7 sports car with his name emblazoned along the side. It really was one of the first instances of marketing a player and showed other footballers where the future lay.

This approach could not have been further away from what Gerry wanted away from football. He would have rather stuck pins in his eyes than drive a car with his name splashed down the side. Kevin's motor led to all sorts of piss-taking in the dressing room as Joe Royle explained, 'I like Kevin, he was a good lad and a great footballer. I used to room with him and he was always asking questions about my time in the game and advice for playing. Rooming with him was great but at times he was a nightmare. He was a good-looking young lad so as you can imagine when we were on tour he always had attention from the ladies, so I'm saying no more than that. The lads did give him light-hearted stick about his car and his roadshow but he took it in good spirit and let's not forget he was doing the business on the pitch so there was no complaints.'

With City still picking up points and seemingly not going to be drawn into a relegation battle, manager Dicks ventured into the European market with the signing of Ajax left-winger Geert Meijer for £80,000 in March 1979. Meijer became an instant success by scoring after five minutes of his debut against Birmingham City in a 2-1 win.

I managed to track him down for an interview over the phone. Today he is coaching amateur Dutch team VW Strijen so I asked him about his time at City and although it was short he has fond memories of the club and Gerry. He said, 'I enjoyed my time in Bristol. It was a lovely place to live, the team were a really good side and the lads were a very good bunch, they helped me a lot and welcomed me. I liked Alan

Dicks a lot. He was a good manager I was very sorry when he left. Gerry was a great man, a terrific footballer and hard as nails, he was captain of the side if I remember right. He took me out to a bar in the centre of Bristol just after I signed with the intention of showing me the city but we had lots to drink. It was probably a mistake as we had training the next day and I was a bit sluggish due to the late night but I was amazed at him; he was running about like a youngster. Yes, he was a great man and a great player.'

The campaign came to an end with City finishing a respectable 13th and Gerry was named player of the year, which again was an incredible achievement considering his injury at the start. The end-of-season tour was in the USA as the lads prepared themselves for another season in the top flight, but they could not have realised that 1979/80 would turn out to be a pivotal season for the club and for many of them too.

12

End Of An Era

THE SUMMER of 1979 would see the building blocks that Alan Dicks had put in place to get Bristol City to the First Division and keep them there fall apart one by one. In the close-season, the experienced Norman Hunter had decided to move on and take a player-coach role under his old Leeds United team-mate Allan Clarke at Barnsley. Norman recalled, 'I just felt it was the right time for me and I wanted to get into coaching and eventually management. City offered me a two-year deal but the move back up north was right for me. I loved my years at City and if I'm honest I would have loved to have come back one day as a manager but the timing was never right for me or the club for that to happen.'

Terry Cooper also left having not played that much due to a reccurring Achilles tendon problem and went on a free transfer to Bristol Rovers. Added to this, rising star Gary Collier was in dispute with the club after continued interest from Coventry City. Collier, who was out of contract, became the first English player to change clubs under the new freedom of contract law. Previously players had been bound to clubs even after their contracts had expired. But new legislation stipulated that players could leave at the end of their deals, so Collier negotiated his own deal with Coventry who then paid the Robins £325,000.

The result of this was that Alan Dicks met with the City board to put through a proposal regarding players' contracts. The club was one of the best in the league when it came to paying wages. Apart from Liverpool and Everton, City were the highest payers with a basic of £300 per week, which was on a par with Aston Villa, Derby County, Leeds United Manchester City and Nottingham Forest. Dicks's plan was to offer players extended contracts to keep them at the club for a longer period, an idea that was sanctioned by the board. Gerry was presented with a seven-year deal at £350 a week, along with Tom Ritchie, while Clive Whitehead was offered an 11-year deal again on a weekly figure of £350. It's clear to see in hindsight the problems that City were going to have on the horizon but at the time there seemed method in the madness of these decisions.

Along with the departures, Dicks broke the club's transfer record by paying £250,000 for winger Tony Fitzpatrick from St Mirren after he had impressed against City in the Anglo-Scottish Cup games.

There was still an air of optimism from the fans regarding the new season even though the team had lost much of its defence. Another bright spark was the return of City favourite Geoff Merrick, although the captaincy still belonged to Gerry. Now the main man at Ashton Gate, the crowd responded to another season of First Division football by chanting his song for the opening-day visit of Leeds United.

THE GERRY GOW STORY

As 'He's here, he's there, he's every fucking where, Gerry Gow, Gerry Gow' echoed around the ground Gerry put his mark on Leeds United debutant Alan Curtis within the first couple of minutes. Alan laughed when I asked him for a few words regarding Gerry, 'Wow, Gerry Gow, I remember he kicked me up in the air the first few minutes of my debut for Leeds United at Ashton Gate. He floored me and just stayed over me as the ref arrived. It was as if he was saying to the ref, "He's fine". I was fine and I do remember him saying, "Come on, get up, taffy." I'm sure he did his homework and knew it was my debut and he wanted to unsettle me, although it didn't really work as I scored two goals. I had played against Gerry a few times when I was at Swansea and he was a tough lad but he was also a good footballer. In the game against Leeds he won three tackles one after another, got possession and hit a 40-yard ball to feet. You can't do that if you can't play.'

The encounter ended in a 2-2 draw and that really set the tone for the start of the season as City had reverted to the inconsistent form that had dogged them throughout their time in the top flight. Only four wins heading into Christmas left them stuck in a relegation battle. As the festive season came and went they could not get a win from anywhere and with tension in the camp, Gerry clashed with Alan Dicks after a 3-0 defeat at home to Ipswich Town. There had been a demonstration outside the ground after the game with fans calling for Dicks to resign. It was rare for the two friends to clash as they thought the world of each other, but City had suffered some heavy defeats at home during the season, including 3-1 scorelines against Aston Villa and Tottenham Hotspur.

Things had come to a head. 'He had a right go after the Ipswich Town game,' recalls Alan. 'We were poor and he just said as captain what we were all feeling really. It wasn't Gerry's style to shout and bawl in the dressing room, he always did it on the pitch and had done it since he was a kid. You got a real sense that the spirit wasn't there that had been before. Silly things like the lads didn't socialise like they used to and I think that had an effect on the team spirit. For people like Gerry, not trying was the worst crime you could commit and maybe he thought one or two were not trying.'

With relegation looking a real possibility, particularly after a 4-0 thrashing at Old Trafford by Manchester United, Dicks announced that a £1m clearance sale was launched and he was prepared to listen to offers for Kevin Mabbutt, Clive Whitehead, Geoff Merrick, Joe Royle, Chris Garland, Tom Ritchie and Gerry Gow. The club also cancelled the contracts of Peter Cormack and Geert Meijer as the clouds over Ashton Gate were getting darker and darker. Cormack ended up at Hibernian, while Meijer returned to Holland in a £50,000 deal with Sparta Rotterdam. There were no enquiries for the rest of the team as clubs were waiting for the end of the season when they might have been able to get a better deal.

The Robins' fate was finally sealed in a bitter, bruising encounter with Norwich City at home, when they went down 3-2 in front of only 16,000 fans. The game will be remembered for a headbutt on City centre-back Dave Rodgers by Justin Fashanu that was basically an assault. Rodgers needed four stitches to his eye in an incident that enraged the whole team and particularly Gerry who had to be restrained after the game when he tried to get at Fashanu in the away dressing room.

Norwich manager John Bond calmed the situation down by talking to Gerry and then entering the Bristol City dressing room to apologise to the players and tell them that Fashanu would be fined.

Gerry's reaction as usual was to support his team-mate but there was an air of frustration that had built up during the season for him to react in the way he did. Years later, in an article for *Shoot!* magazine, Fashanu was asked the question, 'What have you done on the field that you're not proud of?' He cited this incident and went on, 'The result being that I had Gerry Gow chasing after me, and if you know Gerry Gow he is a man you don't want after you.'

City were relegated and their fate was sealed after a 5-2 away defeat to Southampton and a 0-0 draw at Tottenham Hotspur. They were four points from safety and were joined in dropping to the Second Division by Bolton Wanderers and Derby County. The supporters voted Geoff Merrick as their player of the season, which was an incredible turnaround for a player who had been written off the previous year. Equally incredible was the award of five-year contracts to Alan Dicks and Tony Collins.

Gerry took the relegation badly. He wasn't really the sort of player who took his results home, good or bad, but it took a few weeks for him to get over the way the season had panned out. It was a case of mooching around the house for a bit before getting away with the family, who pulled him back together ready for another season. A summer with his kids Chris and Rachael, along with wife Julie, soon put him back on track, although conversations between the players during the close-season were of what would happen in the following year and whether there be more departures. They were on the mark as Joe Royle left in a £60,000 deal with Norwich City. Donnie Gillies also left although it was a move the likeable Scot didn't want, 'I didn't really have much choice to be honest. Alan Dicks told me he couldn't play me and the club couldn't afford my wages. He said there was a move on the table to Bristol Rovers and it was a case of take it or stay in the reserves so I took it and left.'

Gerry missed the two opening games of 1980/81 due to knee problems. The start had been rather uninspiring for many fans with 1-1 draws against Preston North End and West Ham. Gerry returned in the heart of midfield for the 0-0 draw at home to rivals Bristol Rovers. The clash brought in a crowd of 16,000 fans which was a far cry from the 26,000 who attended their last league game against each other four years previously.

After another defeat away at Watford, things came to a head for Dicks following a 1-0 defeat at home to Swansea. The Welshmen were more skilful and city were devoid of any ideas throughout the game. Fans turned on the board and Dicks and demanded that the manager depart. The club offered Dicks the chance to move upstairs but he refused and on 8 September 1980 he left after a tenure of one month short of 13 years. Gerry was devastated and had words with various board members but to no avail.

Talking about his time at Ashton Gate brings mixed emotions for Alan, 'I loved my time at the club and I loved the players. I received criticism towards the end that had been harsh and some of the things said were deeply hurtful. It had been a long and enjoyable road, the reaction of the players was incredible; even players who had left contacted me and wished me well. I remember Gerry being very upset and we spoke a few times on the phone and his kind words meant a lot to me. I had some great players and what we achieved together was immense. I hope the fans remember that.'

Dicks went on to have coaching spells in Greece, Cyprus, Qatar, USA and Fulham where he was assistant to Ray Lewington. Today he lives in Bristol and still attends the odd City function.

It was clear that City were in a state of freefall and despite relegation they couldn't get a win from anywhere in a division they should have more than held their own in. They had lost players and recruited players before and it had always worked but now Gerry and the more senior players felt they were on a rollercoaster that was heading only downwards. Team spirit seemed at an all-time low and gates were dwindling fast. Coach Ken Wimshurst, along with Tony Collins, took over the hot seat until a replacement could be found, but they could not stop the rot with three defeats on the trot.

As City sat at the foot of the table the board unveiled their new manager and on paper at least it looked a tremendous appointment. Bob Houghton was a former Fulham and Brighton player. He had been coaching abroad with Greek club Ethnikos after taking Swedish club Malmo to four national titles and also guiding them to a European Cup Final where they were beaten by Brian Clough's Nottingham Forest.

Houghton, however, was not the club's first choice. That had been Norman Hunter who spoke of his dilemma regarding the job, 'I was assistant at Barnsley when Allan Clarke, the manager, moved to Leeds United, then I got a call from the Bristol City board offering me the job. It was a really difficult decision at the time but I made the right one as things went from bad to worse at City and I'm not sure any manager could have stopped the rot. It would have been great to see the supporters again, but it was not to be as I went for Barnsley which worked out in the end for me.'

Houghton arrived and called a meeting at the training ground where he set out his plan for survival with the players. City were going to play a more direct approach as opposed to building up from the back four, through midfield and towards the strikers, which had been their familiar style. They were now going to effectively bypass the midfield and get the ball up front as quick as possible. Gerry had serious reservations about this and how this would impact his own game but he kept them to himself as if it got the club out of trouble it would be worth it.

Houghton's first game in charge was a 1-0 defeat away at Grimsby, but City rallied a week later when they beat Luton Town 2-1 at home in front of only 7,571 supporters. It was their first win in ten games and they followed this with another victory at home to Newcastle United. Although City were off the bottom of the table, for Gerry the games had been a nightmare. He phoned Alan Dicks and told him how unhappy he was. Alan remembers the call, 'He rang me and he was really down; he said it was like being in a basketball team as the ball was always in the air and the midfield hardly got a touch. I asked him if he had spoken to Houghton about his concerns and he said, "Yes, every training session, but he wasn't concerned. All he wanted was results, and that was how they were going to achieve it." We spoke a couple of times and I asked him bluntly, "What do you want to do?" "I'm not sure," he replied. I hated the thought that Gerry was unhappy at the club as it was so unlike him, so I made a few calls, one in particular to John Bond who had just taken over at Manchester City. Bondy was a really big fan of Gerry, when he was manager of Norwich City he was always asking me if he was for sale, so I just told him, "You might be able to get him."'

Gerry's frustration continued as City drew 1-1 away at Bolton Wanderers with the same route one display. During the week Gerry was informed by club officials that an offer had been made for him. He was flattered that it was a club the size of Manchester City who were in the First Division, but leaving Ashton Gate would be a massive wrench personally as it was all he knew. Gerry turned out for the 1-0 defeat away at Wrexham but inside he knew this was going to be his last game in a City shirt. Jonathan Pearce, who at the time was working for Radio Bristol, remembers the emotionally charged interview with Gerry after the game, ' He came over to do an interview and I asked him if the rumour was true that he was leaving and he said yes. I think I was crying on air and he was the same. I will never forget it.'

Gerry went to talk terms with John Bond in a hotel just outside the centre of Manchester. There were no agents and no hangers-on – just Gerry, Bond and City chairman Peter Swales. Bond laid down the terms and thinking with his head rather than his heart Gerry decided to sign for the Manchester giants. He phoned Julie and explained that he had agreed a deal and he would be home in the morning. The move then depended on Gerry passing a medical and with this in mind Bond phoned Dicks asking what his knees were like. Alan responded, 'Knackered and he won't pass a medical but still sign him as he will give you 100 per cent and you will always

END OF AN ERA

be able to rely on a player like Gerry.' Incredibly Bond signed Gerry without a medical for £175,000. The Scot had played nearly 450 games for the Robins and netted 55 goals.

When Gerry returned to Ashton Gate, he said his goodbyes to the lads. They were a good bunch but it just wasn't the same as the old days and he knew it was the right thing to do. With finances tight at the club he waived his signing-on fee, reputed to have been £20,000, so City could have it. It was money he could have done with as he had moving expenses and a house to buy but he knew it was the right thing to do for the club he loved. Gerry shook Bob Houghton's hand and they wished each other well. He felt no ill feeling towards Houghton, who was there to do a job and he didn't really know the young coach so there was no emotional tie to him.

Before walking out of the ground he strolled around the Ashton Gate pitch and in his head he could hear his song, 'He's here, he's there, he's every fucking where, Gerry Gow, Gerry Gow.'

Memories came flooding back – arriving as just a kid, his debut, the FA Cup games against Leeds United and Liverpool, along with the night they clinched promotion. As Gerry looked up to the Williams Stand he imagined all the lads singing and drinking, celebrating with the fans, and if he closed his eyes he could still hear John Sillettt's voice booming around the ground telling the youth team to run faster.

Gerry knew the move was right for his own career, but he knew his heart would always be at Ashton Gate.

13

The King Of Maine Road

IN THE modern game Manchester City have been trailblazers with their state-of-the art facilities and their work in the local community. The money the club sits on has not only been spent on bringing the best players in the world to the Etihad but also on reaching out beyond the local area to all parts of the world, turning City into a global business. Although the takeover in 2008 by the Abu Dhabi United Group has put Manchester City at the very top of the footballing tree, we must never forget that this has always been a massive club.

From the days of Billy Meredith, Don Revie, Roy Paul and Bert Trautmann through to the sublime skills of the great Joe Mercer and Malcolm Allison team of Bell, Sumerbee and Lee, City have always won trophies and put bums on seats. Even in the dark days of 1998 when they languished in the Second Division, they were still getting home gates of over 25,000 fans.

The Manchester City that Gerry Gow signed for in October 1980 was however on the verge of dropping out of the First Division for the first time since 1965/66. In the previous season they had seen the return of Allison to become number two to manager and legendary former skipper Tony Book. Allison had then become the main man at the start of the season when Book moved upstairs as general manager. Allison decided to get rid of a clutch of experienced players such as Dave Watson, Brian Kidd, Gary Owens and Peter Barnes and bring in a nucleus of young relatively inexperienced faces. He also spent a few million in the process on several players who were not really up to the job. The strategy failed and chairman Peter Swales relieved Allison of his duties in October 1980 with City one place off the bottom of the First Division.

Swales was a local businessman who made his name in the electronics business. He was a flamboyant character who enjoyed the limelight given to him by the very nature of his position at City. Swales appointed a manager who was not a million miles away from his own image of fine suits and readiness to involve the media – John Bond. Bond had made over 400 appearances for West Ham United during the late 1950s and early 1960s when he was also a team-mate of Allison. A master technician of the game, Bond cut his teeth in management with AFC Bournemouth before taking Norwich City to the 1975 League Cup Final and also promotion to the First Division. When taking the job, he said, 'When a club like Manchester City come calling you don't say no.'

The task for Bond was huge and he immediately realised that the team needed a spine of steel if the already turbulent season was to be turned around. He made three signings, who would all prove pivotal. Bond went straight to Coventry City where he signed Scottish pair, full-back Bobby MacDonald and forward Tommy Hutchinson, for a combined fee of £320,000, knowing that both players had fallen out with Coventry manager Gordon

Milne. His next purchase was to strengthen the midfield and having been a long-time admirer of Gerry Gow he enquired about the Scot and to his delight he found he was also unhappy at the club. Gerry signed for a bargain £175,000.

Bond knew that Gerry had problems with injuries and persuaded Swales to take a gamble and sign him without a medical. The manager later said, 'Gerry Gow was one of the best players I ever bought.'

In my research for this book, I eventually tracked down Bobby McDonald who told me that he didn't really get involved in publications or reunions at his old clubs as he felt his career had now gone and he had moved on. But when I mentioned that this project was about Gerry Gow, he said, 'Of course I will do it. Gerry was a great player and great man.' Bobby recalled with real affection the time the three players all signed for Manchester City, 'Tommy and me were unhappy at Coventry as we had been promised certain things that never materialised so the move to City was great for us as we felt like it was a new challenge for us. I had always rated Gerry and when I played against him in my Aston Villa and Coventry days I always thought, "God, I wish he was on my side."

'Bristol City were a team you did not look forward to playing against and although they were a side with few stars they were really disciplined and had a great team spirit, so I was over the Moon when I found out from John Bond that he was going to be the third signing. In a way I suppose Gerry thought the move was a new challenge for him also as Bristol City had just been relegated.

'We all hit it off right away and the club put us all in a local hotel until we found houses to move our families into. We had some great times in the hotel. Me and Tommy shared a room but Gerry had a room to himself and we would go to training and when it was finished we would hit the hotel bar for a chat and a few beers. John Bond would also join us some nights to make sure we were happy. I remember one night when we were having a few drinks with some travelling salesmen that were staying in the hotel, we were drinking and talking football until well into the early hours. Anyway we went to bed and apparently Gerry, who was a bit the worse for wear, got up in the night completely naked and totally disorientated. He went out of his room thinking it was the toilet then somehow got into one of the salesmen's room who was asleep in bed. Thinking it was his room Gerry dived into bed and straight on to the poor fella. It woke the whole floor up as both of them were screaming. Me and Tommy couldn't stop laughing at breakfast along with everybody else while Gerry sat there shaking his head which was bright red. The salesmen never came down for breakfast and we had a great story for the lads in the dressing room before training.'

Bond's first game in charge was a 1-0 home defeat to Birmingham City. He had been at the club for just one day and could already see the size of the task as City had now gone 12 games without a win. But his effect on the playing staff seemed to have a quick impact with a 3-1 win at home to Tottenham in their next game. McDonald and Hutchinson were drafted in for their debuts the following week as City won 2-1 away at Brighton but Gerry had to wait a week for his first appearance, a 1-0 victory against Bond's old club Norwich City.

The new faces on and off the pitch drove an immediate improvement in City's fortunes as the fans took to the new line-up, especially Gerry, whose never-say-dive attitude and strength in the tackle was a far cry from what they had witnessed under Allison. Before the Christmas period City had climbed the table by losing only twice in a 12-game run, with Gerry finding the net five times in the process.

For the rest of the squad the signings were just what had been required. Goalkeeper Joe Corrigan, a veteran of over 600 games in his distinguished Manchester City career, explained their impact, 'It really was all about experience. We had a young side, particularly in the back four, so to have Bobby Mac alongside them and Gerry Gow sat in front of them worked a treat. Put that with Tommy Hutchinson who was always capable of snatching a goal meant we really had something for the fans to cheer.

'I had played many times against Gerry when he was at Bristol City and he was a real difficult opponent. He was hard as nails and never shirked a challenge. Our dressing room was always talking about Gow in City's midfield whenever we visited Ashton Gate. Our fans took to him and he looked like a "wild man" with his frizzy grey hair and his moustache. He wasn't the typical Manchester City midfielder like a Colin Bell but he had a connection with the fans from day one.'

Gerry's neighbour and former Bristol Rovers player Phil Bater recalls how much the fans thought of him, 'Gerry had just signed for City and I went up from Bristol to see him when he was staying in the hotel with Tommy and Bobby. We went out and in Manchester and I couldn't believe how popular he was with the fans up there. They are a tough crowd who have seen some great players but he really was appreciated by them.'

THE KING OF MAINE ROAD

Gerry's ability was there for all to see and lifelong Manchester City season ticket holder Peter Williams remembers one game in particular, 'We were away at Crystal Palace and I travelled down with the supporters' club. There was a sense of optimism about travelling to games now with John Bond at the helm. If I'm honest I wasn't that keen when he was appointed but I will be forever grateful to him as he brought Gerry Gow to the club. We won the game 3-2 at Palace and it was off the back of a 3-0 home win against Southampton and a 3-0 home win against Coventry City. Gerry had been incredible in all our games since signing and that day at Selhurst Park he ran the show. He was box-to-box, he won every tackle in midfield and scored two goals to go with it.

'I will always remember the coach journey home where we were all chatting about what a bargain he was and how we should have bought him years ago. I don't mind admitting when we signed him I was one of the ones who thought he wouldn't be able to cut it with Manchester City, but I, like a lot of fans, was proved wrong. He will always be one of my favourite City players.'

Off the field, Julie and the children had moved up from Bristol which at least at put an end to the high jinx in the hotel with Tommy and Bobby, much to the delight of John Bond. The family moved to the Somerfield estate in Wilmslow, just outside the city. There were a few of Gerry's team-mates on the estate, including Tommy Hutchinson and his family who moved in across the road from the Gows and Bobby MacDonald who bought a house around the corner, with Bobby joking, 'I had to go around the corner as I wasn't on as much money as Tommy and Gerry.'

For Julie and Gerry, Manchester was certainly more high profile as they were invited to different events around the city, although Gerry was now a relatively small fish in a very big pond as opposed to at Bristol where he really was the top player at the club. The family settled in well as Julie had the other wives to call on whenever she wanted and they would organise things for when the players were away. She didn't have to worry about Gerry though as he had become such a hit with the fans and he really was the 'King of Maine Road'.

Bond was certainly the right type of manager for Gerry as Bristol City's Alan Dicks had been. He believed the ball should be played through the midfield and he allowed Gerry to express himself on the pitch. He, like Dicks, was always there for a chat after training or of an evening if Gerry needed it. Bond had built a good team spirit, which had been there under the surface but with the depressing run under previous manager Allison things had got low.

The squad were a much more talented group than Gerry had experienced at Ashton Gate but he did comment in later life, 'I would give the Bristol City promotion team a chance against anybody but the Robins side I left was a shadow of that team.' Gerry certainly established himself in the First Division but the relentless schedule took its toll on him. It was well documented that Gerry had problems with his knees or his ankles and they could very well have put an end to his time at Maine Road before it had even got going if Bond and Swales had gone down the medical route.

Throughout Gerry's career, one thing that could always be said about him was that he was consistent. Right from his early days with John Sillett in Bristol City's youth team he always played regularly and was a virtual ever-present for the Robins. Former manager Alan Dicks used to say, 'He was the first name on the team sheet.'

At 28 years old he was still an amazing trainer but the use of cortisone on his knees and ankles before and after games was becoming more frequent. Hydrocortisone was essentially a steroid that was injected into the painful or swollen part of the body. The steroids dampened down the immune system and relieved the pain. They effectively masked the initial problem for a period of time and they were widely used on footballers throughout the 1970s, 1980s and 1990s, and although the practice is safe and better controlled today its overuse can still mean cartilage damage, joint infection and nerve damage in later life.

Joe Corrigan explained how it affected Gerry, 'When I saw Gerry play and train I, like a lot of the players, wished we had got him a few years earlier. He was great with us so he must have been something else with Bristol City. Like a lot of us at the time the club used cortisone injections to get us through games if we had injuries. There were a lot of different factors that caused this. Pitches were heavier, squads were smaller and we played so many games. I think Liverpool won the league and European Cup using 14 players back in the day.

'There was also the financial implications for us as players. We all had to play. Don't get me wrong, we were relatively well paid compared to the average man on the street, but that was only if you had your wage, added to your appearance money, your win or draw bonus, or your goals bonus, and playing was all we ever wanted to do so you never wanted to sit on the sidelines.

'Gerry was always having injections, he would have trouble recovering after games, so it was a wonder he was playing so well for us because I'm sure he was in real pain during games as he had no chance to rest before the next game was upon us.'

Not only was the John Bond rollercoaster taking Manchester City up the league to safety, they were also holding their own in two domestic cup competitions. As the season headed into spring, City were dealt a blow when they were knocked out of the League Cup by Liverpool in a controversial two-legged semi-final. They were defeated in the first leg at Maine Road 1-0 in front of a 48,000 crowd, with many City fans and neutrals believing they should have seen a goal stand which had been ruled out by the referee. They drew the second leg at Anfield 1-1, which sent Liverpool to Wembley where they eventually defeated West Ham United.

The disappointment was not lost on the City squad and although Gerry was cup- tied for the competition he and his team-mates vowed that they would do something in the FA Cup where they were due to play Everton in the quarter-final the following month. As City consolidated their league position the excitement about the FA Cup started to build and the encounter at Goodison Park drew a crowd of over 52,000 for a tough 2-2 draw. Gerry once again put in a stellar performance, covering every blade of grass and getting one of the City goals, with experienced defender Paul Power scoring the other.

The replay some four days later once again drew a crowd of over 52,000 to Maine Road where a scintillating display by City steamrolled Everton 3-1 with two goals from Bobby MacDonald and another goal from Power. Bobby remembered the dressing room afterwards, 'We were on cloud nine as they say: we were in the FA Cup semi-final and we were really full of confidence. I remember poor old Gerry could hardly walk. He had given everything during the game, as we all had, but he was just coasting on adrenaline, and when that died down I'm sure he would have been in agony. We had a home game in the league against West Bromwich Albion in three days' time so it was a case of patching ourselves up and going again.'

For Gerry the match against West Brom would prove one too many as after the 2-1 victory his right knee had ballooned up and was a real cause for concern. Physio Roy Bailey, assistant boss John Benson, and manager Bond agreed that this would not be a case of a quick injection of cortisone to fix it; it would need rest as City had a semi-final against Ipswich Town in four weeks and if their star midfielder was going to have any chance of playing he would need complete rest. Gerry agreed as the thought of missing the chance to get to Wembley was unthinkable.

14

Dad

AS A youngster growing up I would watch Gerry Gow from the terraces at Ashton Gate. He was terrifying to look at with his long frizzy hair and regulation 1970s moustache; in fact he looked as if he had stepped straight out of a spaghetti western film. In a way that was his role in the City team – the enforcer, an outlaw who would kill a man as soon as look at him, but in Gerry's case, if you had a football he would come looking for you on the pitch and invariably the opponent would come off second best.

It certainly was an image that many fans have of this City great. At school we would all play football in the playground and shout who we were going to be, and it's no surprise that the 'hard' kids would always want to be Gerry as it gave them a green light to kick their opponents up in the air, safe in the knowledge that it was what Gerry would have done. I grew up in the Whitchurch area of Bristol and would see Gerry at the shops and just around the neighbourhood. I knew where he lived but again that reputation of his meant my mates and I were too scared to ask for his autograph or knock on his door.

This changed in later life when I met Gerry at a few Bristol City reunion events and it always left me with a sense of regret as when I did actually speak to him I realised how completely different he was to that image and how he really would have made my day as a kid had I plucked up the courage.

Working on this book and talking to people who knew Gerry has confirmed that he was a genuinely nice guy off the field, as many of football's 'hard men' are. Most importantly, I wanted to know what he was like as a dad which is why when I sat down with his children Chris, Rachael and Jenny in Portland I was intrigued to know more. It was plain to see that his exit from their lives left a massive hole in the family that rippled right through all areas of their life. Chris explains, 'He was my best mate, always on the end of the phone and always calling to make sure the whole family were okay and safe. I miss him every day, we all do, but we have some great memories of him growing up.

'It's funny that fans had this image of him. I understand it as he was tough out on the pitch but once he was off all he was interested in was us kids and my mum; irrespective of the result he had, he switched off at home. I knew dad was a footballer from a young age and I would go and see him at Bristol City from about four years of age. I would go with my mum and my grandparents who were City season ticket-holders and had been for years. Growing up I never really knew how big he was. I remember the fans singing about him but I'm sure my mum blocked my ears halfway through his song for obvious reasons.

'I went to Bridge Farm School in Whitchurch and we were such young kids that I don't really remember my friends being that bothered as to what my dad did. I think they would probably have been more impressed if he had been a policeman or a fireman; I know I would have been. It really kicked in for me when the club got promotion in 1976. I was about six or seven and I remember his picture, along with the rest of the team, being all over the local paper. Soon after we moved to the Hanham area of the city, I can still remember all the neighbours watching us move in and smiling and waving at dad. I just thought he knew everyone.

'A memory that comes back is the day we had to get a phone line installed by the GPO and obviously it was noted that the owner of the house was Gerry Gow. Three vans turned up with GPO men who were obviously City fans. One bloke did the work and the others drank tea talking about football with dad. He loved chatting to fans.

'I used to love playing football with him in the back garden and he never ever pushed me regarding football. Other people assumed he would want me to be a footballer, but all dad wanted was for me to be happy in whatever I did and that was the same for Rachael and Jenny. Those times when he was at Bristol City were really special for us growing up. Many of the players had kids, my own age and after matches when the fans were gone me and a few other players kids along with Jonathan Pearce and Patrick Dicks, would have a kick about in the Ashton Gate car park while dad was having a drink with the players in the bar. They would come out and join us, and you appreciate now how special those memories are.

'I know he took the relegation of the club really hard but at the time he tried not to show it. It was only in later life when we talked about it that he told me he felt he had let the City fans down which was nonsense really but that was how he felt.

Dad was a really quiet man off the field, and it's really difficult for people to imagine that due to his image. He would go and take our dog for a walk, chat with the neighbours and go for a pint, or a meal with mum, just normal things really but I have to say people were great with him and as a young kid I never ever witnessed any hostility towards him, which could have happened especially being in a city with two clubs.

'Another memory is of him and mum sitting me and Rachael down and telling us he was going to Manchester City. I was thrilled to be honest. I loved Bristol City but I always had a soft spot for Manchester City after seeing the likes of Bell, Summerbee and Lee on television. Dad asked us if we were okay with it, which was typical of him. He said we would have to move so it would be new school and new friends and if we were not happy he wouldn't sign. Me and Rachael looked on it as an adventure and an adventure it was.

'Dad moved up and stayed in a hotel for a few months and we moved up then into a new house on the Somerfield estate in Wilmslow just outside Manchester. It was great as there were a few players and their kids on the estate which really helped us all settle in. Dad was really paranoid that we were all happy and enjoying our time there and I think once he knew we were all settled he could enjoy his football. He would always ask us how school was and were we enjoying it.

'I remember my first day at my new school in Manchester. I was about nine or ten and I was introduced to the class by my teacher as Gerry Gow's son which was a bit embarrassing but it certainly made me very popular with the Man City fans in the class. As for the Manchester United fans, well, I won them over in the end.

'I recall my PE teacher being very impressed with the new addition to the school. In fact he rang my mum and asked if she could bring my football boots up to the school as there was a game that evening and I was immediately catapulted into the team. I'm not sure looking back if the teacher was disappointed that he didn't get an absolute clone of Gerry Gow with blistering tackles and an engine that went box-to-box, but I didn't let myself down staying in the team at least. Dad thought it was hilarious though.

'His time at Manchester City will always be precious to me. He loved the club and, like Bristol City, the club and its supporters loved him and it was something he was very proud of. Manchester City gave me the chance to see my dad play in an FA Cup Final and that will always be a very special moment for me. At the time the FA Cup Final was the biggest game in the country. Typical dad, although he was so disappointed to lose the match the first thing he asked about after was how was mum and the kids and had they had a good day.

'I was gutted when he left City and I remember the moment well. I was coming home from school with my mates and our house was the first house on the way home so we would stop, I would get changed and then we would move on to the next friend's house, and eventually we would stay out playing. When we arrived at my house Rotherham United manager Emlyn Hughes was sat in the front room with mum and dad. I was introduced to him and told he was signing dad. Bitterly disappointed, I ignored him and went upstairs. When dad did sign and played his first game I went to the match with a Manchester City scarf on as an act of defiance. Emlyn later forgave me and him and his family became very good friends of our family.

'He was a lovely bloke, although I remember him and dad giving me one of my most embarrassing moments. We stayed with Emlyn and his family one evening and he had a massive corner bath. I had been out playing and was about 14 I think, anyway I had a bath and while I was in there Emlyn and dad had come back from the pub a bit the worse for wear. They heard I was in the bath and thought it would be funny to come up and see me. Anyway I had made the fatal error of not locking the door and suddenly the two of them crashed into the bathroom armed with a loofah each and they proceeded to stick it into me and hit me over the head. They were laughing like two kids. I was absolutely mortified by it before Emlyn's wife and my mum came up and told them off like naughty boys.

'It's strange when I see a picture of Emlyn Hughes today, I don't think of him captaining England or lifting trophies with Liverpool, I think of him, along with dad, attacking me with a loofah.

'I think dad knew after his time at Rotherham and later Burnley that maybe the knees and the ankles had given up the ghost, so when he was offered the chance to be player-manager of Yeovil Town he jumped at it. He loved it and we moved back to the West Country.'

This time marks the first real memories Rachael has of her dad, 'I was really small when we were at Bristol and Manchester. I am about five years younger than Chris but he has an encyclopaedic memory when it comes to dad's career. For me I remember his time at Yeovil Town and that's when I knew he was well known. He would be on television and when we were out and about people would be interested in us as a family, often stopping dad in the street. I was a real daddy's girl and I often recall him going away due to football and in some ways when he wasn't playing it was as though I got him back.

'I really cherished the time he was at home as he was only interested in us kids and he gave us 100 per cent attention. Dad was head of the family and any troubles we had he would want to know about. When he and mum divorced, me, Chris and Jenny were devastated, but they were an amazing couple whose only thoughts were for us kids and eventually our kids. The way they handled the divorce is testimony to what wonderful people they are. And it was great that mum found love with her husband Peter and dad later found love with Joolz. These two have become wonderful additions to the Gow family and I can't really express the love we have for them both.

'When dad gave up football completely I think he did struggle, but he never really talked about it. He, like a lot of players, just seemed to think, "Right, what shall I do now?" He did a few things here and there but his main priority was the family, especially as he had grandchildren. I don't think I have ever seen love like it, the way he was with the grand kids.'

These thoughts are echoed by Gerry's youngest daughter Jenny, 'I had no recollection at all of dad being a footballer as I was born in 1986 and I am told he only just made the birth due to football commitments. I can only talk about him as a dad and he was everything to all of us. I know he had this reputation as a hard man on the field and that is maybe true but he was kind and loving and always there for all of us. He idolised my four kids as he did with Rachael's and Chris's. He certainly left a hole in the family but I know he is looking down on all of us.'

The legacy Gerry has left in football terms is not lost on the family and in particular Chris, who recalls how touched he is by the level of love shown towards his father, 'It's incredibly humbling when I see how loved he was by Bristol City fans and Manchester City fans. Even the Rotherham supporters acknowledge how committed he was to their club and it really means a lot. I go to the odd game at Ashton Gate and I still see some fans with shirts on with Gow on the back, and recently I was contacted on Facebook by a lady who told me a story of how after the Cup Final the Manchester City team arrived back at Maine Road where they were swamped by supporters. Dad had a Man City top on and he gave it to a guy; well, that guy was her father and the shirt had been passed down to her. The shirt had become a family heirloom which was so nice and it's great to hear how people had met dad and the effect he had on them.

'I never get tired of hearing stories about dad whenever I meet fans. He was a special man who meant a lot to many people, but at the end of the day he was dad and a very special one at that.'

15

Wembley

AS GERRY desperately tried to get fit for the FA Cup semi-final it was no surprise that in the five matches he missed leading up to it, City didn't win one. City's opponents on that April afternoon at Villa Park were Ipswich Town, managed by Bobby Robson, and the team from East Anglia were fighting out the title with Aston Villa. As far as the press and pundits were concerned, Ipswich were stonewall favourites to get to the twin towers. Their side featured a midfield of quality that included two talented Dutchmen, Arnold Murhen and Frans Thijssen, who along with Scotsman John Wark had been carving teams up all season.

Robson was a big fan of Gerry's and had enquired about him seasons previously during his Bristol City days, so with this in mind Robson knew how important Gerry was to City's chances of winning the midfield battle that day.

Gerry had a fitness test with physio Roy Bailey in the grounds of the team hotel under the watchful eye of John Bond and his assistant John Benson. Gerry was desperate to play and they all agreed he would be okay providing he had a few cortisone injections before kick-off. This was a dream come true for Gerry as he had lost a semi-final before in the League Cup with Bristol City in the early part of his career and he was ecstatic that the chance to get to Wembley in a major final had come round again.

Manchester City's journey to the semi-final had seen them dispatch Crystal Palace, Norwich City, Peterborough United and Everton after a replay. Gerry's presence on the team sheet gave a real boost to the rest of the City players, including young striker Dave Bennett, who said, 'I always felt we had a chance when Gerry was in the side; he was so committed. We could be 3-0 down or 3-0 up and he never changed, he always gave everything to the cause.

'John Bond reminded us how important the midfield battle was going to be that afternoon, so you can see how desperate the club were to get Gerry in the side.'

The game in front of a crowd of 47,000 was certainly no classic. In fact it was a typical battle between two sides who gave nothing away, and the deadlock was broken in extra time when City received a free kick on the edge of the Ipswich box. Skipper Paul Power stood over it and crashed a shot into the Ipswich net, sending the travelling City fans into total rapture.

City held on and when the final whistle blew the adrenalin and joy of the occasion filled the players as they embraced each other, while the defeat emptied the Ipswich players as they sank to their knees. Gerry, who was in pain all through the game, found enough strength to cling on to his team-mates and City had done it – they had reached the FA Cup Final just months after seeming to be destined for relegation. Bond took the applause in the stand before joining his team on the Villa Park pitch.

The atmosphere and importance of the game wasn't lost on the young Chris Gow, who says he still gets goosebumps when he thinks about the occasion today, 'I was about ten at the time and I remember seeing all these Manchester City fans in Villa's Holte End. They sang all game and I loved it when they sang about my dad. As the whistle blew I just hugged my mum and grandad with everything I had. Even at that young age I knew how important the FA Cup Final was and here was my dad reaching the final. I recall a man who was sat behind me tapped me on the shoulder and gave me the Man City badge he was wearing, and I still have it today. It was a magical day.'

The other semi-final had been between Tottenham Hotspur and Wolverhampton Wanderers and was drawn 2-2, so four days later the players and fans found out that Spurs were to be their opponents when they won the replay 3-0. The excitement in Manchester was at fever pitch leading up to the final as fans scrambled around for tickets and the players were mobbed by supporters wherever they went. City fans were used to success and going to Wembley, but maybe this was different as they could not have dreamed of the season ending like this during the dark days with Malcolm Allison. With the final approaching Gerry was rested for three games as extra time in the semi had certainly taken its toll on his knees and ankles. He came back a week before the showpiece occasion in a 1-1 draw with Crystal Palace and told Bond and his backroom staff that he was raring to go.

Saturday, 9 May 1981 was the day of the 100th FA Cup Final. In the build-up the story was all about Spurs' Argentinian midfielder Ossie Ardiles and his dream to win the cup for, as he put it, 'Tottinam'. The story was the backdrop to the Londoners' Cup Final song which they had recorded along with fans Chas and Dave. The single even peaked at number five in the charts, combined with the media latching on to 1981 being the year of the cockerel in the Chinese zodiac, plus Spurs often winning a cup when the year ended in one. It was plain to see that for the majority of the nation Manchester City were just there to make up the numbers, although this view was plainly not felt by City fans or the players.

The FA Cup was always the biggest game in the country. It was the prize every player, fan and manager wanted to win, and viewing figures were huge as it was one of very few live matches shown on television at the time. The build-up started on the Friday night with an ITV show called *Who Will Win The Cup* where host Brian Moore along with a chosen panel of ex-players or current managers dissected the teams' runs to the final and each individual player in the process. The prediction of the show was that Spurs would be victorious.

For viewers at home the day's TV started on both ITV and BBC at 9am with items such as *FA Cup It's a Knockout*, *A Question Of Sport*, introductions to the wives of the finalists, and also cameras following the teams on their coaches from their hotels to the stadium.

Gerry and the City squad had left Manchester earlier in the week for London, before doing the interview rounds and also being measured for their obligatory suits, which were a light sky blue in colour. The players were in the Selsdon Park Hotel in Croydon which was about an hour's drive from Wembley. While the team were relaxing, with light training sessions and the odd card game or round of golf on the Friday, the families and some of the club officials made their way to their hotel right next to the stadium.

For Gerry's son Chris the whole experience was unreal, 'I went up with my mum and grandparents. I was so excited I could hardly get to sleep on the Friday night. I particularly remember being in the hotel with Tommy Hutchinson's son and we were walking round the hotel exploring all areas when we called a lift and when it opened there were three men inside who I recognised. They were Zico, Socrates and Junior all in their Brazil tracksuits. We entered and they smiled before they continued to talk in Portuguese; it was the most surreal lift experience I have ever had and when we got out we couldn't wait to tell everyone. The Brazilian team were staying in the hotel as they had a friendly against England at Wembley on the Wednesday night as preparation for the World Cup in Spain the following year.'

As the City team made their way towards the twin towers there was an atmosphere of relaxation on the coach. Bobby MacDonald was sat next to Gerry and the mood was good, as he recalls, 'We were really up for it. I think we all thought we had nothing to lose really. In the press it was all about Spurs so I think that did us a favour if I'm honest. On the way me and Gerry chatted about our families and if they were okay. I had played at Wembley before in the League Cup Final for Aston Villa back in 1975, so I drew on that experience and talked with Gerry about that day. Suddenly when we got to Wembley Way and saw the City fans and a sea of blue, there wasn't much chat on the bus; it was all about us being in our own little world getting ready for the biggest game in our career.'

The players walked around the dressing room while all their kit and a match programme was laid out for them. At 2pm the players of both sides had a walk about on the pitch and maybe an interview with the various TV stations covering the game. As the players came out, the noise of the fans was incredible even though there was still an hour to kick off. Gerry spoke to ITV and described the feeling as 'incredible'. The reporter also pointed out to him a banner which read 'GERRY GOW MAKES GLENN HOBBLE'. Gerry laughed and shook his head.

With the walk about over, the players returned to the relative calm of the dressing room where John Bond went over a few tactics.

Steve Perryman, who captained Spurs that day, was incredibly open when he told me about manager Keith Burkinshaw's real worry, 'Keith told us that Gerry Gow would be all over us, particularly Ossie [Ardiles] and Glenn [Hoddle]. He pointed out that if City stood off us and let us play we would murder them in midfield, so he expected Gerry Gow to get among us right from the word go. He told us not to retaliate and not get bullied by him. I remember lining up in the tunnel and looking over at Gerry. Our paths had crossed many times right from that FA Youth Cup semi-final all those years ago, and the look on his face told me we were going to be in for a tough afternoon.'

After the traditional singing of 'Abide With Me' the players walked out to a cacophony of noise from all around the ground, with an estimated 23 million people watching on TV in the UK alone while the match was being beamed across the world. As Gerry strode out with his team-mates in their sky blue tracksuit tops every player puffed out his chests and looked ten feet tall.

THE GERRY GOW STORY

In the crowd were Julie and the children along with Gerry's brother Willie, all of whom shed a tear of pride. Also tucked somewhere among the 100,000 fans was Gerry's old youth team colleague Dave Bruton, who says, 'When Manchester City got to the final I was always going to go so I could see Gerry in the cup final. I took my dad who knew Gerry and we were just so proud of him.'

Across the country streets were empty as everyone, no matter who they supported, settled down to watch the game. Bristol City fans watched with a sense of pride as 'one of their own' took part in the season's biggest fixture. Gerry's old teammates from his days at Ashton Gate watched glued to the TV irrespective of where they were now in the country. Some of their careers had gone from strength to strength like Gerry's but for some they had faced relegation and an uncertain future in the game; nevertheless they were all rooting for the man with number eight on his back.

As the players lined up in front of the Royal Box they all glanced up and wondered if they would be going up those steps as winners or losers later that afternoon. The teams were presented to Elizabeth The Queen Mother before breaking off towards their supporters in an eruption of sound.

City started the better and won four corners within the first five minutes. Gerry had already introduced himself to Ossie Ardiles with ITV commentator Brian Moore saying, 'Gow will have to be careful of challenges like that today.' His co-commentator Jack Charlton laughed and replied, 'There's nothing wrong with that challenge, Brian.'

Gerry also frustrated the talented Hoddle, hassling him with every touch the Spurs man got, and with 20 minutes gone Gerry was certainly running the midfield. With every one of his challenges, the City fans got louder and louder as they sang, 'He's here, he's there, he's every fucking where, Gerry Gow, Gerry Gow.' The chant reverberated around the cauldron of Wembley and probably in many Bristol City fans' houses.

On the half-hour, some intricate passing between Dave Bennett and Kevin Reeves led to a pinpoint cross by Ray Ranson. The ball curved on the edge of the box and from nowhere Tommy Hutchinson met it with one of the best headed goals ever scored at the twin towers. It screamed past Milija Aleksic in the Spurs goal and the City end of the ground just erupted, as did the players, who all jumped on Tommy.

Tommy was difficult to get hold of regarding research for this book as today he lives in the Stirling area of Scotland. I was fortunate to interview him back in 2011 for another book I was writing, which wasn't about his time at City but I couldn't help talking to him about his goal. After all, you don't meet many players who have scored in the FA Cup Final. He told me, 'It was a fabulous ball from Ray Ranson. I gambled on the ball missing out Spurs defender Paul Miller so when it did I threw myself at it, and from the moment I connected with it I knew it was destined for the net. It's like if you hit a ball at golf, tennis or cricket, you know instinctively if it's going to be good and I just knew. The goal came at the right time for us as we were in control and to be honest Spurs and their fans were quiet.'

Throughout the first half City were in control although the BBC pundit Jimmy Hill was more concerned with their number eight, pointing out to commentator John Motson, 'Gow must be careful in this game. His enthusiasm in the tackle is starting to draw the eye of referee Keith Hackett.'

Pundits and armchair fans across the land were surprised by the control and confidence of the City side. Hoddle and Ardiles had no room to create and Ossie's fellow Argentinian Ricky Villa had hardly touched the ball. Spurs had a few chances but Corrigan was immense in goal and looked like nothing would get past him.

City's young side had certainly won the first half, but Spurs came out desperate for an equaliser in the second. Spurs pushed and pushed, but Corrigan was a safe pair of hands and Gerry and City's midfield continued to hassle and break up any move the Londoners made. As the clock ran down, it became more and more likely that the cup would be heading north, so sensing this the City fans sang with all their hearts, drowning out any noise coming from the Spurs end. It was as though the team from north London had become resigned to their fate.

With 80 minutes on the clock and the City fans singing, a procession of policemen made their way around the dog track around the outside of the pitch, always an indicator that the game is drawing to a close. Gerry won a tackle just outside his own box and looked up for somebody to pass to but nobody showed; with that Ardiles nipped the ball away from him and headed across the outside of the box to the opposite wing. Gerry gave chase and floored the little Argentinian. Referee Hackett blew for a free kick on the edge of the box. ITV pundit and 1966 World Cup Winner Jack Charlton enthusiastically bellowed, 'This shows what Gerry Gow is all about. He lost the ball because nobody showed for it then he ran after it to win it back but he fouled Ardiles in the process, but the fact that he is there is what he's all about. What a player.'

The next couple of minutes will always be one of the great moments in the competition's history. Hoddle stood over the ball alongside Ardiles. They spoke while City made a wall about 20 yards out and as the referee blew his whistle, Hoddle struck the ball towards Corrigan's left-hand post. As the City keeper came across to save it, Hutchinson left the wall and headed back towards Corrigan but as he did the ball struck him on the shoulder and diverted towards the City net, leaving the stopper helpless. Spurs were saved, their fans at last found their voices that had been missing all game, and Tommy rested on his haunches as the whole team looked at each other in disbelief.

After the restart, Spurs seemed to be a different team, moving the ball quickly as they sensed City's shock, but the men from Manchester held out as the final whistle blew. Both teams were out on their feet as they sat on the Wembley pitch with John Bond and his coaching staff administering drinks and words of encouragement to the players. Gerry was in agony and he felt he had lost a yard of pace already, and deep down he was seething at getting caught with the ball by Ardiles which led to him giving away the free kick. But this was not the time for a post-mortem as they had half an hour to go.

Extra time saw both tired teams cancel each other out but Gerry almost broke the deadlock minutes from time the end; his shot just went wide of the goal As the whistle blew both teams trudged off in what was a bizarre situation with no outright winners. The replay was booked in for the coming Thursday, back at Wembley, which would be the first time a final replay would be taking place at the national stadium. It was clear to everyone that City were the better side and Spurs were let back into the game due to the own goal.

Having interviewed various City players for this book, they all had an opinion on the goal. Corrigan says, 'We had a meeting at the hotel on the Thursday and we discussed putting a man on the post for free kicks. John Bond was keen to do it but I thought they would be in the way. I thought if they beat me from distance then fair play, so the decision was made that we wouldn't. Anyway, when we were setting up the wall, the lads heard Hoddle tell Ardiles that he was going to put it into the top corner. Hearing this, Tommy left the wall and tried to get to the post but he got caught in no man's land and the rest is history.'

Dave Bennett, who would win the FA Cup six years later as part of the Coventry City team that defeated Spurs in the final, backs up the story, 'We heard Hoddle tell Ardiles what he was going to do and I grabbed Tommy and told him to stay there but he just broke free and left us. I always mention it to him when we meet up that he cost me a winner's medal; after all, we were much the better team on the day.'

Speaking to me in 2011 Tommy Hutchinson recalled the moment and said he felt sick to the pit of his stomach, 'It was a freak goal. I tried to get back but I was too slow, and what really hurts is that Joe had it covered in the goal and we were so on top it was incredible. I also felt sorry for Tommy Booth who had to postpone his testimonial game due to the replay. It took me a few years to get over it, but now I just think it was just part of the day.'

There was a massive anti-climax for both teams after the crowds had gone home. They both had banquets organised but it was strange for them knowing there was no result at the end of the day. The players met up with their families and that seemed to recharge their batteries. Gerry stayed in the hotel with his family as most of the side did, and on the Sunday morning the papers wrote in praise of the City team and the various writers went to town on the Spurs side, with some of them claiming the side lacked heart and desire. In particular they focused on Ricky Villa, who was substituted and cut a lonely, forlorn figure as he walked off the Wembley pitch.

The FA decided to put tickets for the replay on general sale on the Sunday morning which left the City fans at a disadvantage as most of them had to return up north straight after the game. The consequences were that on the Thursday night there were clearly more Spurs supporters than City at the stadium, desperately hoping for a better performance from their team. Gerry's family were again in the crowd except for brother Willie who had to return to Glasgow due to work. He said, 'I was gutted that I had to return but all the family crowded round the TV to watch the game. I think everybody in Drumchapel were Manchester City fans that night.'

The 1981 final may well have been an anti-climax in terms of a result but the replay will go down in history as one of the best finals. It was a warm May evening as the teams walked out on to the Wembley pitch. City knew they had come so close to winning and for Spurs it was as if they had been given a second chance, which was very much the view of captain Steve Perryman, 'Manager Keith Burkinshaw had told the press he was happy in the end with a draw. He also told the midfield that they had to be stronger and how Gow had intimidated them in the centre of the park. We just had to show a bit more steel.'

City defender Bobby MacDonald had a great sense of fate going into the game, 'I'm a great believer in fate and that everything happens for a reason. Obviously I wanted to win but I just thought we had missed our chance. Certain things happened in the first match, notably Tommy leaving the wall. I had played with Tommy for many years and he never left a wall yet on Saturday he did. I just had this feeling in the pit of my stomach that it wasn't going to be our night.'

Gerry was in real pain going into the replay and he was injected with cortisone to get him through. Joe Corrigan recalls, ' It was a real dilemma for Gerry. Obviously he wanted to play and we needed him, but that's why I say I wish we had him at Manchester City a few years earlier. I think he would have easily got in the Scotland squad then. Gerry's time at City was great but after every great game he had he was patched up and that's what happened in the replay. He played through the pain barrier and its testimony to him that not many people noticed. The only indication was a few of the tackles on the night were late and he just was missing the pace to get there like he did in the first game.'

The replay kicked off at a ferocious pace and the ball was squared to Ardiles but in an instant both Gerry and midfielder Steve MacKenzie caught the Argentinian with a double tackle, sending him to the ground. The City fans erupted with chants of 'Gerry Gow, Gerry Gow' and Ardiles got up and, along with his team-mates, remonstrated with refereee Keith Hackett. The early incident showed City's determination to win the midfield battle and also demonstrated Ardiles standing up for himself as in the first game; if he was fouled he just walked away.

With around five minutes gone, Ardiles evaded Gerry on the edge of the City box and his shot found Steve Archibald who spun and forced Corrigan to push the ball out only for Villa to smash home the rebound and put Spurs 1-0 up. City fought back immediately and three minutes later with Spurs fans screaming around the stadium, a ball was headed out of their box by defender Graham Roberts. It found its way to Hutchinson who had the presence of mind to head a perfectly weighted ball across the box for MacKenzie to volley into the Spurs net. The goal was an incredible piece of skill and thrust the men from Manchester back into the game at 1-1.

The noise in the stadium was ear-splitting and just ten minutes in two goals had been scored. For the rest of the half both teams went close to breaking the deadlock and it was pretty even in midfield as Hoddle showed touches of brilliance but Gow was never far away the action as the first 45 ended 1-1.

Midway through the second half, Dave Bennett was played through into the Spurs box, where he was brought down by Paul Miller and Chris Hughton. Keith Hackett pointed to the spot much to the protests of the Spurs players. The responsibility for the penalty fell to striker Kevin Reeves and he didn't let the blue half of Manchester down by striking the ball into the corner.

The goal seemed to invigorate the game; tackles started flying in from every angle and, as Hackett was brandishing yellow cards to players on both sides, it seemed he had lost control. Sensing things were slipping away from them, Villa and Ardiles remonstrated with Hackett on every City challenge, then as Ardiles moved the ball across to the touchline Gerry caught him with a challenge that sent him to the ground and incensed him and his team-mates. Ardiles got up and thrust his arms into Gerry's chest, Gerry retaliated in kind and it was as if somebody had lit the blue touch paper. Players surrounded the referee and then suddenly a Spurs supporter found his way on to the pitch where he ran up to Gerry to have a go. Gerry just stood there while the fan thought better of it and was led away by police.

Hackett called Gerry over to lecture him and book him. Ardiles's reaction in that split second came from all the frustration that had built up during the first game. Every time he had the ball Gerry was there. Gerry was no respecter of reputations and Ardiles may well have been a World Cup winner but he was not going to win the midfield battle on this occasion.

The game continued at a frantic pace and with 15 minutes left Spurs pulled a goal back through Garth Crooks, giving them a new sense of importance as they chased the victory. With ten minutes to go, Villa picked the ball up outside the box and headed for the City goal. Gerry was about five yards behind him but it was plain to see his legs had gone and he was not going to catch the Argentine. As the City players backed off Villa went around three of them before putting the ball in the net and winning the FA Cup for Spurs with one of British football's most iconic goals.

As the ball hit the net, Gerry dropped to his haunches and put his head in his hands. He knew the final was over. As the whistle blew Spurs celebrated but not before all the players shook hands. Perryman and Hoddle ran towards Gerry to commiserate and although the Scotsman was sick to his stomach with defeat, in later life he appreciated the gesture they had shown.

Full-back Bobby MacDonald relives the defeat, 'We were on the floor. I had won a League Cup at Wembley and it's the best place to win but its also the worst place to lose. We just couldn't wait to get off the pitch and a lot of the lads were in tears. We had some young lads in the side like Ray Ranson who was 20, Tommy Caton who was 18, Steve MacKenzie who was 19 plus Dave Bennett and Nicky Reid both in their early 20s. They were distraught and it was up to us more experienced pros to pull them through.'

As Spurs danced away on the pitch holding the cup aloft, the City players waved to family and friends in the stand and acknowledged the fans who were still singing loudly for their club. Gerry just wanted to get to Julie and his family and when he did she never forgot it, 'It was the only time I had ever really seen him upset after a game. He was inconsolable. He told me and my dad that he would rather have been beaten in the semi-final. My dad told him that was rubbish. He explained to him that he had played in the biggest game in the UK and played well and he should hold his head up and how we were so proud of him, but he was still on the floor. He gave me a gold necklace that he had bought for the occasion and on giving it to me he said, "I thought we were both going to get something gold today." He really was heartbroken by the defeat.'

The game really was Gerry's swansong in a City shirt. He was a footballer who thrived on being tested, he had got the better of the Leeds United midfield of Billy Bremner and Johnny Giles in 1974 with Bristol City when Leeds were the best team in Europe and at Wembley he had outplayed one of

THE GERRY GOW STORY

Britain's most skilful players in Glenn Hoddle and a World Cup-winner in Ossie Ardiles. His reputation had increased tenfold but whether his body could keep up would be a question for the following season.

Young Gerry

Gerry as a first year pro

A young Gerry in 1972

Bristol City, 1972; (L-R) Back Row: Gerry Sweeney, Joe Durrell, Martin Rogers, Paul Crowley, Clive Whitehead, Don Gillies. Middle Row: Alan Dicks, Gary Collier, Tom Ritchie, Ray Cashley, Len Bond, Bob Wardle, Dave Rodgers, Bobby Gould, John Sillett. Front Row: Eddie Woods, Kevin Griffin, Trevor Tainton, John Emanuel, Geoff Merrick, Keith Fear, Gerry Gow, Brian Drysdale

Gerry Gow in action

Bristol City promotion squad of 1976

Trouble ahead: from left to right Gerry, Gerry Sweeney, Tom Ritchie, Donnie Gillies

The wild man of Ashton Gate

Gerry sends Stan Bowles of QPR tumbling to the ground

The King of Maine Road

In action for Manchester City

Gerry in the FA Cup Final suit

Bobby MacDonald and Gerry celebrate with Tommy Hutchison as Hutchison puts Manchester City 1-0 up in the 1981 FA Cup Final

Ossie Ardiles with Gerry in pursuit during the 1981 FA Cup Final

Gerry chatting to the ref in his Rotherham United days

One of Gerry's rare Burnley games

Enjoying life with Joolz

Gerry signs Ian Botham for Yeovil Town

Gerry with the man that discovered him, Tony Collins

Gerry and Joolz are always at each other's side

Gerry back in the Bristol City home dressing room before his testimonial game against Manchester City in 2012

16

Moving On

DESPITE THE disappointment of losing the FA Cup Final, Manchester City finished the season in a respectable 12th position. Given where they were when John Bond took over it, was a remarkable achievement for all concerned. Bond wanted to push City on but after the Malcolm Allison era, when spending was at its height, chairman Peter Swales and the board were finding finances tough. Having said that, they still managed to find £1m for the capture of striker Trevor Francis from Nottingham Forest and significantly for Gerry; Bond also secured the services of midfielder Martin O'Neill from Norwich City. It had been rumoured that O'Neill was an obvious replacement for Gerry as he loved a tackle and played in the same position. City had also sold youngster and FA Cup Final scorer Steve MacKenzie to West Bromwich Albion and Dave Bennett to Cardiff City to free up some cash.

During pre-season Gerry's knees were causing him all sorts of problems, although when he was at home with the kids he just got on with things and never complained. In the back of his mind, however, he knew things were not right. He spoke to Bond and his backroom staff and he came in during the summer to work with physio Roy Bailey on the knee. It was clear that he was having trouble and Bailey referred him to a specialist in Manchester. After examinations and various scans it was plain to see that the right knee had deteriorated with the rigours of First Division football. The surgeon decided to remove the cartilage, just as had happened on Gerry's left knee when he was at Bristol City. He agreed to an operation and knew that he would really have to work hard to start the season.

During his time off Gerry focused on strengthening the knee and getting fit. There would be no end-of-season tour or family holiday for him; his main focus would be on starting the new season with his team-mates in August. He missed the pre-season friendlies but he came through a game against the reserves with flying colours, putting himself in the shop window for the opener at home to West Bromwich Albion. Everybody at the club was impressed by his commitment, including team-mate and friend Bobby MacDonald, who said, 'Gerry worked really hard that summer. I would see him at the ground working with the physio all on his own. He would also run around the area keeping fit. There was nothing to him anyway but he did look in great shape, and when we talked all he was concentrating on was getting back into the team.'

Unfortunately, Gerry didn't make it against West Brom. Bond sat him down and explained how well he had done but the manager said he wanted Gerry to sit it out. Gerry was gutted but took the news on the chin. He found himself back in the side the following game, away at Notts County. He sat in midfield with O'Neill, Kevin Reeves and Paul Power. He felt fantastic and it was a credit to him that he could work so hard and come back to get in the first team after such a major operation. In the back of his mind, and manager Bond's, were doubts about whether the knee would hold up against the rigours of the season. Only time would tell.

Gerry had a six-match run in the side during which City won twice, lost twice and drew twice. At the end of the last game, at home to Spurs, he was in agony with the knee and knew he was in trouble. It was apparent the knee could not meet the demands being asked of it to play week after week. It was now the start of October and the season had barely started so Gerry sat down with Bond to discuss his future, not only at City but as a professional footballer. Despite Gerry's denial at first, both he and Bond agreed that he would not be part of the first team plans. He was heartbroken but he was a fighter on the pitch and he would fight this to save his career. Bond told him he would still train when he could with the first team lads and he would try and use him when the opportunity arose. Gerry said that he would prefer to make a clean break and try to get a new club. Bond understood his feelings and said he would help in any way he could. Goalkeeper Joe Corrigan remembers Gerry's final days at Maine Road, 'It was terrible for him. He was a big part of the dressing room and especially in training. He still trained like a madman but his knees were inconsistent ...'

While at a Bristol City function early in 2019 I was informed by one of the club directors of that time that Gerry almost returned to Ashton Gate. The director told me that Bond phoned Bristol City manager Bob Houghton, who was putting out fires with City as they were in free fall down the league. The Robins were now in the Third Division and at the wrong end of it, staring the Fourth Division in the face. Apparently Houghton was keen to see a return for Gerry even though he and the Scotsman hadn't hit it off previously. Both managers agreed that Gerry would be a great influence on the young players that City were now relying on to see them through the season. The move would also have a great impact on the fans who were staying away in their droves.

Houghton put it to the board but as the director explained to me, they were more concerned with keeping the club alive than making any new signings. Apparently, Gerry was keen on the idea but nothing happened. It would have been a great move for everyone, provided that the time was right and Houghton used the midfield a bit more in games rather than getting the ball forward as quickly as possible. I mentioned the story to Gerry's son Chris and he confirmed it, 'As far as I know yes there was some talk of dad going back to City but, yes City were in no real state to have moved forward with it. It would have been great though.'

It's well documented that in the early part of 1982 Bristol City needed Geoff Merrick, Trevor Tainton, Peter Aitken, Gerry Sweeney, Julian Marshall, Dave Rodgers, Chris Garland and Jimmy Mann, most of whom had played with Gerry, to tear up their contracts in order to save the club. This they did and the Robins lived on.

There were several approaches for Gerry. First Division Stoke City offered a six-month deal but Gerry was not interested. Third Division outfits Reading, Preston North End and Portsmouth all enquired about a one-year deal. While Gerry mulled over the offers, he was back in first team action for Manchester City as they started their League Cup

MOVING ON

campaign at home to Cardiff City. He was thrilled to be back in the side, particularly when the 31,000 supporters at Maine Road started singing his name. City won 3-1 with a brace from Trevor Francis and one from Bobby MacDonald. Gerry returned to the team for the next round at home to Coventry City and found himself playing at right-back after Ray Ranson was suspended and his successor John Ryan was cup-tied. Gerry found himself severely out of his depth and City withdrew him at half-time during a 3-1 defeat in front of 32,000 disappointed fans. It was a game too far for Gerry as he never had the pace to make the runs a full-back should make, and it also proved to be his last in a Manchester City shirt. After that appearance, the FA Cup Final seemed a long way in the past. But, a few days after the disappointment, Gerry was given the news that Rotherham United manager Emlyn Hughes wanted to see him about a two-and-a-half-year contract. Gerry agreed and knew it was time to move on.

Gerry agreed to meet Emlyn at his house, which was a change from the motorway service station where it seemed every transfer negotiation during the 1970s and 1980s had taken place. Emlyn had won everything as a player having started out at Blackpool and then moving to Liverpool under the great Bill Shankly. At Anfield he made 665 appearances and won four league titles, an FA Cup, two UEFA Cups and two European Cups as well as captaining England. He had only recently been appointed player-manager at Rotherham and took over a side that had just won the Third Division title under Ian Porterfield. Gerry knew Emlyn from playing against him and they had socialised on an end-of-season tour in Spain in 1976 when Bristol City had won promotion to the First Division.

Emlyn was an infectious character and he told Gerry that he needed a bit of steel in the side as Rotherham were starting to slump down the league. He also said that the fans would love Gerry. Emlyn and the board knew all about Gerry's fitness and the manager told the Scot that he had agreed with Bond that he could train at Manchester City then travel the 50 miles to Rotherham, and stay the night before the game. Emlyn also told Gerry about Shankly's take on injuries, saying to his new signing, 'I remember I couldn't walk after a game once and told Shanks. He replied, "Emlyn, I don't want you walking around the training ground, I only want you on the pitch so whatever it takes for you to be fit for the game then so be it."'

It was music to Gerry's ears as Emlyn was happy for him to spend time at home and train when he wanted just as long he was fit for matches. The men shook hands and a £50,000 fee was agreed along with Gerry's wages and contract. Rotherham rushed through a medical without any real problems, which was a relief for Gerry. It was a great deal for the Scotsman and his family as he would see more of the kids, they didn't have to move and it was just the challenge he needed at that point of his career.

South Yorkshire-based Rotherham were about 50 miles from Gerry's home in Wilmslow and played their games at Millmoor. Their claim to fame was that they had been beaten in the very first League Cup Final in 1961, when they lost a two-legged affair 3-2 to Aston Villa. They had been knocking around the lower divisions for all of their life, but the Third Division title a year earlier and the recent appointment of Emlyn Hughes in his first managerial role had brought a new wave of optimism.

MOVING ON

After I approached the club, they immediately put me in touch with John Breckin. John is a legend at Millmoor having played over 400 games for Rotherham between 1971 and 1983 before appearing for Bury and Doncaster Rovers. Later, John was the Millers' manager before becoming honorary life president. He said, 'Of course I remember Gerry Gow. He was a great friend to me in his time at the club; he was a popular lad in the dressing room and outside the club. I had many a beer with him. When he arrived he looked like an assassin with his wild hair and large moustache. I think some of the younger lads were a bit scared of him. I had played against him a few times notably down at Ashton Gate where me and him had a right battle. He was just what the club needed at the time. And of course if you ask any of the fans they will say, "Gerry Gow, legend, and what about that game against Derby County?"'

Another player who remembers Gerry with fondness is goalkeeper Ray Mountford, who made more than 120 appearances for Rotherham. He said, 'Gerry came to us with a fierce reputation. He had no ego and he was a real asset to the young lads in the side; he would talk through games, winding up the opposition and also encouraging our own lads. Although he was tough, in training he couldn't kick his way out of a paper bag as he would take it easy due to his knees being shot.

'I always fancied myself as an outfield player, like most goalkeepers do. I used to take the ball off him now and then and he would just look at me with those piercing eyes and say in his Glasgow accent, "Go steady, son." I would think, "Right, okay, whatever you say, Gerry." I also always remember him having really nice suits and he was always well dressed. He always carried a money clip with him and sometimes when we were at training he would say to Barry Claxton, the physio, "Hold this for me please, Barry, would you?" and then give Barry a wedge of money, about a thousand pounds. We had never seen that much but that was Gerry. He had a few quid but he was so generous with it, always buying the lads drinks when we were out. We used to call him "Champagne Charlie" as he really looked the part but as I said with no ego.'

The Millers looked candidates for relegation as they sat third from bottom in the Second Division at the end of January. Gerry was a ball-winner, whose mere presence in the dressing room and out on the field instilled a bit of belief among the players and a certain amount of dread in the opposition. Gerry made a good debut at home to Watford and that gave him a real boost of confidence. He and his family were staying at Emlyn Hughes's house as the club also had a game on the Tuesday night. The introduction of rest and light training had certainly paid off as he was like a new player despite the 2-1 loss.

His next game has certainly gone down in Rotherham United folklore as well as being in the odd pub quiz for the quickest sending-off. Defender Paul Stancliffe was in the Rotherham side and says the story of the game has kept people entertained at many sporting dinners over the years, 'I knew of Gerry's reputation when he came to the club and if I'm honest I was a bit wary of him as I was a few years younger than him. It was an evening game at Millmoor and we really need a result against Derby County as our season was starting to slip away. We had played well with Gerry in the team on the Saturday against Watford but we needed the points. Gerry and John [Breckin] were geeing us all up in the dressing room as that was the type of guys they were. Derby kicked off and the ball went to the Derby forward and Gerry came from nowhere and clattered the lad on the deck. He was booked after 30 seconds and the ball had not even left the centre circle. The crowd were on their feet singing "Gerry Gow, Gerry Gow". A couple of the Derby lads tried to get in his face but he just stared at them in that way he had.'

That look was not lost on lifelong Rotherham fan Sam Bingham who was a great fan of Gerry and met him on various occasions, later becoming friends with him. Sam said, 'He had quite a soft Glasgow accent that could be quite soothing yet he still carried an aura. It was all in the eyes; he would test you, probe you, letting you know if you did upset him he still had this ability that he would invite you to step outside. We loved him on the terraces.'

Stancliffe continues 'When it all died down, Derby had a free kick which they knocked back to the full-back, a lad called Steve Emery. He controlled it then Gerry came from the side with a sliding tackle that makes me shiver today. He broke the lad's leg and was duly sent off after two minutes and we hadn't even touched the ball. The fans loved it, but Christ it was a bad challenge. The game was in uproar as he just walked off the field. I remember thinking, "I'm glad he's in our team." He left with the fans singing his name but the Derby team and supporters wanted to lynch him. We went a goal down but battled back to win the game 2-1, and when we got to the dressing room at half-time he was sat there and apologised to us all but the Derby players and staff wouldn't go near him.'

The grief after the game Gerry experienced from the rival Derby players was nothing to what Julie was preparing to give him. She explains,' I was sat in the stands with our son Chris.

THE GERRY GOW STORY

We were sat next to Emlyn's wife and some of the other players' wives, and when he got sent off I just wanted the ground to open and swallow me up. I was so embarrassed by it all. I gave him what for after the game even though we were staying at Emlyn's house.'

Goalkeeper Mountford recalls how the game always gets a mention even today with his friends, 'I was playing in the game and I obviously remember it and in particular Gerry. After the match he was contrite. I think it was a case of him just trying too hard. Although somebody breaking their leg is not a laughing matter, I always think of my mate who was a long-distance lorry driver and had to make a trip to London and back that day. He raced down to London so he could get back for the Rotherham game as like a lot of fans he wanted to see Gerry Gow in action for the first time. He arrived at Millmoor ten minutes late, took his place on the terraces, and asked the lads which one Gerry was. He had already been sent off, and we still laugh about that today.'

The incident was never mentioned by Gerry to his teammates and they knew he certainly never intended to break somebody's leg. He was visibly upset by it as he probably had memories of the Gerry Sharpe leg break all those years ago. Maybe it was that desire to make his mark and show the game that he was not finished as a player that drove him to be reckless when it came to the challenge. It certainly was not his finest hour, although it was exactly what the supporters had beemn expecting of Gerry.

The challenge was the catalyst for Rotherham to go on a remarkable run of games as John Breckin explains, 'We were third from bottom just before February and we went on a run of ten games in a month due to re-arranged games. We won nine on the spin and drew one, and ended up third from top at the beginning of March. It will never be repeated again.

'Gerry was magnificent, he knew the game so well and he played things simple. He had his moments after games with pain but Emlyn handled him just right, giving him time off and letting him tell Emlyn when he was ready for matches. The treatment worked as he ended up first on the team sheet. All Emlyn wanted was him out there playing as he brought so much to the team.

'He was a real character and I really miss him. I remember one game when the linesman used to come into the dressing room to check your studs. If you had your boots on, you just showed them too him and if you didn't you would hand him the boots you were wearing. The studs had to be of a certain size and made from a plastic/resin. He got to Gerry who handed him a pair of boots which the linesman checked. When he was happy that they were okay, he moved on to another player. Gerry then put those boots in a bag and got another pair out that had aluminium studs and were a half an inch higher than the regulations. We just fell about as that was him; he was desperate to let the opposing midfielder know he was there.'

If anything, Gerry's reputation as a hard man was still growing when he signed for Rotherham. He could certainly play – you wouldn't have had the career he had if you couldn't – but even though he was struggling with the pace of the game and arriving for tackles late he was certainly the man to beat if you were in the midfield. At times he found himselfs living up to the hard man image as a tool of intimidation against the opposition.

THE GERRY GOW STORY

Veteran player and manager Neil Redfearn, speaking to reporters after Gerry's death, certainly remembers his first encounter with him, ' I was 17 and making my Bolton Wanderers debut against Rotherham United. Gerry Gow was my immediate opponent in midfield. He introduced himself by coming up to me and saying in a gruff Glaswegian accent, "Son, I am going to break your fucking leg today." I was shocked so I asked another of my team-mates, Tony Henry, who was a senior pro, about what he had said and Tony replied, "Just ignore him, he does not mean it." Only for Gow to return and assure me, "I do fucking mean it." I never went near him again.'

Rotherham finished the season in seventh place, just missing out on promotion to the top flight. Unfortunately, Gerry's penalty prowess that he showed so often at Bristol City had deserted him at Millmoor and in a late-season game at home to Luton Town Gerry missed from the spot. The score was 2-2 at the time and Gerry stepped up but changed his mind over the direction of the kick and two priceless points were lost. Gerry was inconsolable after the game but the fans sang his name around the ground.

Gerry had played 21 games out of 23 after signing for Rotherham and in that period they had only lost four times. Gerry even managed to get on the scoresheet in a 2-1 victory over Cardiff City. It had been a good season but it was so close to being a great one.

The team left for an end-of-season tour of Jersey and Gerry was in the thick of things again. He was enjoying his football once more and the Rotherham fans had connected with him, just as the supporters of Bristol City and Manchester City had done in previous years. With the new season came optimism for Rotherham and Gerry, although manager Emlyn Hughes decided to move some players on, notably John Breckin. It was a bold move, but it backfired on him as the side struggled to score goals at one end and keep them out at the other. Hughes was asked to resign, but wouldn't so he was sacked in March 1983.

The new man was George Kerr who had played for Barnsley, Bury and Oxford United in the 1960s and he had managed at Lincoln City and Grimsby Town. Although Gerry was a regular in the side, it was plain from the off that Kerr thought Gerry was finished and he also had no intention of continuing the regime that Hughes had started regarding keeping Gerry fit for games. Kerr demanded every player lived within the Rotherham area and Gerry refused as he said he joined the club on the understanding that he would continue to live and at times train in Manchester. It was a stand-off that the new manager could not afford to lose, so he placed Gerry on the transfer list.

Gerry still played until the end of the season, but it was clear to both parties that he would be better off away from Millmoor. The following August, Gerry was told by Kerr that Burnley had come in for him with a loan deal and an option to sign him permanently. Although seething at the way Kerr had treated him, Gerry agreed to the move – mainly because the Burnley manager was John Bond.

17

A Club Too Far

BURNLEY FOOTBALL Club is built on sound traditions. It was founded in 1882 and was one of the founding 12 members of the Football League in 1888. Their honours include two First Division titles, one FA Cup and two defeats in finals. Throughout all their various promotions and relegations they have always lived among their means and produced some of the best players the country has ever seen, usually selling them off at a high price.

At time of writing, Burnley sit in the Premier League and unusually they are one of the few top-flight outfits in Britain still British-owned. From the 1950s through to the early 1980s they were owned by local butcher Bob Lord who ruled with an iron fist. He was very much against paying high wages and was a keen advocate of getting rid of TV cameras at games, which he thought affected revenue. Burnley were the love of his life and he made sure during his time as chairman that things were done very much his way.

Gerry's time at Burnley is best forgotten. It was plain to see that his days as a driving force in the midfield of the team were behind him. In later years he made no secret of his dislike for his time at the Clarets, and the feeling at Burnley was mutual. The injuries had caught up with him and unfortunately he also became a target for the negativity aimed at manager John Bond, a manager he had links with from his Manchester City days. It would be easy to gloss over his time in Burnley in a couple of paragraphs as his failure there doesn't fit with the narrative of this story, but it would be doing Gerry and the fans of the club a disservice if the season he spent there wasn't probed a little.

Bond arrived at Burnley in June 1983, having left Manchester City after an embarrassing cup defeat at the hands of Brighton. Bond's resignation was hard for the City fans to stomach as during his reign they had always finished in mid-table, but Bond felt that finances and decisions from board members had not given him the support he needed to take City to another level.

His appointment at Turf Moor was surprising as Burnley had been relegated the season before to the Third Division and it was the first time that they had appointed a manager who had not played for them previously. Usually any appointments were made from within.

Bond promised that he would get Burnley promotion right away, although his first signing, of the 36-six-year-old Tommy Hutchinson, didn't lift many spirits. Bond culled the dressing room on arrival, selling defender Brian Laws, letting a young Lee Dixon leave on a free transfer and also sidelining fan favourite Martin Dobson, even calling him 'Colin Dobson' in a radio interview. Midfielder Dobson was, and still is, revered in Burnley after gaining five England caps in the 1970s and making over 400 appearances for the Clarets over two spells ... Many fans thought he would be groomed by Bond to take over one day.

It really was a time of change after relegation the previous year. The Burnley way had always been to produce their own players instead of buying and it was a system that up until recently had served them well. Bond brought in a lot of players on high wages, including many from Manchester City such as Tommy Hutchinson, who had been made captain at the expense of Dobson, Kevin Reeves, and Dennis Tueart. Gerry arrived one game into the season for the sum of £15,000.

Researching this period in Gerry's life, I contacted Burnley Football Club and they put me in touch with Tony Scholes. Tony was in his late 60s and a lifelong Burnley fan who at the time of Gerry's stay at Turf Moor was secretary of the supporters' club. I phoned Tony and explained the book and asked him about his memories of Gerry. He replied in his thick Lancashire accent, 'Gerry Gow, bloody hell, the worst signing John Bond ever made and by god he made some terrible ones.' After we had both finished laughing, Tony went on to explain his views on Gerry's move, 'I think Gerry was about 32 when he joined and his legs were gone. I wasn't expecting the Gerry Gow I had seen and admired at Bristol City years ago but he was dreadful for us. It's a shame to remeber him like that considering the career he had.'

Burnley started their 1983/84 season with a 4-1 thrashing at the hands of Hull City, so Bond signed Gerry who made his debut in a 5-1 victory at home to Bournemouth. A further 2-0 win followed against Newport County before Burnley played away at Oxford. The 2-2 draw at the Manor Ground was, according to Tony, Gerry's finest hour in a Burnley shirt, 'He was great in the game against Oxford. I remember we were 2-0 down with about ten minutes left and we pulled it back to 2-2. He did well and there was the odd glimpse of the Gerry we knew, but his distribution and control still let him down at times. Ask any Burnley fan of a certain age and they will tell you Gerry's best game was Oxford away.'

It's quite ironic that the game many Burnley fans feel was his best came out of a late-night drinking session with Tommy Hutchinson and Bobby MacDonald. Bobby takes up the story, 'I had moved on from Manchester City and was at Oxford United. We were due to play Burnley and I was looking forward to it as Tommy and Gerry were at the club. With Oxford we used to go to the hotel sometimes on the Friday night before a game and we did so on this occasion.

'Unbeknown to me, Gerry and Tommy had left their hotel to come to ours and find me. They did and turned up at the hotel room armed with beer, so we drank it all and reminisced about old times. It was a great night, just like the old days when we were staying in a hotel at Manchester City. They also informed me that Tommy had won the fans over, but Gerry pulled no punches when talking about how things were going for him, telling me that he was in pain every game and the fans were on his back. The lads left late at night and it was great to meet up.

'Looking back, it was one of the last times I saw him although I do remember being invited by the Manchester City Supporters' Club to a match along with Tommy and Gerry. This was a few years ago now but I only went because I knew Gerry was coming. They really looked after us and we walked out on the pitch and the City fans stood and all sang our names.

It was very emotional for all of us. They were brilliant and certainly recognised what we did for the club. I think all three of us were in tears at the gesture.'

Despite his form, Gerry played the next five games as Burnley picked up two wins in the process. Although he joined in September, his last full appearance was at home to Gillingham in October and in total he played just nine times for the Clarets. The Gillingham encounter was the basis of a story Gerry told in later life. He said, 'I hated my time at Burnley as it was a club too far for me, and the fans didn't like me either. I remember playing Gillingham at home and I was barracked during the game as usual. Just before the final whistle I had enough of this one particular bloke giving me stick all game, so when I got chance I went over to where the hoardings were and looked him in the eyes and pointed to the players' bar and said, "After the match, me and you." He agreed and the whole section of the fans cheered.

'We lost the game 3-2, so I went to the players' bar and I was seething and couldn't wait to see the guy. I thought, well, he's my size so if it kicked off I can handle him. As I walked into the bar I saw him and he was at least 6ft 6in. What I didn't know was that area of the Turf Moor enclosure dips down over a foot, so when we were staring eye to eye he was standing in a two-foot hole. Well, I took a deep breath and went over, and in the end we shared a pint.'

The hostility of the fans was certainly something Gerry had not experienced at any of his clubs previously. He could take a barracking from the opposing supporters as it was a sign of how they really respected you, but this was a new one on him and it took big shoulders for him to deal with the situation.

Tony Scholes reflects on Gerry and Burnley, 'It really was the signing that shouldn't have happened. He was awful at the club because his legs had gone and it's no wonder with the type of player he was over the years. I remember when we signed Tommy Hutchinson. He was 36 and we all thought, "What the bloody hell is this?" but Tommy never missed a game in two seasons for the club, plus over, the years his game was different to the type of things Gerry had to put up with in midfield. Tommy won the fans over but I think Gerry came and we expected so much that season with Bond, who in my dealings with him at the time was that he was a real gentleman but his reputation at Burnley will always be on the floor. And I think that didn't help Gerry as he played him for eight or nine games and then he was out of the team, except for a game at home to Orient in May at the end of the season.

'John Bond had gone missing for a few games. He said he was away scouting but us supporters felt he was playing golf, so anyway he put his number two John Benson in charge. About an hour before kick-off, Burnley player Wayne Biggins was too sick to play so we had no substitute as it was the days when you only had one, so the call goes out to some players who are obviously at home. In the end Gerry answered the call and I can still see him walking to the dugout to sit on the bench with the game already 20 minutes in. The rumour was and still is among the Burnley fans is that they got hold of Gerry in the beer garden of his local pub. I would love to believe it but somehow I don't think it's true.'

As the season came to a close there seemed to be a light at the end of the tunnel for Gerry as he found out through his contacts that Yeovil Town were looking for a manager. Gerry had originally had no thoughts of being a coach or manager during his career but there was something about this job that he really fancied, He knew he still had a few games left in him but certainly not at Football League standard, so he would not be relinquishing his playing registration. He talked the job over with Julie and also John Bond and both of them thought he had nothing to lose, especially Julie who could see that Gerry was unhappy at Turf Moor. It would also be a chance to go back to the south-west.

Gerry contacted Yeovil and was granted an interview. He didn't know who else was being spoken to but he knew there would certainly be a lot of interest in the position as they were one of the biggest clubs outside of the Football League and had aspirations to move into the professional game. Gerry met chairman Gerry Locke and the two of them hit it off. Locke outlined the vision for the club, which was to reach the Fourth Division and also to get more bums on seats. He also explained that Yeovil in the future would be moving from their Huish Park ground, with its famous slope at one end, to a new stadium down the road.

All of this sounded perfect for Gerry and he knew it was a perfect platform to get into the world of management. The pair shook hands and Gerry left to go back up north with Locke telling him he would be in touch in the next few days. As Gerry got excited at the prospect of a new career the realisation of his own situation dawned on him. He knew that Burnley were not going to offer him anything in the summer, so he had to get a new move sorted out. Two days after the interview, Gerry received a call from Locke to tell him that he had been unsuccessful and the job had been given to Ian MacFarlane.

MacFarlane had been a full-back in the 1950s with Aberdeen, Chelsea and Leicester City, and he had also managed Carlisle United, Sunderland and Leicester City in the 1970s. Gerry was gutted to say the least and took positives from the fact that he was granted an interview and had come close to getting the job but MacFarlane did have a wealth of experience on his side. Gerry thanked Yeovil and sat out the remaining games of Burnley's season.

The Clarets finished 12th and Gerry was let go as he had expected. Gerry had a lot of time for John Bond over the years but their relationship with each other and their reputations were tarnished by the move to Burnley. Admittedly, Gerry wasn't fit enough to do himself justice and he felt that he had also let Bond down. Bond had tried to make too many changes in a short period of time and surrounded himself with ageing players he knew, rather than blooding Burnley's younger prospects, which aggravated the fans. He had spent big and thought that maybe the experienced players he believed he could trust did indeed let him down. In hindsight, both of them felt that maybe it was a signing that should not have happened. Bond was sacked at the end of the season and made way for his number two, John Benson.

With no club on the horizon, Gerry kept himself fit at home but he had not given up on his thoughts of going into management. As 1984/85 started, it was the first time in his career that Gerry had not had a club to start the season with. He was down but typical of Gerry, he never passed those obvious anxieties and worries about his future on to the family.

With the season a few weeks old, Gerry received a call at home from Gerry Locke. He asked Gerry what he was up to and received a reply, 'Well, you should see my garden. It's in a fantastic state.' Following that, Locke said, 'Do you want the manager's job as MacFarlane has left the club for his own reasons.'

Gerry accepted then went into the front room to find Julie and the kids, asking them, 'How do you fancy moving to Yeovil?' The Burnley nightmare was over and the Gows prepared for a new challenge in Somerset.

18

New Challenges

IT WASN'T hard for Gerry to say goodbye to Burnley. The players were great but he didn't really have any sort of connection with a lot of them. He was still living in Wilmslow, as were Tommy Hutchinson and his family, and that was probably the toughest goodbye Gerry had to make as both families had become close over the years. He thanked John Bond for everything and Bond told Gerry as he stepped into management for the first time that he would always be on the end of the phone should he be required.

Gerry also spoke to Alan Dicks and Emlyn Hughes about the job that awaited him. He asked if they had any advice and each obliged in his own way. The main point was, 'Make sure you are your own man.' Gerry had learnt a lot from all of his managers and there were rumblings, particularly in the south-west, that maybe the 'hard man' footballer was not really the right type to be a manager. But Yeovil chairman Gerry Locke believed in the appointment and that's all that mattered to Gerry. With the family now relocated in Yeovil, Gerry looked forward to taking the reins at his new job.

Yeovil Town were a massive club in non-league terms and had a big history in the FA Cup, remembered mainly for their exploits of the 1940s when they knocked out First Division Sunderland on their famous sloping pitch at Huish Park. It did slope, by the way – 17 feet to be precise from one end to the other.

The arrival of Gerry had certainly raised local interest and this was one of the points that Locke wanted Gerry to grasp. He told Gerry that the club at the time were drifting along, failing to excite the supporters, and they needed a team that played attractive football to bring the fans in. Locke explained how Gerry would be full time but the players would be part time with the dream that they would reach the Football League. Gerry was also informed that Yeovil were in negotiations with a supermarket to buy the old ground and build a new one in the distant future.

He knew Gerry had a tough challenge and both of them knew the team just were not good enough to do anything in the coming season and in fact relegation was a real possibility as they were struggling at the foot of the table, but Locke would give Gerry a bit of money and most of all he would give him time to build his own team, even if they did go down.

It was music to Gerry's ears as he set about getting his contacts book out. Initially, Gerry went for the John Bond approach and brought players he knew he could trust and to a certain extent he wanted players who would build a team spirit that was certainly lacking. Gerry got former Bristol City teammate Chris Garland in to help him with coaching. Chris had been out playing in Hong Kong with Geoff Merrick after the two of them had been made redundant by Bristol City back in 1982. Gerry had a decent group at his disposal but he needed some experience, particularly of the Football League. With this in mind he recruited his old Bristol City mates Tom Ritchie, Paul Cheesley and Jon Economou.

Tom had left City a few months after Gerry in a big-money move to Sunderland, but things had not worked out for the striker and he returned to the Robins in their hour of need as they fell through the divisions. I asked Tom about the move to Yeovil and he recalled how Gerry knew he was leaving City before he did, 'Gerry rang me really late at night and told me apparently there was a chance that City would be letting me go. Well, this was the first I had heard of it. He asked to see me in the morning which I did after I had spoken to the City manager, Terry Cooper. I think he had already spoken to Gerry about me. I agreed and decided to give it a go.

'A lot of people ask me whether I thought he was managerial material and if I'm honest I thought he would struggle but he was great.'

Paul Cheesley was another player who arrived at Yeovil through the non-league scene, and explains, 'After my injury I played a bit of non-league football, so when Gerry called I was really happy to take him up on his offer. The set up was great at Yeovil and although we were struggling with relegation looking a real possibility Gerry and the board knew we would give it a real go but if it did happen we would bounce back. Gerry looked after me in terms of my knee and as you can imagine when we finished games I don't think we left the club bar.'

Gerry thought Cheese would bring that buzz and team spirit to the dressing room, and it certainly worked, while another addition to the team caught the interest of not only the local press but also the national media. Ian Botham, the great England and Somerset cricketer of the time, was born and bred in Yeovil. His parents still lived in the area and were Yeovil fans. As a youngster Botham was a talented footballer who had trials at Crystal Palace, but he had to choose between football and cricket, and despite his decision he had also played some games for Scunthorpe United a few years earlier.

Gerry went to chairman Locke's house and put the idea to him that maybe they could get Botham to sign for a season at Huish Park. Locke thought it was a great idea as it would certainly get fans through the turnstiles. Gerry contacted Botham's mum and dad and asked if the cricketer could ring him, which he duly did. Botham loved the idea, so signed for the winter as a centre-half or striker. The media loved the story and Gerry was happy to do any interviews about his new signing, always making the point that Botham could actually play. Botham's first game for Yeovil almost doubled the crowd, which was Locke's intention.

Tom Ritchie remembered Botham in the dressing room, 'To be honest we were all a bit in awe of him for what he had achieved in his sport, but he was really down to earth and a really good bloke who dished out banter and took it in good spirits. He wasn't with us for too long but he could certainly play and handle himself on the pitch. I think he doubled the home gates for us.'

Paul Cheesley is another who was with Botham at Yeovil, 'He was great for us, although when Gerry decided to play him at centre-forward I had to sit on the bench which wasn't great especially when Ian would get the ball from the halfway line and try and shoot for goal. I used to say to Gerry, "Put me on first. Let me get a goal then take me off," so the fans could see

Ian, but he never did though. Ian was really down to earth. He was one of the lads and you can imagine what he was like in the bar afterwards. We had a real giggle at the time it and was as if F Troop had returned.'

Throughout the campaign, Gerry demonstrated particularly to his old team-mates that he had taken to management well. He also proved that he really did have an eye for a player. Gerry spotted young midfielder Micky Tanner in the Bristol City reserves on one of his many scouting trips up to Ashton Gate. Tanner was a tough tackler who City manager Terry Cooper felt would benefit from playing at Yeovil rather than the second string. Gerry stole the march on a few other clubs and got Micky on loan for eight games.

Micky recalls his time at Huish Park with great affection and above all his devotion to Gerry, 'I loved the bloke. When I was a schoolboy at Bristol City, Gerry Gow was my idol. I loved the way he played and I loved to try and emulate him. When I was asked to go down to Huish by him I was overjoyed. Yeovil were a great club who had a brilliant set up and although they were struggling at the bottom Gerry had created a great team spirit. They were also getting gates of 3,500 which was brilliant for a youngster like me.

'He had signed Ian Botham for a few games and I think that's what sparked the stayaway fans interest. I had a great time, scoring seven goals in my eight-match stay. In that time I got to know Gerry and he was really supportive to me and helped me in any way he could. When the loan was over he wanted me to stay and part of me did too, but I explained to him that my dream was to pull on the shirt of Bristol City and going back was hopefully going to make that happen. He understood and kept in touch with me throughout my career. He was a legend.' Micky achieved his dreamy playing over 20 games for the Robins before being sold to Bath City.

Another youngster who unfortunately escaped Gerry's clutches was brought to his attention after Yeovil took on Weymouth Town. In Weymouth's team that day was Martyn Rodgers who had been Gerry's apprentice at Bristol City back in the day. Martyn takes up the story, 'It was great to meet up with Gerry again while I was playing for Weymouth. He came over to me after the match and asked about the young midfielder in our side. I told him his name was Andy Townsend. Gerry said he would be making an approach to get him. I don't know why the move never happened, but Andy went on to Southampton, Chelsea, Villa and even played in a World Cup with the Republic of Ireland. At the time nobody had shown any interest in Andy. It showed how Gerry could spot a player.'

Although gates were high and Yeovil's performances had improved, Gerry could not prevent relegation to the Isthmian League. It was a blow but it was one that chairman Gerry Locke had expected. Everybody knew that Gerry was building something at Huish Park and the following season his recruitment was second to none. Ian Botham had left and Gerry knew the importance of building on that initial fan base by playing attractive football and getting back into the Alliance League, which became the Football Conference. Gerry had spent the summer watching pre-season games and scouring the country, and with Locke's blessing he recruited an unknown midfielder from Dulwich Hamlet called Alan Pardew. Another recruit was from Scotland in the shape of striker John McGinlay. Both players were incredible for Yeovil, with Pardew sometimes playing in midfield with Gerry and Tom Ritchie. Tom said, 'Alan did all the running, Gerry did all the tackling and I did all the passing.'

To round it all off, Gerry felt he needed another striker to complement McGinlay. Gerry made an audacious approach to Bristol Rovers for their star striker Paul Randall who was out of favour with manager Bobby Gould. In his autobiography, *Punky*, Paul said, 'There were all sorts of rumours about clubs coming in for me as I had always scored goals but things were quiet, then suddenly, out of the blue, Bobby told me non-league Yeovil Town wanted to talk to me. I was a bit surprised. I was only 28 and no league club had come in. I wondered if my details had really been circulated but I will never know.

'To go and play non-league would be a massive decision as I would have to find a job to supplement my earnings, and in the end I thought I would give it a go. I met Gerry and the chairman at the Rovers training ground and both clubs agreed a fee of £5,000 for a two-year deal, which would be worth £120 a week to me with a £20 win bonus and a £10 draw bonus. Gerry also told me he would find me a job in the commercial department of the club which he did. I will always remember hearing him on the phone to the local press saying, "You aren't going to believe who I have just bought."'

After capturing Randall, Gerry also secured the services of talented Bath City centre-half Tony Ricketts and his old Bristol City pal Donnie Gillies, while also persuading one-time Manchester City team-mate and million-pound striker Kevin Reeves to sign even though it was just for eight games. The team clicked from day one and McGinlay and Randall started scoring goals for fun as the Glovers headed into a two-way fight at the top of the table with Sutton United, while along the way Gerry was picking up Manager of the Month awards every other month.

The 1985/86 campaign was Gerry's first full season in the Huish Park job and he had created a side that played attractive football with a great team spirit, not unlike the Bristol City team of the 1970s. Yeovil finished second that season, four points behind Sutton. Gerry was gutted but everyone could see how the club had improved under his stewardship. What did aggrieve Gerry was that although he had done well to bring in the kind of quality he had, he knew he was fighting an uphill battle given the Glovers' wage budget and Somerset location. Many of the teams in the Football League and the Alliance League were full time and as Yeovil were still part time with training sessions for the players on Tuesday and Thursday evenings after their day jobs. With a lot of Football League clubs also being in the London area, they had the pick of players who had been released by London's professional clubs. It was certainly an obstacle for Gerry but frustrated though he was, he gave the next season another go.

Yet again Yeovil hit the ground running with some great results, notably a 4-1 away win against league leaders Wycombe Wanderers. The game is remembered by Tom Ritchie for the on-pitch events and Gerry's reaction afterwards, 'We were great that night. Every move we made came off and they were the leaders yet we bossed them on their own doorstep in front of their own fans. I remember when we were on the coach to come home, Gerry was chatting to one of the Wycombe directors, Alan Parry, who used to commentate for one of the

TV companies. When Gerry got on the coach I asked him what Parry had said and he replied. "He just told me that was the best footballing display he had ever seen by a non-league team." Gerry was so proud. I think it was one of his proudest moments in the game and I will never forget his face.'

Then as 1987 arrived with Yeovil neck and neck with Wycombe in the league, Gerry went to see Tom and told his old team-mate that he was resigning as manager. Tom recalls his shock, 'I still to this day have no idea why he resigned. He was doing a great job at the club, with a chairman who loved him, as did the players and the fans. I know he was frustrated we couldn't get to the Football League and that we were not full-time but I thought he had a real future in management. He had proved what he could do in terms of finding players. Alan Pardew ended up at Crystal Palace and John McGinlay played for Bolton Wanderers and Scotland yet Gerry found them for virtually nothing. He managed on a shoestring so imagine what he could have done with a club with a few bob. It was very sad but that was Gerry: when he made his mind up it was made up.'

Gerry's son Chris also remembers his dad leaving the Glovers, 'I was gutted when he resigned. I loved it at Yeovil, they were a good club who thought a lot of dad. I used to go to away games with the supporters and we had a ball. I remember Gerry Locke, the chairman, being in tears when he left the house after dad told him he was going. We never really spoke about why he left but I just think he got frustrated that success couldn't come sooner.'

The Yeovil board reluctantly accepted his resignation, telling the media it was for personal reasons. As Gerry threw himself into his family he also made a decision that he was finished with football and maybe it was time to try something else. We will never know how far he could have taken Yeovil Town and he was certainly carving out a career in management that would have seen him take a job at some point in the Football League.

Gerry's time at Yeovil is remembered with affection by Steve Sowden who writes for the *Yeovil Press*. He told me about when he first met Gerry, 'When I was younger I had the opportunity to go on work experience from school. Me and my mates put down that we wanted to go to Yeovil Town FC as we were all fans. I was no footballer but I was up for spending a day at the club and meeting Gerry Gow, so me and a few mates went to the club and were looked after by none other than Gerry Gow. He got us doing some chores around the ground like sweeping the terraces and the main stand.

'Gerry then got one of his players, Paul Thorpe, who was a larger-than-life, mean defender, to take part in a penalty shoot-out competition with us. It was great fun. And then after that Gerry took us into the social club bar where he got us a drink – lemonade, I hasten to say – and took us on in a pool completion. It was amazing how he had the time to make some young lads' day when I'm sure he had better things to do.

'His legacy at the club in my opinion is huge. A generation of Yeovil Town supporters will remember Gerry and the players he brought to the club, the way he energised the club and made people want to go to Huish again. He also reinvigorated the club within the local community. His time at Yeovil Town was all too brief, but eventful and I for one am delighted to have experienced it.'

Away from the game he had known for over a quarter of a century, the next few years would see Gerry looking for something to fill that void. When the dust settled on everything Gerry was able to look back on his time at Huish Park with pride. He had brought in some great players, not forgetting the money the club made from the signings when they moved on. In the season Gerry left, Yeovil missed out yet again and finished second to Wycombe Wanderers who gained promotion to the Conference.

Gerry, though, would still not be persuaded to change his mind when it came to returning to football, even in the face of various offers coming his way. Despite all the enquiries, he wasn't interested and looked for something outside the game.

Throughout the 1970s and the 1980s there appeared to be an unwritten law that said when footballers retired they were required to become publicans. I can understand why breweries encouraged this practice as what better draw was there than to have a well-known publican behind the bar telling stories of old football matches as eager regulars hung on their every word while sipping pints? It's a cliché now but back then it was a real opportunity for a lot of former players to earn a living and, for Gerry, that change came at The White Horse Inn in Bedminster.

The pub lay deep into Bristol City country, in fact from it you could have thrown a stone and hit Ashton Gate, so somebody like Gerry was perfect as the new landlord. Gerry had no experience on that side of the bar but he had spent a lot of time on the other side. The family moved into the large, red-brick pub and lived upstairs. Gerry's son Chris was now starting a career in the building trade, so he helped get the pub up to scratch and ready for opening.

The White Horse, which is now flats, was a well-known pub in the area but like many around Bedminster it had fallen victim of dilapidation and lack of investment since the closing of the Wills Tobacco factory in the early 1980s. It was a million miles away from the vibrant, bustling area of Bristol it is today. Nonetheless the pub became popular, especially on matchdays as everybody wanted to see Gerry Gow. It was during this time that Sean Donnelly became friends with Gerry.

Sean is a well-known figure around Bristol as a businessman and owner of the Three Lions pub in Bedminster. He is also a 100 per cent Bristol City nut. The Lions, as it is affectionately known, is 50 yards from where the White Horse stood back in the day before it became flats. On a personal note, I have known Sean for nearly 50 years as we went to the same school together and he is never short of a good story regarding Gerry.

He says, 'I was really privileged to get to know Gerry. When I started to go to watch City as a youngster, he was my idol. I would stand on the terraces along with my mates and sing his name and his song. We loved him but didn't know him. Then he got the White Horse and we just all flocked to the place. It would be rammed with all us City fans; it was a great atmosphere in there and no trouble because we all loved Gerry.

'I remember one of the first weekends we were in there we did a charity party where we all shaved our heads and Gerry did it too and that really integrated him with the fans on a personal note. They knew him as a player but not as a bloke and the fact that he shaved his head along with us really meant a lot to us all; it showed he was one of us. Anyway we all got absolutely smashed and the pub was packed bear in mind that before he took it over the pub it was dead. So we all spilled out on to the street and climbed on to the bus stop roof outside singing, "He's here, he's there, he's every fucking where, Gerry Gow, Gerry Gow". He was trying to get us off the bus stop when all of a sudden the roof collapsed along with the rest of the bus stop, with us all ending up on the floor. I don't think Gerry could believe what was happening. I know he took two weeks' money in a day though.'

With Gerry behind the bar and the White Horse quickly becoming the place for City fans to go to, Sean pestered Gerry to come and play for his football team whenever he got the chance. Sean takes up the story, 'It's true. I kept on to him all the time about playing for us. Our team was Eagle House and we were sponsored by Avon Glass. It was only local parks football but he was such a great guy and one of the lads, so we thought it would be great if he said yes. He relented and agreed, so I had to get some signing-on forms for him, and on the forms you have to put down clubs you had played for. Well, Gerry, being the bloke he was, he just put Yeovil Town down on the form, so in theory he had gone from Bristol City, playing in an FA Cup final with Manchester City to being a new signing for Eagle House Football Club, Knowle West. It was hilarious.

'With the form in hand I have to go to see the secretary and give him the forms. So I go up to his house and I'm buzzing to show Ron, our secretary, who I have got to sign. I knock on the door and give him the form, and say, "I got a new player, mate." He replied, "Cheers," then asks me how I am. Now I'm desperate for him to look at the name on the form but he's still chatting about all sorts so I say, "Have a look at the form," and he goes, "FUCKING HELL, are you serious? He must be good if he played for Yeovil Town." I shouted, "Never mind about fucking Yeovil, look at the signature. It's Gerry fuckin' Gow." I will never forget the look on his face when he realised who it was.

'So Gerry did play a few games for us and the press loved it, sometimes writing more about our game with Gerry in the side than Bristol City's game. And if Gerry didn't fancy a game we told the press he was injured after dropping a barrel on his toe, although he ran out of toes in the end as we kept using that excuse. But when he did play, and he was brilliant, he would shout for the ball and we were just in awe of him. We had a great time.'

The family worked tirelessly behind the bar. Both of Gerry's daughters were still at school and after a while the Gows realised that maybe living above a pub wasn't the greatest of environments for the girls, while the long days were also putting pressure on Gerry and Julie's relationship. During this time he was also doing some scouting work for a few of his contacts, which entailed the odd Saturday or evening game at Ashton Gate. The scouting work and the occasional game for Eagle House seemed to have ignited his enthusiasm for football once again and, after 18 months behind the bar, Gerry was contacted by a representative of Weymouth Football Club asking if he would like to become their next manager. Gerry thought over the proposition and decided to go and meet them.

The club were languishing in the relegation zone of the Beazer Homes Premier Division, which was the seventh tier of English football, and plainly there wasn't any money about to splash out on players, but it was a nice part of the world and there was something about the offer and the club that got Gerry thinking.

NEW CHALLENGES

Gerry left for Bristol and told the board that he would give them his answer after he had spoken to the family. Julie and the kids were keen, so Gerry phoned the club and accepted the job. The Gows moved down to Portland, so Gerry could be nearer his work. He knew it was a tough task and Weymouth certainly had a fight on their hands to stay up. Sean and the regulars at the White Horse were gutted but they knew football was Gerry's life. And, with Sean being a decent amateur player, Gerry enticed him down to Weymouth for a few games. Sean explains, 'I loved it down at Weymouth. He got me a few quid for playing and there were a lot of lads from Bristol there which created a really good atmosphere at the club but if I'm honest I was way off the level required.'

As well as Sean, Gerry also signed his former Yeovil Town team-mate Micky Tanner, who explained what it was like to get the call, 'I had been doing really well at Cheltenham Town who at the time were in the Conference. They changed their manager and I just wasn't in his plans. Anyway Gerry called me and said he wanted somebody to make a spark in the side on and off the field. I was flattered to be honest, so we worked out terms and I signed. It was a great time at Weymouth for me. They were a good bunch of lads and we had some fun off the field, but mainly it gave me chance to really get to know Gerry who after all was my idol. Me and Gerry would have loads of chats over a pint about the game and looking back, especially now he's gone, those times are really special to me.'

It was a real struggle for Weymouth, as results initially didn't go their way. Gerry even had to pick himself against Maidstone United after he couldn't name 11 fit players for the team sheet. They then had a desperate 2-1 Boxing Day defeat at the hands of local rivals Dorchester Town. Despite the result the fans still stuck with Gerry and the team and it was plain for all to see that he had got his enthusiam back for the game.

The Dorchester result gave them a lift as they then went on a four-match unbeaten run which lifted them to mid-table. On the horizon was an FA Trophy game against Barnet who were second in the Conference, some two divisions higher than the Terras, as they were nicknamed. This tie remains Gerry's finest afternoon as manager of Weymouth and it's still talked about today among supporters.

Barnet manager Barry Fry had assembled a decent side who were heading for the top of the Conference, so they were the clear favourites for the game. A crowd of 1,235 squeezed into Weymouth's Wessex Stadium and they were not disappointed as the Terras put on a display that had Gerry Gow written right across it. They hustled and bullied Barnet at every challenge and to a man they never stopped running. The 2-1 win brought fans on to the pitch and had Gerry beaming with pride. Speaking to the press afterwards, he said, 'I am so proud of the lads. We outbattled Barnet and certainly matched them for skill. The team's belief in their ability has come back to them. It was a good result for the club and at last the supporters have something to cheer.'

Fry was also glowing in his praise for Gerry and the team, 'We were outfought today by the better side. They hassled us and we couldn't take it. Gerry really has something good going here.'

Unfortunately Weymouth went on to lose in the next round to Dover Athletic. Gerry managed to keep the club up that season but it wasn't enough for the board and they sacked him

NEW CHALLENGES

in April 1990. Gerry was devastated and he vowed that he was finished with football for good. He understood how the game worked but he thought he would at least be given another season, although he was given barely one.

With no football in his life, Gerry proceded to do different jobs to earn a living in and around Portland. Unfortunately, he and Julie had grown apart and they decided to divorce. The pair had been a great team and she had supported him when times were good and when they were not so good. The children had grown up and were embarking on lives of their own and it's to the couple's credit that they remained friends right up to Gerry's death.

They had come a long way since their first meeting in a Bristol nightclub all those years ago. They took comfort in the fact that they had produced three great kids in the middle of the crazy world of football, but now their lives were going to be different, not as husband and wife but as the best of friends.

19

Where's Gerry Gow?

THERE WAS a certain irony in the fact that although Gerry's famous chant told us, 'He's here, he's there, he's every fucking where,' the subject of the song had gone off the radar completely when it came to team-mates and supporters. I don't think it was intentional; it was just a case of him living what for him was a different life, away from the game and everything that went with it.

He was still in his kids' lives, but there were many former colleagues who told me during their interviews for this book that they just lost touch with him and had no real idea where he was. I for one struggled to try and find him for a book I was doing about the Bristol derby in 2006, and in the end I had to leave him out of the final chapters, much to my annoyance. Gerry, apparently, was working in the Portland area and living alone. He didn't have much contact with the game or any of his old team-mates.

As it turned out, I wasn't the only person looking for Gerry at that time. His old Manchester City mate Bobby MacDonald spoke with real disappointment about trying to find him on one occasion, 'It's one of my great regrets that I wasn't able to track Gerry down. My son, who was in the army, was stationed down near Dawlish and I thought it would be a great idea to go down for the weekend and visit my son and also go along to Portland to surprise Gerry as we had not seen each other in years. I had no number for him or address but through a friend I found out that he would drink in this particular pub so I went along to see if he was there or the locals could point me in the right direction. I found the pub and asked around but nobody knew where he was or where he lived. I stayed for hours in the pub drinking orange juice hoping he would turn up but he never did so I had to leave. It was one of my biggest regrets that I never got to meet him again and I think that's what made it so hard when he passed away – the fact that I would never see him again.'

It was a quiet life in Portland for Gerry. He did various jobs such as working in Tesco and warehouse work and many of his colleagues had no idea that he had been a famous footballer. But that was typical of Gerry – he was never going to brag about his exploits in the game. If somebody asked, he would tell them but he would never offer the information first. People liked him for being Gerry, not for being an ex-footballer.

But things did change for Gerry around 2009 as not only did he meet his wife Joolz, he also had an encounter with his old mate Sean Donnelly that would once again put him in the Bristol City limelight. Sean explained, 'I had lost touch with Gerry as a lot of people had. I remember going to a Bristol City pre-season friendly down in Southampton. There was a load of us on the train down and when we got there we took over a boozer near the ground. We were all having a laugh when I noticed Chris Gow at the back of the pub. I left my mates and went over to him, and we hugged and I said, "Where's your old man?" "He's over there," he replied. "Where?" I said. "Over there, by the wall," and sure enough it was Gerry.

'I went over to him and we grabbed hold of each other; it was great. I then said to him, "What have you done to your hair, you silly bastard?" "Nothing," he replied. "It's jet black." "You must have done something, mate," I said. We were laughing and he said, "It was always this colour." "Bollocks," I said. "It was bloody grey when you played for City."

'We had a great time and had a few drinks after the game. I took his number and on the way home I decided that I was going to organise something for him at my pub, The Three Lions. So I got a few of the old '76 side together, people like Paul Cheesley, Brian Drysdale, Donnie Gillies, etc., and invited Gerry to the pub. He came with his wife Joolz and when they walked in the whole place sang his song and you could tell he was really moved by it.

'I remember Joolz saying she didn't realise how famous he was in Bristol. The night was great; we had local comedian Stoney Garnett there, and he did a few jokes and invited Gerry on stage with him. The players were so pleased to be back in touch with him, although they all asked where his grey hair had gone. The night was a real success as he spent the evening chatting to the fans and his old mates. I loved doing it for him as it was a recognition of the affection all the City fans had for him and I think he was a little overawed by it. The place was rammed and it just showed how much they loved him.'

In the autumn of 2010, Bristol businessman Chris Bradfield met up with his friend Adrian Ashby for a coffee in the Bedminster area of the city. Both being lifelong Robins supporters, they talked in between sips of cappuccino about the good old days and the latest Ashton Gate gossip. Chris had run Radio Robin, the music programme broadcast each matchday during the heady days of the 1970s when City were in the First Division. They both agreed that for City to have stayed in the top flight for four years like they did was incredible.

Adrian, like Chris, was a DJ during those days and he ran the Avon Soul Army, an evening playing soul music from the Guidhall Tavern in the centre of Bristol. They shared a love of music and football and today are entrepreneurs in their own right. As they chatted and laughed about the 'old days' they realised that the following spring would be the 35th anniversary of that famous promotion and they could not let that go unnoticed. Chris, the owner of Bristol-based production company Sounds Commercial, had already been responsible for producing a number of supporter-led events at the club, so he suggested they put on the 'Spirit of 76', which would get the lads together and celebrate their achievement. They contacted all the media outlets and tickets sold like hot cakes.

On Saturday, 5 March 2011 every player from that promotion-winning team was at the Marriott Hotel in Bristol along with supporters to celebrate the success. It was the first time Gerry had been part of the team in a long while and it was a very emotional night for everyone. Even centre-half Gary Collier was there with his wife after flying in from San Diego, California. It was a wonderful evening.

Manager Alan Dicks led the team, all smartly dressed in tuxedos, into the room to a rousing standing ovation. City were represented by Marina Dolman, the wife of former club president Harry Dolman, and she presented all the players with an engraved glass plate inscribed with their achievement. The night also saw Kevin Mabbutt join the celebrations via satellite from his home in California and he said a few words about how sad he was that he couldn't be there in person. The audience were also treated to a compilation of the goals that City had scored in their time in the top flight, which was provided by Jonathan Pearce and Mark Tovey of the Supporters' Trust after hour upon hour of searching through the archives.

For Gerry, the night was fantastic. He laughed and joked with his old mates and had his photo taken with supporters, and although he really wasn't one for the limelight it was clear to see that he was among his friends and he loved every minute of it.

In the weeks that followed the successful event, Chris contacted Gerry and offered to run a testimonial year for him. Gerry was blown away by the offer as despite his 11-year career at Bristol City he had never been granted a testimonial. Chris explains, 'After the success of the '76 night I just thought it was fitting for him. He had left the club when we needed the money and he even waived his signing-on fee at the time to again help the club. He was such a popular player on the night with his team-mates and the supporters and he had time for everybody, so I just contacted him and said I would get some people together to put a testimonial year on for him. Typical of Gerry, he wondered whether anybody would come.

'I visited him and his wife Joolz along with their dog Mina down in Portland and they were living the dream to be honest. It was plain to see that they were very much in love and he was so different to the image I might have had of him when he was playing. He was a real gentleman and a very special guy. We reminisced about when I was running Radio Robin for the club and I used to interview him sometimes and how I got used to his Glaswegian accent over the years.'

So with Gerry's permission it was now time for Chris to get together a team that would run events over the year, culminating hopefully in a match at Ashton Gate against a Manchester City Legends team. Chris continues, 'I decided to have the meetings at the Three Lions pub in Bedminster so Sean Donnelly, the landlord, was a must to get on board. Sean is a real character and he has a fantastic knowledge of all things Bristol City as well as running a true Bristol City pub. Another important member of the team was Tim Hill, a former Granada Television and Manchester United TV producer. Tim was originally from Henleaze in Bristol and again is a big City fan. We also added James Ryan who had written an excellent book about former City star Chris Garland. I contacted the wonderful Derek Partridge who organised the Manchester City Legends team and he said yes straight away.'

Armed with a full events team and a game planned, Chris approached Bristol City and told them of his intentions. To his dismay, the club were unsure about holding the event and they turned down the idea. 'I have to admit I couldn't believe it,' Chris explained. 'After all, Gerry was a god to a lot of the fans and I was taking the financial risk in the venture not them. Anyway, it probably made me more determined to make this happen.'

Chris dusted himself down and the committee approached Clevedon Town Football Club to see if they would be interested in holding the event at their Hand Stadium. They were in the Western League and the ground, about 13 miles from Bristol,

THE GERRY GOW STORY

held 3,500 supporters. They jumped at the chance. The word spread and interest in the event was amazing among fans, and suddenly Chris got a call from Bristol City who asked him to the club for a meeting. They had thought long and hard and decided they could put the event on after all. They would give Chris a stand, but he would have to pay for Manchester City's transport, all security costs, and everything else including programme sellers, stewards and food outlets along with first aid cover.

Chris had a new dilemma, 'I talked it over with Gerry and first of all I must say that I felt incredibly sorry for Clevedon Town as they had backed us when City didn't but I knew how much Gerry wanted to be on that Ashton Gate pitch after all those years, so I was really going to agree to anything Bristol City wanted. I couldn't deny Gerry his moment.'

The committee agreed and the game was set for 28 July 2012. The first event in Gerry's honour was a black tie dinner at the Bristol Marriott Hotel. It was hosted by Jonathan Pearce and during the evening there were glowing tributes via video link from Sir Alex Ferguson, Peter Reid, Joe Royle, PFA chairman Gordon Taylor and Richard Scudamore who at the time was chairman of the Premier League.

At the start of the festivities, Jonathan invited Gerry on to the stage to ask him how it had all started for him. After the applause, which seemed to go on forever, Gerry explained that it was legendary scout Tony Collins who had discovered him playing schools football in Glasgow and he had invited him down to Bristol along with Billy Menmuir and Steve and Tom Ritchie, both of whom were in the audience. Jonathan then asked if Gerry had seen Tony recently, to which he replied,

'No, I have not seen him for years.' With that, the doors opened and Tony came into the room to a massive standing ovation. It was a fantastic moment as the pair embraced, and there was certainly not a dry eye in the house.

Chris commented, 'I was disappointed there was only Colin Sexton, the chief executive of Bristol City, there to represent the club, particularly as I knew what the club meant to Gerry, but I was very impressed when Bristol Rovers bought a table and filled it with Gerry's old adversaries such as defender Frankie Prince whom he had many a battle with during Bristol derbies.'

Later in the year a golf day was organised at Shirehampton Golf Club supporters alongside City players from different eras. Chris also invited businessman Mark Jakeways to help raise money for a local children's hospice. Mark brought along some fantastic sporting memorabilia and an auction raised thousands for the charity. There were also several 'open mic' events where Gerry was able to tell a few footballing stories to fans and they were able to meet him and watch clips of his career. All of the events were incredibly well supported by fans and local businesspeople.

With the game against Manchester City looming, Chris and his team were busy sorting things out for the big day. Chris organised for former Bristol City and Manchester City player Shaun Goater to come and play even though he was living in Bermuda at the time. Chris looks back at those days before the game, 'It was really hectic. Derek Partridge had sorted out the Manchester City side of things and they were ready to go. I paid for Shaun to come over with his wife and stay for the week then it was a case of organising for Dariusz Dziekanowski to

THE GERRY GOW STORY

come over from Poland and get Brian Tinnion to come back from Spain, which they both did.'

The game attracted a crowd of 4,100. It was mainly fans of Bristol City and Manchester City fans along with a contingent from Yeovil Town. As Gerry led the two team out on that hot sunny afternoon, the crowd sang, 'He's here, he's there, he's every fucking where, Gerry Gow, Gerry Gow.' It was another emotional time for everybody watching and probably the most emotional event of the testimonial year as it saw Gerry walking back out on to the pitch at Ashton Gate, the ground he loved, and the ground where he had gone from a boy to a man in the red shirt of Bristol City.

When I spoke to Joolz about the event, she said, 'Gerry and myself were really nervous before the testimonial match, more nervous than any other event. Gerry even said he was more nervous than the [FA] Cup Final. I think we did not know how it would go. Even after all the adulation he had experienced from City fans he never really thought he was worthy of it.'

Manchester City's squad included Joe Corrigan, Andy Dibble, Eric Nixon, Peter Beagrie, Paul Dickov, Gary Bennett, Dave Bennett, Asa Hartford, Kevin Horlock, Peter Barnes, Jeff Whitley, Fitzroy Simpson and Shaun Goater.

Bristol City had Gerry Gow, Dariusz Dziekanowski, Brian Tinnion, Bob Taylor, Junior Bent, Rob Newman, Gerry Sweeney, Gary Owers, Brian Drysdale, Trevor Jacobs, Chris Honor, David Moggs and a host of local celebrities. Manchester City won 2-1 and the crowd witnessed a very special occasion that they would never see again.

Chris recalls, 'It was a great success although I am still disappointed that no bigwigs from Bristol City attended the afternoon. Gerry was in tears at the end, saying he couldn't thank me enough. It was ironic as it should have been me thanking him for all the joy he gave me watching him over the years. The game was a long time coming, but it was a fitting tribute to a true icon of Bristol City.'

Gerry had now been truly recognised by the fans who loved him at his various clubs and maybe the testimonial year did bring him out of his shell and show him how much everybody thought of him both as a player and as a man. With some of the money the testimonial year raised, Gerry and Joolz took the opportunity to go to Australia to visit his sister Agnes and her family. She had emigrated from Ireland in the 1980s and it was wonderful that the year of events dedicated to Gerry allowed him to go and see her.

While doing research for the book I also stumbled upon another accolade for Gerry – his name appeared in the 2014 single 'This One's For Now' by Liverpool indie rock band Half Man Half Biscuit. I tracked lead singer Nigel Blackwell down and asked him about the reference to Gerry. It goes:

> 'See how it unfolds when I try to include you
> I'll fit you in someday somehow
> A thousand words but not right now
> I've got a few lines on Gerry Gow
> I had three in a packet in '78
> I went back to the shop in a manner irate'

Nigel explained, 'I am a Tranmere Rovers fan but growing up I used to collect the football stickers of teams and I was for some reason fascinated by the Bristol City team and in particular Gerry Gow who looked like he was a real wild man. If I remember Bristol City was the first team I completed, so for some reason I had a soft spot for them. I also won't lie: that Gow is a really easy name to use when you're looking for something to rhyme with the word now. Anyway, he just popped into my head when I was writing the lyrics.'

Although Gerry had enjoyed his day in the sun with almost his second wave of fame, he was really at peace with Portland and Joolz, although what lay ahead for the pair was the biggest battle they would ever face.

20

Joolz

DURING THE research for this book, another name kept popping up when speaking to friends and family – Joolz, who was Gerry's second wife. Everyone said, 'Speak to Joolz, she's great, her and Gerry had a blast when they were together.' After our long conversation on the phone I wasn't disappointed. Her personality shone through as well as her love for Gerry. It was also really refreshing that all her recollections and emotions were based on knowing Gerry the man as opposed to Gerry the footballer, who was somebody she had never met.

When I asked about Gerry, Joolz spoke with passion and obvious love for him, 'Wow, meeting Gerry, where do I start? I came down to Portland from my home in Stourbridge in the West Midlands for a wedding with my friend Anita. We loved the area so much that we decided we would come here every year for a holiday. We made friends with people around the island and loved it. On our fourth trip we were invited to a BBQ at a friend's house. I remember the date, it was 14 June 2009, and that's when I met Gerry. He was a friend of the hosts and we spoke and hit it off right away. There was a real connection; we chatted, drank and laughed right into the early hours of the morning. It was like a spark had gone off inside me. He asked me if he could see me the next day and I said yes. And we were inseparable all week.

'I remember my friend Caron telling me that Gerry was a famous footballer, and I should Google him. Well, I had no interest in football at all so that was lost on me; however if she had said he was a rock singer or from a rock band I probably would have been impressed. I returned home on the Thursday and while I was there I did Google him, even though I said I wouldn't. I even went online and bought a signed photo of him from a web site, where he looked like a 1970s porn star with a big moustache. I drove back down to see him on the weekend, a four-hour drive at least, and showed him the photo. We both just fell about laughing; he was in fits, saying he could have signed it for me. As a relationship we really hit the ground running.'

It was obvious that Gerry meeting Joolz was certainly meant to be. By Joolz's own admission she had not had the greatest success in meeting the right man, and explains, 'Blokes I had met in the past had usually turned out to be bastards but Gerry was different. I had never met anybody like him. He didn't want to hold you back or suffocate you; he wanted you to live your life. He really was extraordinary.'

Gerry had got divorced from Julie several years previously and it was a worry for his kids that he did seem to spend a lot of his time on his own. He had also just been made redundant from an engineering company in Portland where he had been working for a few years, and although he was between jobs at the time Gerry's attitude to work was very much how he played football – he was a grafter, so it would not be long before he found work.

As far as football was concerned, he was still involved to a small degree by doing a bit of scouting for his friend Paul Hart at Portsmouth now and then, as well as watching the progress of his daughter Rachael's two sons Josh and Brennan, who were showing promise in the game. Defender Brennan later signed professional forms for Bournemouth, has been capped for Scotland at Under-19 level and is truly following in his grandfather's footsteps.

Three weeks into their relationship Gerry asked Joolz to marry him. 'I said no but I would if he wore a kilt. He asked me again but not with the kilt and I said yes,' she said. Despite the 12-year age difference between them, the following August Joolz got a transfer from her civil service job to Portland and in September the pair moved in together. Joolz certainly got the seal of approval from Gerry's family as they all said she was the best thing that had happened to him for a long time. Even Julie, Gerry's first wife, became great friends with Joolz and they remain so to this day.

The pair were married August 2010 at Eastern Methodist Church, Portland. It was a wonderful day and one that Joolz will never forget, 'It was magical. All the family was there as well as our friends, and unbeknown to Gerry as we signed the register I got a piper to play for us. He played "Flower of Scotland". I told Gerry I don't like the words as they are anti-English but I like the tune, and he just fell about laughing. The piper marched us and all the guests across the road to the Conservative Club where we had one hell of a party. We were so happy; I couldn't believe my luck as we were surrounded by all our loved ones, his kids and the grandkids. Yes, it was a very special day for everyone.'

Gerry and Joolz lived an idyllic lifestyle; in fact to their friends they were called 'The Olympic Torches' as they never went out. Joolz explains, 'We were so happy in our own company and we loved to do the garden and have a few drinks while relaxing with some rock music, which we both loved. I felt calmness about being with Gerry and I think he felt the same. I remember once we were in Gerry's daughter Rachael's garden and a bee was on the grass so she asked her dad to kill it as it might sting her dog Scooby, who was running around the garden. Gerry refused and picked it up on a leaf and placed it on a wall. Rachael looked at me and her face just creased with laughter as she said, "What have you done with my dad? He's like a hippy?"'

Gerry was becoming rather bohemian and I remember a story his brother Willie told me when I met him in Glasgow. Willie said, 'I picked him up once from Glasgow airport when he was flying up for a few days. I was waiting for him to appear from Arrivals when all of a sudden in through the double doors came Gerry with a t-shirt on, shorts, sandals and beads around his neck and wrists. I remember hugging him then taking a step back and saying, "What the fuck have you got on?" It's fucking November." He just laughed and told me to chill out. I thought, "Chill out, chill out, no fucker chills out in Glasgow."'

Gerry was now working at Tesco in Portland and it appeared that the story of an ex-footballer doing a 'normal' job seemed to have sparked interest from the national newspapers as the *Daily Mirror* ran an article headlined 'Wild-haired 1970s footballer Gow works nights in Tesco'. It really was a non-story and Gerry just thought it was funny, but what it did was show what the man himself was really like. He wasn't in hard times, he had just finished playing football and got a job like anybody else. Just because he had been a footballer he didn't think that work was too demeaning for him or that somebody owed him a living. At the store Gerry was popular and hardly talked about his career, which was why people liked him. He didn't think he was better than anybody.

As well as the supermarket job, Gerry also did some work in the building industry with his son Chris, who said his dad was a hard worker, 'Dad was a grafter. He would work sometimes in the day and even do a night shift at the supermarket. I used to think, "Christ, I can't imagine what he must have been like when he was training as a player." Even then he seemed to go on and on.'

Even though the couple loved Portland, Gerry had always wanted to live in Spain and he and Joolz discussed the possibility. Joolz said, 'He always wanted to move to Spain. For me especially, coming from the Midlands I loved Portland and it was enough for me. The climate was great and the beaches were breathtaking, but we talked about it and planned it. We thought that if I took early retirement, and Gerry had his small football pension along with his Tesco pension we could do it. We wouldn't want a flash lifestyle as that wasn't our way.

'We started to plan for it and it took around two years in total but then he started to become really tired and was falling asleep. We just thought nothing of it as he was doing loads of work to get the money together for Spain plus he wasn't getting any younger. He started to lose weight, and bear in mind there was nothing to him anyway. We went back and forth to the doctor's without any definite answers for us as to what was wrong with him. In the meantime, we had set a date for Spain and we would be leaving on 2 May 2016. Although Gerry was poorly, he still kept saying we will be going and we started to pack some stuff for the move, then he became really ill at Christmas and collapsed. He was then diagnosed with lung cancer. As you can imagine it ripped a hole not only in us both but the whole of the family.'

Gerry found himself in and out of hospital as the illness took hold. On 10 October 2016 Chris issued a statement from the family, which read, 'Today the world fell apart for our family. My beautiful dad passed away in the early hours of the morning, 64 years young he lost his battle to the most disgusting disease. Me and my family are broken hearted and nothing will ever fill the void in our hearts. RIP my hero, my best mate, my dad xxx.'

Gerry left behind his wife Joolz, three children, nine grandchildren and a great-grandchild, and since then the Gow family have a new great-grandson who has aptly been named Gerry. It was notable that while interviewing various opponents and particularly former team-mates for this book their tone and demeanour changed when talking about their friend's battle with this terrible disease. When we reached this point in the interview, many just shook their heads and said, 'What a waste, it's not how I want to remember him.' It's a view that I for one share and I knew that in the process of writing this book I would have to cover Gerry's battle with cancer.

Speaking to family and friends, it was plain to see that any words I wrote would not be able to express the grief and trauma they all felt at his death. I particularly did not want to document the numerous heartbreaking trips to the hospital the Gow family made during his illness. All I would say is that Gerry fought many battles and was scared of none of them. He took on this dreadful illness with the same guts and determination he showed on the football field, but unfortunately it would be a battle he couldn't win.

The news of Gerry's passing erupted through the world of football and his clubs issued statements. Bristol City said, 'Everyone at the club sends its condolences to Gerry's family and friends at this sad time.' Manchester City added, 'Everyone at Manchester City is saddened to learn of the passing of Gerry Gow following his brave battle with illness. [He was] A cult hero in his short spell at Maine Road in the '80s.' Rotherham United wrote, 'Rotherham United are deeply saddened to hear of the passing of Gerry Gow. Once a Miller, always a Miller.' Burnley said, 'We are saddened to hear the news of the passing of former Claret Gerry Gow. Our thoughts go out to his family.' Yeovil Town and Weymouth also both added their condolences to the family. The clubs also held a minute's silence for Gerry at their next home games.

Son Chris remembers the tribute at Ashton Gate before Bristol City took on Blackburn Rovers, 'It was very emotional for all of us at the Ashton Gate game. We were all on the pitch, us as a family and his other family, the former Bristol City players he played with, you could have heard a pin drop. The club showed clips of dad playing games throughout his career and there were loads of banners with 'GOW' written on them. They even sung his song, 'He's here, he's there, he's every fucking where, Gerry Gow, Gerry Gow.'

'I want to pay my respects to the City fans that day. They really gave him a great send-off and it was apparent how loved he was by them. I also want to thank the Blackburn Rovers fans that day who also remained silent.'

Rotherham United's John Breckin looks back on the Millers' tribute, 'I went on to the pitch and said a few words. I was choked up to be honest as he was a real mate and I loved playing with him and being in his company. The supporters were brilliant; they showed their respect to him which was really moving.'

Gerry's funeral took place at Easton Methodist Church in Portland. It was especially tough for Joolz who had stood with him in that same church on their wedding day some six years previously. A lone piper played the coffin out and it was a sad day for all concerned as everybody who knew Gerry attended to say goodbye and also to celebrate him. Fans from his former clubs were present too. Many of them had never spoken to him but they just wanted to show their respects to a player who always gave everything on the pitch, irrespective of who he was playing for at the time.

Joolz lit a spark in Gerry and he in her, so it's best to leave the final words to her, 'Words can't tell you what a wonderful man he was. My friend Anita described him as the toughest of men with the kindest of hearts. I did not have enough years with him, but for those I had I am deeply grateful. He looked out for all his family over the years so he will always be, as his song goes, 'here, there and everywhere,' especially with us. He was Gerry Gow and there was nobody like him.'

Career statistics

Clubs

Years	Team	Appearances	Goals
1969–1980	Bristol City	445	54
1980–1981	Manchester City	36	7
1981–1983	Rotherham United	58	4
1983–1984	Burnley	9	0

National team

1974	Scotland Under-23	1	0

Clubs managed

1984–1987	Yeovil Town (player-manager)
1989–1990	Weymouth Town

Bibliography

Stevens, M. and Woods, D., *The Four Seasons* (Stevens & Woods Publishing, 2018)

Woods, D., *Bristol City The Modern Era* (Desert Island Books, 2000)

James, G., *Manchester City The Complete Record* (Breedon Books, 2006)

Lee, E. and Whalley, P., *The Pride and The Glory* (Burnley Football Club, 2002)

Randall, P., and Palmer, N., *Punky* (DB Publishing, 2013)

Cope, Q., and Collins, S., *Tony Collins Football's Master Spy* (The Book Guild, 2016)

Watson, D., *Millmoor Personalities 1946–1986* (Metropolitan Borough of Rotherham, 1986)

Powell, M. and Burlton, C., Harry Dolman – The Millionaire Inventor Who Became Mr Bristol City (Bristol Books, 2007)

Hopegood, T. and Hudson, J., *Atyeo – The Hero Next Door* (Redcliffe Press, 2005)

The author's interviews:
Willie Gow; Phil Dwyer; Chris Gow; Don Murray; Alan Dicks; Pat Rice; Sarita Collins; Don Megson; Joolz Gow; Sammy McIlroy; Julie Gow; Derek Partridge; Rachael Gow;

BIBLIOGRAPHY

Barrie Hole; Jenny Gow; Joe Royle; Mike Gibson; Jonathan Pearce; John Galley; Norman Hunter; Gordon Parr; Colin Rapesey; Micky Tanner; Martyn Rodgers; Trevor Tainton; Chris Bradfield; Dave Bruton; Geert Meijers; Jimmy Mann; Alan Curtis; Paul Cheesley; Phil Bater; Geoff Merrick; Joe Corrigan; Tom Ritchie; Dave Bennett; Donnie Gillies; John Breckin; Gerry Sweeney; Paul Stancliffe; Steve Perryman; Tony Scholes; Ray Cashley; Ron Clayton; Bobby MacDonald; Harold Jarman; Tommy Hutchinson; Bryan Drysdale; Keith Fear; Ray Mountford; Clive Whitehead; Howard Pritchard; Steven Sowden; Sean Donnelly; Neil Grigg; Jim Lees; Pete Jeffin; Peter Williams; Tom Phillips; Bob Cullingford.

About The Author

NEIL PALMER is a freelance writer based in Bristol. *The Gerry Gow Story* is Neil's tenth book to date. Others have included the popular *Derby Days* series as well as the acclaimed biography of Welsh football maverick Trevor Ford. Neil has also written for various sporting publications and websites.

Also available at all good book stores

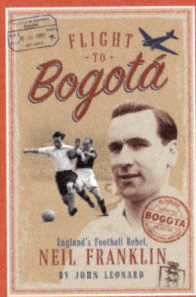
9781785316548

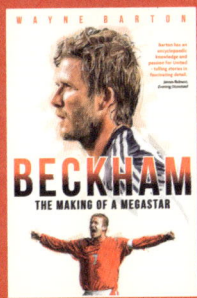
9781785316760

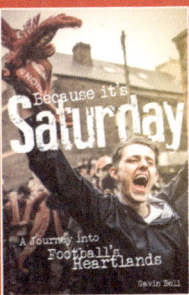
9781785316463

9781785316531

9781785316791

9781785316708

9781785316289

9781785317194

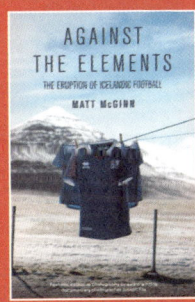
9781785317200